What
SOCIAL
IMPACT?

ILDIKO ALMASI SIMSIC

Cap de Nice Press

ISBN: 978-1-7384321-0-3

TABLE OF CONTENTS

CHAPTER 0

WHAT IS A SOCIAL IMPACT?

Social impact and social impact measurement have gained significant momentum in recent years, particularly when environmental, social, and governance aspects (ESG), corporate social responsibility, and impact investing became mainstream for many banks and financial institutions. Each approach, each instrument we have to facilitate the creation of this magical social impact has its purpose, scope, and limitation. We very rarely speak of this though. In fact, over the past two years, I have seen the term *social washing* thrown around in mainstream news articles, the same way we talked about the inflated green or climate change impacts reported by companies. What makes social impacts unique in my view is the lack of robust, legally regulated, standardized measurements and the fact that many social impacts remain subjective and hard to quantify. We have tools that are compliance based and tools that aim to proactively create a positive social impact. We also have different layers of impact creation, whether we examine it on the corporate level (employee well-being), the operations level (community health and safety around main manufacturing plants), or the investment level (is our portfolio sustainable or managed sustainably?). The concept of social impact is defined in a generic way that means different things in different contexts. There are methodologies used to identify indicators in an attempt to standardize the ways we measure social impact, through qualitative and quantitative indicators, that are still subject to interpretation in many cases. Without giving everything away in the first chapter, this book aims to provide a comprehensive overview of the concept of social impact from a social performance practitioner's perspective to open an honest conversation about what each instrument can and cannot achieve.

I am a social development specialist or social performance practitioner. Defining social impact from my perspective is very different from, for instance, indicators you would use for macro-level ESG ratings, impact investing, corporate social responsibility, social bonds, or the other instruments currently in use. When looking for a good definition I also encountered challenges, as they all seemed vague and different depending on the context I used for the search. I did ask ChatGPT what a social impact is in January 2023 to see if the AI is more up to date, and the answer was:

> A social impact refers to the effect that an action or decision has on people and communities, and the broader society. This can be either positive or negative and can include changes to culture, economy, environment, and well-being. Social impact can be a result of the activities of individuals, organizations, and governments, and can have long-lasting effects.
>
> A social impact is the effect that a person, group, organization, or activity has on the well-being or state of society, communities, or individuals. It refers to the positive or negative changes made to society as a result of an action or influence.

There are various ways to measure social impacts, including:

1. *Surveys and questionnaires: gathering information directly from individuals who are affected by the change.*
2. *Qualitative research: gathering in-depth information through interviews and focus groups.*
3. *Quantitative data analysis: using numerical data, such as statistics and metrics, to measure changes over time.*
4. *Case studies: exploring the experiences of specific individuals or communities in depth.*
5. *Impact assessments: evaluating the overall impact of a specific project or initiative taking into account both the intended and unintended effects.*

It is important to note that measuring social impact can be challenging due to the complex and dynamic nature of social systems and the long-term effects of changes. The best approach often involves a combination of methods to provide a comprehensive understanding of the impact.

It is a challenge to not be sarcastic and conclude that everything has a social impact, right? In my opinion, this is because we have not been up front about what our social impact means in the given context, and we derived far-reaching positive impacts on all of society for interventions that, in fact, benefited only a select few. This is not a criticism nor a complaint, more like an attempt to look at the tools and instruments for social impact creation in a systematic way where we acknowledge the opportunities and shortcomings as well. What we can achieve through corporate social responsibility, we might not be able to achieve through ESG or sustainability, simply because these are different tools with different scopes and purposes.

When ESG and sustainability became the hot topic in the financial sector, I wondered how people like me with vast site-level experience on operational impacts would be utilized to better understand asset-level impacts—impacts of the investment or project on the environment and the people. I spare you the suspense: my skillset and experience was pretty useless in the first 5-7 years of the ESG era, and only recently became more valuable as investor interest shifted to social impacts. While the assessment of environmental impacts has been a standard practice for the permitting process for decades now, the difference between international standards and local legal requirements remains significant. Social impact assessment has not been a standard part of any permitting process for any new project or operation in general. It is only in the past couple of years that some countries, including Australia introduced legal requirements for social impact assessment.

Creating the impact is the first step, but the focus now seems to be on demonstrating and reporting it. There are professional networks and organizations that provide guidance and methodology for impact measurement. There's the social return on investment (SROI) that can quantify some impacts in monetary terms. I have not seen social impact assessment and SROI used for impact reporting in ESG documents. I also understand that ESG is more of a high-level reporting on corporate performance, as opposed to an aggregate of the assets in the portfolio—at least for the social aspects. Typical ESG reports include waste management, recycling, energy use, proxy voting, and board composition. Some indicators are for the corporation, while others are for their operations and portfolio. On the social side, the topics typically covered include employee well-being, labor and working conditions, contractor and supply-chain management, antibribery and anticorruption policies, and any impacts on communities. As a field specialist, I wondered who those communities were—communities around corporate headquarters, customers, or communities impacted by operations. I also had questions as to how the impacts were measured and how the indicators were selected. Were they using a baseline study to show preintervention status for comparison? I was not alone in questioning the contents of the *S* in ESG. The CFA Institute—the institute that offers the three-level exam to become a chartered financial analyst for investment professionals— also issued a comparison study of eighteen different ESG frameworks and their inadequacy when it came to capturing and reporting on social impacts. To address gaps in the social impact creation market, the CFA Institute started to also offer a course on ESG with the potential to obtain the ESG Investing Certification in 2021.

Sustainability and sustainability reporting are other terms that are used almost interchangeably with ESG in the mainstream media. Now, nearly every company has a sustainability policy or strategy that largely covers the same topics that have been listed under ESG. How is sustainability different from ESG? If they are the same, why don't we use just one definition? What does social sustainability mean? Is this another high-level initiative that looks at the corporate-level sustainability of the business based on the social aspects only? With the ever-changing and increasing requirements for companies worldwide (but especially within the EU) to report on corporate sustainability, it is time to make sense of what should and should not be covered under this heading. The new EU Corporate Sustainability Reporting Directive requires companies to report on human rights due diligence, covering their operations and their supply chain even if they're outside the European Union. What is human rights due diligence, and how is it different from a social impact assessment? A guide has yet to be developed, and there has yet to be a discussion on the implementation of such a directive. Who will be the human rights due diligence experts who decide whether an assessment is thorough enough and covers the relevant players in the supply chain? Looking more into the supply chain and using terminology that deviates from previous reporting requirements means an additional burden of establishing internal management systems for the collection and analysis of data. Or are we repackaging already existing requirements?

If we wanted to gather all the sustainability reporting requirements that companies need to fulfill, it would be an endless circle of acronyms all created for the green transition, for the good of society, and to achieve a sustainable future for all of us. If the reporting requirements and contents of the report are confusing even to people working in the industry, how can it be informative for the general public or nontechnical stakeholders? Larger companies have to employ a team of data analysts to prepare all their annual reports to fulfill each requirement they have. Lufthansa Group, for instance, employs a team of six for the sole purpose of putting the data into the right format for each sustainability and nonfinancial report. Is it time to start the discussion of how we can make the reporting on social aspects meaningful? Can we use the resources that are already committed to doing good and reporting on it in a more efficient way? I sure hope this book gives you a taste of what that would look like.

We don't have to go far from the corporate-level reporting requirements for ESG and sustainability to find another tool for social impact creation—one that has been in use for a long time: corporate social responsibility (CSR) initiatives. CSR is widely understood as the responsibility of a company to *do good* for society and the environment. It involves creating policies and initiatives that respond to community needs, providing some sort of benefit. CSR initiatives are usually long-term, ongoing engagements with communities. Its most well-known representations are probably community service, charitable giving, environmental stewardship, or community investment. While the previous reporting requirements and programs are all related to compliance with legal requirements, CSR is largely undertaken on a voluntary basis. No company is legally required to proactively invest in their communities, though it does help with relationship management, especially for companies with controversial operations or significant environmental or social impact. Think of mining companies, companies with manufacturing facilities in poor countries, traditional fossil fuel–based power plants, or companies in industries with a track record of human rights violations (mainly forced labor and child labor). These companies are under stakeholder and public pressure to take care of the communities around them and contribute to economic and social development. CSR is not a direct response to project or operational impact and can include a variety of activities, from building sports halls, schools, or hospitals to subsidizing computer labs, language classes, glasses, and shoes to providing apprenticeship opportunities for members of the local community.

Impact investing is another relatively new approach to *doing good* beyond the compliance element. In practical terms it means investing with the purpose of creating a positive social or environmental impact, while also having financial returns. This is another type of voluntary proactive impact creation activity that evolved into having a more standardized set of guidelines, yet it remains free of legal obligations. Impact investing is strongly connected to CSR initiatives that could be turned into a profit making business or investment. Since then, impact investing became a category of its own, separate from the CSR-type activities. If impact investing is doing good while making money than how does it differe from other types of social impact businesses, such as a social enterprise?

Social entrepreneurship has evolved to use business principles to create positive social change, serve underserved communities, and solve social problems through innovation. Social entrepreneurs often focus on addressing social issues such as poverty, healthcare, education, and environmental sustainability using innovative and sustainable approaches in either for-profit or nonprofit business contexts. These businesses are driven by the desire to form a more just and equitable society and create long-term, bankable solutions to social problems. We see how the different types of social impact products cover similar areas with similar purposes. If the majority of businesses need to comply with ESG frameworks and report on sustainability—including social sustainability—and if investments are made with the primary goal of making a positive impact, then is it time to revisit the notion of what a social enterprise is? Finding a market gap or underserved community is the goal of any business, at least as far as I could gather. It's what every business wants to do. What makes some businesses social enterprises and others not?

I think the market and the sector have matured enough to look at these instruments as tools, each with its own uses, limitations, and timing in the investment and business cycle. If we understand what each product can do, we can better optimize for the desired social outcome. We will be able to have a better definition of affected people, targeted communities, or just communities in general, and we will be able to avoid the artificial inflation of positive social impacts in our reporting. This has already started happening in the environmental and governance aspects of ESG, and it is time that we continue with the social aspects. The scope of these products and instruments is not well understood, and there is a lack of useful resources that can point out the social indicators or actual social impacts in a pragmatic manner. This lack of standardization and the increasing pressure from civil society, governments, shareholders, and communities has led to an increase in social washing. This has resulted in several instances where companies have multiple amazing ESG and sustainability ratings from major agencies, yet they are affected by scandals around working conditions in the supply chain.

What I noticed is that there is a lack of differentiation between the mandatory social safeguards and the voluntary or *extra mile*–type activities. This resulted in several instances where a company is given a favorable ESG rating for working conditions and employee well-being when in fact their only achievement is complying with national legislation and ratified International Labor Organization (ILO) conventions to avoid forced and child labor. Can we truly celebrate companies for their voluntary CSR activities when they fail to comply with supply chain management legislation? In my world, the basis of any assessment is compliance with the international best practice in environmental and social risk management regarding project or operational impacts. In my current role, I am not able to sign off on a disbursement or financing unless the company complies with the requirements. Even if they spend a few million dollars on CSR initiatives, such as building women's shelters for victims of domestic violence. I am not here to argue what social impact is *better,* I am simply pointing out that being a *good* company in CSR terms doesn't always translate to being a *good* company when we use a different lens for our assessment.

Measuring social impact is a critical and often debated component of the whole movement to *do good.* Standardization attempts have been made that allowed rating agencies to compare and rank companies. One popular methodology is the SROI, which involves measuring the social, environmental, and economic benefits in monetary returns. I have seen a few examples of this methodology being used for impact investing and even for social enterprises. Again, this is a methodology that might be appropriate to measure the social impact of certain instruments but not others. In my line of work, we focus on monetizing the risk of the impact for compensation purposes as opposed to looking at any returns on the community investment. Again, I'm in the compliance game, with limited (but existing) options for additional impact creation.

Despite all the challenges, there is a clear interest from investors and civil society to use financial capital for social sustainability and positive impact creation. There is an increasing demand for businesses to mitigate the risks of their operations on environmental and social receptors (their stakeholders) and address social challenges such as poverty reduction, education, healthcare, and environmental sustainability. This shift in doing business has led to a number of innovative and creative solutions in both the nonprofit and corporate sectors, driving the development of new approaches to address social and ecological issues. My industry has stepped out of its isolated and niche role and has provided professional help for financial institutions to develop Environmental and Social Impact Assessments (ESIA), due diligence, and management plans as part of their standard business practices for assets they own or companies they invest in. There is a desire to comply with the international industry best practice that is often equated with the IFC Performance Standards.

These standards cover:

- PS 1 Assessment and Management of Environmental and Social Risks and Impacts
- PS 2 Labor and Working Conditions
- PS 3 Resource Efficiency and Pollution Prevention
- PS 4 Community Health, Safety, and Security
- PS 5 Land Acquisition and Involuntary Resettlement

- PS 6 Biodiversity Conservation and Sustainable Management of Living Natural Resources
- PS 7 Indigenous Peoples
- PS 8 Cultural Heritage

Other international financial institutions (IFIs) have largely similar standards and policies, though minor differences apply. For instance, the European Bank for Reconstruction and Development (EBRD) has Performance Requirement 10: Stakeholder Engagement and Grievance Management, while for the IFC, this topic is covered under PS 1. Other industry standards also build on the IFC and World Bank Group guidelines for environmental, health and safety, and industry-specific guidance notes.

Several countries introduced legislation to look at labor issues in the supply chain. One of the first ones that I had to apply to the projects was the UK's Modern Slavery Act (2015). This legislation was aimed at preventing human trafficking, exploitation, and forced labor in the supply chain. In practice, a lot of companies need to have better management systems for their supply chain and report on the implementation of the act. I remember when we started having the conversation around supply chains over ten years ago. We had limited tools for enforcement, and clients had a limited understanding of the issue and its relevance to their operations and projects. How much the world has changed since then! Now all I seem to work on is projects with sensitive questions around supply chain management and mapping, traceability, and potential forced or child labor risks. The common practice I see implemented seems to be the focus on the main suppliers and their supply chain and contractor management systems. In some rare cases, depending on the contextual risk, we might look at the suppliers of the main supplier, the so-called Tier-2 suppliers. EU-wide legislation, the new EU sustainability directives (see Chapter 9 for details), would require this type of due diligence as standard practice for any European company that meets the requirements. Based on conservative estimates, this equates to around fifty thousand companies.

Even if I was trying to be skeptical and critical of this increased interest in the social aspects, I would have to conclude that it all seems to be going in the right direction. The only issue I see is the lack of guidance on what, specifically, this human rights due diligence should look at in detail. I remember how, over ten years ago, we had several internal conversations about how to approach the inclusion of human rights in the performance requirements for clients. One idea was to have them as a separate requirement or standard under the policy. The other idea was to mainstream the relevant human rights in the existing performance standards. The decision was to mainstream partly due to client reluctance to use the term, partly due to the lack of international good practice on the practical implications of separate human rights due diligence—especially when we had the social impact assessments (SIA) as standard requirements. Although there are differences in scope, an SIA would cover most of the key human rights topics. The approach was also to use language that was not offensive or foreign to clients when describing human rights. We talk about the prohibition of child labor or forced labor in PS 2, as well as supply chain and contractor management and freedom of association. Freedom of association refers to the trade unions and other worker representatives who can lead negotiations on collective bargaining for workers. This is an excellent example of the practical implications of the human rights or social performance requirement.

So, yes, despite spending the past fifteenish years working with social impacts, I started to wonder how to define them and improve our understanding of what they actually are. This book aims to explore the concept of social impact and its applications in various contexts from a social performance practitioner's perspective. By examining the theoretical underpinnings of social impact, the challenges of measuring it, and its role in the nonprofit, corporate, and government sectors, the book can provide a broad understanding of the concept and its potential for positive change. The instruments for social impact creation will be explored with their limitations, scopes, challenges, and timing in the investment or business cycle. I also aim to bring you several great initiatives that demonstrate the wonderful benefits of these instruments if used in the right context.

The book is intended for a wide audience, including scholars and students in social sciences, practitioners in the nonprofit and corporate sectors, government policymakers, and any fund-investment management company that works tirelessly to make sense of shareholder expectations. Though the book has technical elements, it is intended to translate the academic and practitioner discourse on social impact assessment, measurement, and management for a wide variety of interested groups, even those without a technical background.

Why Does Social Impact Matter Now?

One of the reasons it is time to open a discussion between social performance practitioners, academics, IFIs, financial institutions, impact investing, and impact-measuring professionals is to clarify the role of each instrument in our common goal of *doing good*. The attention is shifting from the environmental impacts, decarbonization, and climate change mitigation (or *green* investments) to the social aspects of our interventions.

Data on CO_2 emissions, fossil fuels, and renewables have been a topic of discussion for a long time to the extent that many of the major investment companies stopped financing fossil fuel–related projects. The new sustainability reporting requirements and initiatives have a stronger focus on what we would typically cover under a social heading in an SIA, namely supply chain, forced and child labor, stakeholder engagement, and grievance management. The COVID-19 pandemic also turned attention toward employment relations, with layoffs, furlough, and a general shift to remote working. The engagement with stakeholders, whether it is internal (employees) or external (customers, communities around facilities) suddenly took center stage.

If we require so much information to be disclosed, and we want to see businesses *doing good*, how come no one has come up with a practical guide that explains the difference between micro (project) and macro (corporate) level risks and impacts? You will see that a project can be managed sustainably even if it is not a *sustainable* or *green* project by the common metrics set out under ESG. At the same time, a renewable or *green* project can be badly managed, where project-level biodiversity and land impacts are not identified and mitigated adequately. We have often seen that ESG frameworks rate funds based on how *green* their portfolio is—or rather, how many renewable projects they have in comparison to fossil fuels—but they fail to look at the management systems on the asset level. This leads to the false understanding that all renewable projects are *good* and a net benefit for everyone, without acknowledging that any greenfield project—that is, new construction—carries project- and site-level risks and potential adverse impacts.

The conversations we should be having now include the difference between doing something to comply with legislation and going the extra mile voluntarily, or whether the community or stakeholder expectations are even within the scope of the company to solve. I have countless examples of developers building small renewable projects with the locals and NGOs shouting for improved infrastructure, subsidized electricity, improved access to entrepreneurship, and improvements in gender equality. While I recognize that having an IFI involved suggests the added value in nonfinancial benefits, it is often completely outside the project scope, especially for private-sector developers. While the company developing the project will most likely invest in the community, it is not a legal or performance requirement. Project scopes are an important concept to frame discussions about adverse impact mitigation and proactive positive impact creation.

The Impact Jobs vs. Social Impact Jobs

The momentum of ESG, sustainability, and social impact initiatives resulted in an increased drive to recruit people to fill these roles. The first big category of impact jobs is around the creation of impact or impact strategy. I have seen countless job adverts for impact officers, social impact directors, ESG reporters, ESG experts, sustainability officers, CSR officers, and various other combinations of well-known buzzwords. The job descriptions are all related to global sustainability strategies and programs, compliance to obtain favorable ESG ratings, and positive impact creation. As someone who has spent almost fifteen years in the social performance management business, I find myself lost in interpreting what *social impact work* means exactly for a global cosmetics brand, for instance. How do impactful leadership and employee engagement across sustainability and social impact translate into action? What is the required expertise? you may ask, and frankly, I am asking the same. What makes someone a social impact expert? We'll talk about this later.

Other social impact jobs focus on impact measurement and reporting on initiatives. These jobs pop up in a greater number now, as the reporting requirements for companies increase. While impact measurement sounds more target driven and pragmatic, the job, in my reading, is more about data collection and analysis rather than designing the social value strategy. Commercial banks and some funds do offer hybrid jobs where the same team is responsible for impact creation, measurement and reporting. These jobs encompass a variety of activities from implementation of impact strategies, ESG screening of portfolios, and climate accounting. My experience has been that the majority of impact and ESG teams were largely made up of credit risk analysts or bankers with an interest in climate change or the environment. Now, I see the shift in recruitment to focus on EHS (environment, health, and safety) type expertise or specific climate change experts, but the social aspects are still under the radar. Guess that's why I never got a job at any of these places.

Several commercial banks have E&S (environmental and social) teams that cover project finance activities under the Equator Principles. Basically, the banks signatory to the Equator Principles (EP) have to apply IFC Performance Standards to their operations that fall within the scope of EP. The people on the banks' E&S (environmental and social) teams typically have similar backgrounds to me, even if they mainly cover the environmental aspects. These teams were typically made up of people who were considered generalists (i.e., people who could cover the majority of the E&S issues to a certain extent). Historically, environmental specialists would cover environmental topics and stakeholder engagement. The other social aspects, including labor, resettlement, and supply chain, were largely unaddressed. This has changed of course, and now many teams include social specialists like me.

The market today is very much divided: there are ESG reporting roles that focus on corporate-level ESG topics, there are practitioner roles in consultancy, commercial banks, and IFIs, and there are other roles in between focusing on impact investing and CSR. The interesting thing for me is the social impact bond and microfinance type work, where I see very few of my colleagues ending up. These jobs are typically banking and finance by nature with aspirations of defining social impacts and social projects. When we look at a typical social enterprise, I must admit I don't see a lot of my colleagues being involved. The profiles of professionals who are engaged in these roles shaped the industry as a whole. The lack of any sort of technical social expertise, whether it is a labor expert, a supply chain expert, a resettlement expert, or a communication specialist, resulted in other aspects of ESG and sustainability getting the spotlight. Regardless of how we got here, we always have the option to challenge our current modus operandi and update the way we approach, define, demonstrate, and measure social impacts.

My hope is that with better definitions and a common understanding of social impact products and instruments, we can contextualize the evaluation process and reporting on real social impact within the defined scope. We need to step away from generic definitions of social impact to avoid social washing and inflating the benefits of our investments. We need to balance them with the project- or asset-level risks and examine the good and the not-so-good in a more holistic way. The reporting on impacts should be meaningful and informative, even for nontechnical audiences. This only happens if the right kind of people are in charge of any social agenda and have access to the resources.

Why Would You Care What I Think?

So many books are written by people working to create social impacts that the majority of readers should now have a pretty good understanding of the general principles and trends in impact creation. The incredible stories from the field touched our hearts—stories about people accessing microcredit and turning their lives around, about kids no longer starving, having access to education and healthcare, and learning to read and write. While these books are inspirational, they only speak about one initiative that worked in a given country and context. Can these stories scale? Are they replicable? Probably not all of them. The other end of the spectrum includes the more technical books for professional audiences. I realized that most of my colleagues in the social performance field have been publishing very technical books. While these are incredibly informative for our peers, they often fail to convey messages to more mainstream audiences. The wealth of knowledge my fellow practitioners hold could greatly contribute to improving social impact creation and measurement practices. Even if you disagree with some of my ideas or arguments, there is merit in listening to the people who have been implementing social performance management plans for the most significant large-scale infrastructure investments in the world.

The main reason you should care about this book is because it is the very first attempt by a social development specialist to take a step into the mainstream and write about social impacts in the different contexts of ESG, impact investing, CSR, and the like. The lens we use in my world to measure project-level impacts provides valuable feedback on where other social impact products such as ESG, impact investing, and the like could draw some inspiration. All the mainstream books I read as my research were written by investment professionals, businesspeople, economists, and academics. They come with their own set of ideas on impact investing or ESG or how development impact materializes in their world, but very few of them have experience with being there on the ground from project design through construction to operations. The majority never talk to the farmers who are worried about land acquisition or lack of pastureland, families hoping for jobs and a better life, or village leaders trying to negotiate new roads as part of the deal. We social specialists are the ones supporting our clients and IFIs to, first and foremost, mitigate the adverse impacts of the project. The understanding of the perspectives of the affected people and their perception of the impacts provides excellent framing for any assessment of impact creation.

We can argue about a fund's *green* or *social* portfolio, but that gives us no information on how the individual assets are managed. How did they acquire the land for a wind farm? Are people consulted on the impacts and safety features of the hydropower plant? Is there ongoing engagement with locals around the project site? Do they have avenues to raise concerns with the company? The majority of the ESG frameworks take a high-level approach and focus on the macro-level impacts, muting the voices of affected people for the *greater good*. Missing such important aspects of operations and project sites leads to biased claims, inflated positive outcomes, and greenwashing. It wouldn't take much to do a quick assessment of the management practices of portfolio companies and their assets to provide more meaningful reporting on *sustainable assets* and *assets managed sustainably*. The difference is significant: typical sustainable assets nowadays include any renewable project, while sustainable projects or asset management includes having the relevant permits, processes, and management plans in place to mitigate site-specific adverse impacts and safeguard the people living around the project. What a difference.

This book reflects almost fifteen years of coffee-table and lunchtime conversations around the world with the leading experts in the field: IFI staff members, consultants (freelance or employed by the big consulting companies), people working in project implementation, and academics. I also echo some of the feedback we receive from clients who are lost in the endless requirements and expectations, often without a clear guide on outcomes and outputs. The reason I have this overview of the industry is the many organizations, companies, and clients I worked with due to short-term contracts being the industry norm now. In hindsight, it is a great advantage that I have worked for almost all the major IFIs over the years, taking on consulting opportunities either as an individual or in consortium with other consulting firms.

I also wanted to make sure that the mainstream audience is aware of the hard work of my peers. There are truly wonderful social development specialists who spend a lifetime doing good with the tools given to them by IFIs. They should be recognized for their contribution to the sustainable management of many of the world's largest infrastructure investments, the largest mines and manufacturing facilities. Maybe this hard work and dedication to being in the field with the affected people is the reason no one has written this book before.

What Is a Social Development Specialist or a Social Performance Practicioner?

What is a social performance practitioner you may ask. It is one of my great disappointments that in this day and age, not many people outside our industry know us, yet we could be a very useful addition to all your ESG, sustainability, and impact teams. A social performance practitioner's job is to look at a company and its operations to identify the risks and opportunities to improve the way it manages a long list of things. This list includes the company's workforce, occupational health and safety, supply chain, community health, safety and security, impacts on livelihoods and land, engagement with communities affected by their operations, impacts on cultural heritage, vulnerable groups, or human rights. If this all sounds farfetched, I don't blame you. Our assessments are usually commissioned in response to requirements from financing institutions that provide their own framework for the assessment. As a social performance practitioner, I am there on the site, working with real people and seeing real project impacts—positive and negative— such as the creation of jobs, loss of land, loss of access to pastureland or the forest, influx of workers who might disrupt the community in a small village, or impacts on sacred sites that are important to the locals. Everything I do in my current role is a response to an intervention, a project, or a construction that benefits the community or country on a macro level, despite carrying risks on the micro level. My job is to identify those risks and impacts and come up with mechanisms, plans, and ideas to avoid, minimize, mitigate, or compensate for those impacts. My scope is determined by the impacts of the project or the intervention. My main tool is a social impact assessment that follows the internationally acknowledged standard or best practice and a specific set of requirements from the lenders. I know that I—and my client—don't have the scope or, frankly, the responsibility to solve all the issues faced by the locals, especially if those are related to areas that are typically part of the government's responsibilities. The approach is first and foremost the mitigation of construction and operational risks. My colleagues and I spend a lot of time on the client site talking to workers and affected communities directly. This is a very unique insight to many industries and their operations as we see both sides: the client who wants to comply and maybe even go the extra mile, and the affected communities that have fears, concerns and expectations.

A social development specialist is also a professional who focuses on creating positive change and addressing social issues within communities and societies. These specialists play a critical role in promoting social justice, equity, and inclusive development. They possess a deep understanding of social dynamics, community engagement, and sustainable development principles. Social development specialists work in various sectors, including government agencies, nonprofit organizations, international development agencies, and research institutions. Their primary objective is to design, implement, and evaluate programs and policies that address social challenges, improve living conditions, and empower marginalized individuals and communities. Sounds a bit vague—exactly what I want to avoid; however, what's true for social impacts is true for social specialists: the scope, context, and purpose of the role define what it is.

The responsibilities of a social development specialist may include conducting social impact assessments and research to identify social issues and needs, developing strategies to address these issues, and formulating policies and programs that promote social inclusion and equal opportunities. They collaborate with various stakeholders, such as community members, government officials, NGOs, and civil society organizations, to ensure participation and ownership of development processes. These specialists work on a wide range of social issues, such as poverty alleviation, education, health, gender equality, social protection, and community development. They employ a multidisciplinary approach, combining knowledge from fields such as sociology, anthropology, economics, and public policy to understand complex social systems and develop effective interventions.

In addition to program design and implementation, social development specialists also monitor and evaluate the impact of their initiatives, using data and evidence to inform decision-making and improve outcomes. They may engage in capacity-building activities, training community members and local organizations to strengthen their ability to address social challenges and sustain positive change in the long term.

How does one become a social development specialist? I've observed that most of my colleagues have degrees in social sciences, sociology, anthropology, development studies, gender studies, or economic development. The social impact topic used to be covered by economists when it emerged in the 1970s, but that was because they had the tools to do calculations and data analysis, as well as having some social background. As we will see, the discipline emerged as a *sister* of the environmental impact assessment, and economists were better suited to step up than environmental professionals. The reality remains that someone with the right background just *becomes* one through the experience gained on projects. If you are like me, working for IFIs, your focus will narrow to the implementation and compliance with performance standards. While this is a real art—balancing compliance with social development—it is only recently that universities designed programs around it.

My journey began when I graduated with a degree in sociology with a focus on social policy and equal opportunity policies. My degree program had strong statistical and research methods components but not much on project management, impact assessments, or the like. It took me some time to learn the tricks of the trade and be able to use my knowledge in a way that was appropriate to the scope of my role. My development in the role was swift because of some great managers

I had early on in my career. I was not only able to learn from them, but they also provided me with opportunities to figure things out for myself. When I first heard about the safeguarding aspects of social development (i.e., mitigating adverse project impacts), I was fascinated by resettlement and livelihood impact compensation. I spent a lot of time researching best practices, reading guidance notes, and understanding evaluation and calculation methodologies. I guess as trends in the social impact field change, more and more of my peers find themselves learning from various sources to understand issues in detail. When I had more projects with labor issues, I did become a bit of a self-taught labor expert. And the same happened with supply chains and contractor management as well.

So how does one become a social development specialist? Nowadays, you can get the title through education, but it is mainly defined by the scope of your job. We will go through the social impact products and the relevant expertise needed for each one. The generic definition of being a dedicated professional committed to creating inclusive, equitable, and sustainable societies needs some update to reflect the many areas that are covered by these experts now.

Assumptions for This Book

When I started writing this book, I was not sure how the categories and aspects would come together, especially as I was looking at a number of different social impact products. I started calling them social impact products because it made sense to me. These are tools, instruments, and financial products (largely) that are created with the intention of *doing good*. You will see that I put *doing good* and other similar phrases in italics. The purpose of this is not to be sarcastic but rather to contrast the more generic terms that are old and outdated with the more polished and better-defined one I want to offer in this book. I know I tend to sound cynical about exaggerated impacts that are generic, where cause-and-effect isn't obvious. I guess it is partly my very narrowly defined scope when it comes to my work. In any case, this book wants to suggest a more uplifting and hopeful view on the future of the social impact market.

The first assumption I had even before I started writing is that most people want to *do good*, but they often don't know how. This is true for companies and organizations and maybe even for governments, though I tend to not go into politics. The assumption that I applied to the whole of the analysis was that these tools or social impact products are created to enable individuals, corporations, and organizations to deliver positive social change. I do not assume any malicious intent behind any of these, even if the product involves the creation of financial returns in addition to the social. The tools that are developed have a historical root in individuals, families, and companies wanting to provide services, money, and opportunities through the means appropriate to the times. While several tools remained in use over the decades and centuries, the core principles of the tools did not change. This is the reason why the terminology and narrative could not evolve to have the words to describe our *social impact* in a more nuanced and meaningful way.

The second assumption I have throughout the book is that we are in the refinement and redevelopment phase of the social impact market, so the terminology I use is relatively new and often unfamiliar to audiences. While several instruments have been around for a while (SIA and some form of CSR since the seventies; ESG for the past fifteen years or so; impact investing, microfinance, and social enterprises for decades; and philanthropy for hundreds of years), they have not been examined in the context I offer, especially not with the focus on their social impact creation and demonstration. They have not been viewed as members of a broader category of products and tools to create a social (and maybe financial) impact. They were viewed as independent methods to channel funds for separate programs. As each area grew in popularity, companies often found themselves mixing products and boundaries and getting lost in the reporting. Initiatives that used to be simple donations to local organizations and youth sports clubs could not go under the CSR heading of the company, for instance. Each of these social impact products evolved over time, and it is time to pause and examine them in the context of the broader social impact market. There are overlaps and similarities, but there are also very strong differences between them. This view is what I am offering in this book.

Next up is the context of mandatory vs. extra-mile efforts for sustainability and social impact creation. I've noticed that there is a limited awareness of the social impact products that are mandatory, and thus we tend to favor companies that undertake them. This applies to several social factors of ESG but also some SIAs or human rights assessments. To a large extent, the labor-related aspects of ESG (or the *S* in ESG) are stipulated in legislation, yet companies report on them as if they were gracious enough to offer this to their employees. I tend to view compliance based tools as a bare minimum a company can do, especially if these are also legal requirements. The extra-mile type efforts get a lot of attention and publicity in general, but compliance should come first! If a company employs vulnerable groups and turns part of its business into a social enterprise, then, yes, that is the extra mile, but it is not best practice if the labor law is not complied with. My hope for the next chapter of social impact products is that we will be more aware of the reported impacts that result from voluntary and involuntary requirements and thus will be able to differentiate those that are proactively creating positive social impacts from those that merely comply with legislation.

The next assumption is an interesting one, and I have been thinking about it for a long time. It is related to the creation and demonstration of impact. When I started looking at these products, I realized that while many have frameworks or references to demonstrate the created impacts (ESG), others have no such thing because those are more voluntary initiatives. It became clear to me that any social impact matters, even those that cannot be demonstrated. You will see this when you get to the philanthropy chapter. I got very biased when I was writing about it because, essentially, I do believe that even small-scale impacts, although challenging to measure and demonstrate, matter a lot in the grand scheme of things. It is only through my lens as a social performance practitioner that I want to measure and demonstrate impacts in the context of my project. We cannot disregard social impact products just because we have not come up with better ways to measure and demonstrate their impacts with the available tools. What works for one instrument may be irrelevant to another. The reality of the current market is that companies are incentivized to report their impacts in the existing frameworks, and that leads to a bias toward the kind of impacts that fit into these frameworks. Initiatives such as providing scholarships to underprivileged kids, access to healthcare for remote villages around our manufacturing plants, or boreholes to nearby villages do not score high on the frameworks we use to measure sustainability.

My next assumption is related to impact measurement and demonstration as well, but it looks more at the scope and scale of the impact. When I started looking at examples for each product, I came across macro- and micro-level impact claims. The micro-level claims were up front about their activities impacting a small section of society (vulnerable people), a smaller geographic area (a village or territory), or a subsection of the issue (access to healthcare for certain groups of people). These micro-level impacts are not minimal at all but sounded more honest in terms of the scope and target audience of the initiative. In contrast, macro-level claims talked about improved economy, improved healthcare, and services for society. While those might be true because we are all interlinked and the small pieces of the puzzle make it a whole, I was skeptical because the demonstration of the correlation between the initiatives and the macro-level impacts was vague or missing. There might be demonstratable and attributable contributions from an initiative to macro level change, but this should be clarified in the reporting. Do we really believe that if a company is funding a local youth sports club, the "next generation will be more active and less obese, leading to decreased healthcare expenditure for the government"? Surely more access to physical activities can make kids more active, and that can eventually lead to fewer obesity-related diseases, but our initiative is only a small part of the larger picture. You will see that although I do speak of our collective effort to create positive social impact as something that could *make the world a better place* and have a macro impact on *all of society*, this is an indirect collective impact of our work in the many areas covered by social impact products.

The next assumption further relates to impact measuring. Each tool has its own set of standards or best practice to set up indicators and use methodology to manage impacts. These are more and more refined as the industry of impact reporting grows and matures. When I refer to lack of standardization or vague impact measurement in the book, I am not disregarding the efforts that have taken place, I simply acknowledge that the majority of these tools originate from economics, finance, banking that are not -yet- suitable to include the social impact measurement tools. Social impacts, as we will see are rather complex and it is challenging to find meaningful ways for demonstration without adding qualitative indicators.

The last assumption for this book is that while there are impact experts working with professional standards in the field, we can not disregard the important contribution that the social development specialists could have. The expertise is a combination of educational background, skills in research, project management, strategy design etc., and practical experience on the field. While several impact professionals have incredible skills in impact measurement, setting up the indicators and determining what is essential to meaningfully demonstrate impacts require the detailed knowledge of social systems and the practicalities of such systems in a corporate environment.

CHAPTER 1

SOCIAL IMPACT ASSESSMENT

I'm starting the book with an introduction to the social impact assessment (SIA) because this is what I'm most familiar with. Understanding field-level impacts, risks, and opportunities for affected people and the wider population is essential to determine what the best approach is to mitigation. In terms of the social impacts, it is easy to get lost in generic statements such as *engaging with communities*. This very simple phrase means very different things depending on the context. From an ESG perspective, it usually means that the corporation is engaging with customers, NGOs near their HQ. For the SIA practitioner, however, it has a very narrowly defined scope of engaging with communities in the project-affected area. It is important to note early on that SIA is typically used as a tool for compliance, though it is usually not part of any national-level permitting process. The SIA emerged in the 1970s next to the environmental impact assessment (EIA), a process regulated by the Ministries of Environment to obtain permits for construction and operations.

The traditional definition of the SIA is the process of identifying, predicting, and evaluating the potential social impacts of a proposed project or policy. The purpose of the SIA is to ensure that a project's social and cultural aspects are considered in the decision-making process and that the project benefits are accessible to all people in affected communities. SIA is a vital tool for sustainable development—or should be—and the sustainable construction of new infrastructure. It helps identify potential social risks and benefits associated with a project and provides recommendations for mitigating adverse impacts while also enhancing positive ones. This assessment determines how a project or policy will affect the well-being of people in the community, including their livelihoods, social relations, cultural heritage, and access to resources. It also identifies a project's potential environmental impacts, such as ecosystem services, that may affect the community's health and well-being.

An SIA is typically conducted in several phases, including scoping, baseline studies, impact analysis, and recommendations for mitigation and monitoring. The scoping step involves identifying the social, economic, and cultural aspects likely to be affected by the project. The baseline studies phase gathers data on the project-affected area's social and environmental conditions. The impact analysis phase identifies and evaluates the project's potential positive and negative impacts on the community. The mitigation and monitoring phase involves developing strategies to mitigate adverse effects and enhance positive ones and monitoring the implementation of these strategies over time. Mitigation measures are usually included in the project-level Environmental and Social Management Plans.

It's worth noting that the scope of the SIA is very well defined. It is aimed to be a snapshot in time reflecting the local conditions before the external intervention—though for livelihood-related impacts, baseline data ideally covers multiple seasons. The methodology as cited by academics includes the analysis, monitoring, and controlling of any social impacts of the planned interventions. It should also be looking at the broader process of social change induced by an intervention. These are not the types of SIAs I usually see in my work; my clients need to comply with a set of standards to get funding. The main principle and overarching outcome are to not leave people worse off because of the intervention. This is of course more complex because some impacts are challenging to measure or express in monetary terms. How do we price-check the impacts on intangible cultural heritage? Or how do we calculate the value of what is lost in terms of lifestyle? I remember a conversation with a Ugandan fisherman on one of my projects. I asked him what he thinks of the livelihood restoration measures of the project. For him, it included low-effort continuous access to the fish farm. He looked at me and started to explain the benefits of the fish farm. He told me about the training they received, that they can decide what fish to farm and have the knowledge to keep different species together without problems. He felt very happy that his family had food whenever they wanted it. He was a smart man and an optimist, so he focused on the benefits. All these activities for livelihood restoration were agreed upon with the community before, so we tailored the interventions mainly to their needs and wants. I then asked him whether there was anything from his old way of life that he missed. He looked at me with a big smile on his face as he told me about the early mornings out on the river with his friends. They go out to fish, but it is more than that, it is bonding with friends and family, forming a community. Some days were better for fishing, while other days they could spend hours without catching enough. Being out on the river was a way for them to connect. It was building a community, and it filled their lives with a sense of belonging. This is what their fathers and grandfathers and great-grandfathers were doing, after all. At the end of the conversation, we just stood there looking at each other, silently understanding that everything in life is a trade-off: you lose something, you gain something else. He chose to appreciate the positives.

This fisherman is one of the many, many people I met through my work that I will remember forever. Standing in the Ugandan sun next to the artificial ponds of fish, I understood the development benefit of providing them with reliable, accessible, nutritious food. Yet, at that moment, I felt like everything I knew about life was challenged. Surely people want access to reliable nutritious food, even if that comes at a price. I was standing there with all my Western beliefs and university education and ethnography classes, and I felt like we'd disrupted something incredibly meaningful. The next step after the site visit was going back to the office, where we celebrated our green loan with a high ESG score and low carbon emissions. There seemed to be a significant disconnect between this achievement and the field and project-level impacts. But how do I explain everything that I learned to a banker? What is the monetary value of sitting on a boat with friends watching the sunrise?

If you're reading about SIAs for the very first time: don't get discouraged if you feel like you still have no idea what it is or what it measures. For the purposes of international financial institution (IFI) financing, an SIA is the typical representation of an impact assessment, and this is carried out for high-risk projects (Category A and B projects that carry significant, irreversible adverse environmental and/or social risks). IFIs include the World Bank Group, the International Finance Corporation (IFC), the European Bank for Reconstruction and Development (EBRD), the Asian Infrastructure Investment Bank (AIIB), and the Asian Development Bank (ADB), among others. The SIA is prepared in combination with the EIA, focusing on the IFI's standards or performance requirements to make sure that relevant project impacts are captured. This usually includes the risk screening of social impacts, management systems, stakeholder engagement, grievance management, labor and working conditions, supply chain management, community health, safety, and security, impacts on land and livelihoods, physical or economic displacement, impacts on indigenous peoples, cultural heritage, and to a large extent, gender and human rights.

In an ideal world, a lending institution needs an SIA that provides coverage on current baseline conditions related to the above mentioned topics, an assessment of the existing or planned management systems of the client, an assessment of potential impacts, and a set of mitigation measures. These magical mitigation measures cover the policies (such as an HR policy or a health and safety policy), management plans (traffic management plan, stakeholder engagement plan, grievance mechanism), and procedures that will be put in place for the construction and operations phase. The management plans typically make up the company's Environmental and Social Management System (ESMS)—ideally on a corporate level but more commonly on a project or operations level. This ESMS comprises the underlying management plans that aim to translate the mitigation measures into actionable tasks with timelines, responsible parties, and completion indicators included. In an ideal world, these plans communicate with each other and consistently contain the same information for the specific project or operations they cover.

I have come across a few other SIAs that were measuring the impacts of policy-type interventions. I do not have a lot of experience with such SIAs, and it is more challenging for me to work with abstract indicators as opposed to real visible impacts at this point.

In any case, the SIA is also designed to create a more sustainable, socioculturally equitable, and economically sustainable environment. The aim is also to foster community development and empowerment, build capacity, and create social capital. The SIA could be a tool to help communities and other stakeholders identify development goals and maximize positive results in addition to the risk mitigation aspects. A good SIA incorporates local knowledge and applies participatory methods to understand the concerns of interested and affected parties. The active involvement of communities ensures that the management policies, programs, and plans address the real and perceived impacts on the given community.

The best SIA practice recognizes that social, economic, and biophysical consequences are intrinsically and irrevocably linked. Any change in one of these domains will result in a change in the other. As a result, an SIA must establish a grasp of the impact pathways that are produced when a change in one area affects the other, as well as the iterative or flow-on implications within each field. In other words, second- and higher-order consequences, as well as cumulative repercussions, must be considered.

While the SIA is often used to analyze the social implications of planned actions, the approaches of the SIA may also be used to consider the social impacts of other sorts of events, such as disasters, demographic change, and epidemics. I am eager to see what's next for SIAs, especially now that the mainstream is so focused on human rights impact assessment that greatly overlaps with topics covered in SIAs.

The SIA is best understood as an overarching framework that encompasses the assessment of all human effects and how individuals and communities interact with their sociocultural, economic, and biophysical environments. As a result, the SIA has strong links to a wide range of specialist subfields involved in the assessment of areas such as aesthetic impacts (landscape analysis), archaeological and cultural heritage impacts (both tangible and intangible), community impacts, cultural impacts, demographic impacts, development impacts, economic and fiscal impacts, influx of workers, access to health care, gender impacts. It also looks at impacts on indigenous rights; infrastructure, leisure, and tourism impacts; political impacts (human rights, governance, democratization, etc.); poverty; psychological impacts; resource issues (access and ownership of resources); impacts on social and human capital; and other societal impacts. As a result, a thorough SIA is typically performed by a group rather than a single individual. Now that you know what it is, next, we'll cover how we do the SIA and how we can capture these complex social structures within it.

What Is an SIA?

We looked at the definition in the intro, so I'll go straight to the practical aspects. The SIA is usually carried out by a qualified consultant based on a Terms of Reference developed by the project company in agreement with the lenders. There's a lot to unpack here, but bear with me. This example will be walking through the SIA process for IFI compliance—my typical day at work.

Most companies start talking to potential financiers in the early development stage of the project. Let us use a very practical example. Let's say company X is developing a photovoltaic plant—that's a power plant that uses solar panels—in country Z. Company X already negotiated with the government of country Z to ensure that the land allocated for the project is designated for such activities. They even negotiate a power purchase agreement. Company X now has the land and a buyer for the electricity. As a next step, company X starts talking to the usual suspects. Since it is a private-sector project, it is most likely IFC, EBRD, AIIB, EIB, or ADB—these are the IFIs—depending on the geographic coverage of the bank. The IFIs allocate a team to cover financial, environmental, social, governance, credit risk, and other aspects of the project. This is where my work begins. The scope is defined by the financing instrument, as leverage differs for project finance, corporate loans, bond deals.

Company X has done this before, so they already have a reputable consultancy on board, who developed some sort of scoping assessment or documentation for this new project. Company X also has corporate-level policies that were accepted by IFIs before for similar projects. They have a set of generic management plans (we call this an environmental and social management system or framework) that need a little tweaking to adapt to the site conditions and project specifics, and then they are good to go.

The IFI team discusses the need for an ESIA given the risk categorization of the project. Because the environment and people are inextricably linked, an EIA and the SIA are frequently performed in tandem. This is the ESIA. Company X already knows that it needs a national EIA for permitting purposes, so it usually tries to save on the cost by combining the two (EIA and SIA). The international requirements are generally more stringent for most of the environmental topics. The IFI team, together with company X, agree on a Terms of Reference (TOR) for this ESIA that provides some background on the project, the objectives and scope of the assignment, and the expected deliverables and reporting.

The social aspects of the SIA typically correspond to the IFI requirements and standards, since the whole purpose of the SIA is to comply with IFI standards and suggest measures that make the project compliant with them. Such requirements look at the general management systems, policies, and processes of company X and/or its project company (it might be a special-purpose vehicle or a joint venture), covering the performance standards I listed earlier. For a reminder, I include the list here: labor and working conditions, supply chain management, contractor management, stakeholder engagement, management of worker and community complaints, community health, safety, and security, impacts on land and livelihoods, potential physical or economic displacement, and impacts on cultural heritage and indigenous people.

This is the point where I need to raise the issue of SIA for IFI compliance vs. the broader implications explained in the introduction of this chapter. The reason some of the intangible social impacts such as community cohesion, voice, and agency are not included in the typical IFI-compliant SIA but sometimes might be incorporated in the TOR. It would be great to be able to capture all kinds of social impacts, but IFIs can only reference their safeguard standards when contractually requiring company X to comply in order to get the investment. Any cost-conscious private-sector company, regardless of their social sensitivity, wants to make sure the services they are paying for will suffice. Fascinating, isn't it? Company X is paying a consultant to identify *half* the impacts? Not quite! They are working on identifying the impacts that are within the scope of the project, that are directly or indirectly caused by the project, and that need to be mitigated.

The definition of *social license to operate* has been around for quite some time now, especially used by mining companies. For these companies, it is important to be on *good terms* with the communities where they operate because of the high environmental and social risks of their operations. They understand the element of compensation for any direct impacts of their projects and in general are looking for additional ways to promote local development in these communities. They engage with representatives of the communities and try to understand the sensitive cultural contexts they operate in. To give you some tangible examples, I was helping out on a mining project where a cemetery had to be resettled in a developing country. The issue here was not only the logistics of moving coffins and tombs but also the spiritual connection to the burial site and the cultural disapproval of disturbing the spirits. In circumstances like this, it is not enough to compensate for project impacts ("we'll build you a better cemetery"). One must also discuss the culturally appropriate ways to make it happen. In some cases, the company has to finance an additional ceremony and accommodate the date and time (around a religious holiday or depending on the moon phases). What is the true cost of delaying construction by five months because you wait for the right moon phase to remove a cemetery? What if the alternative is locals protesting and delaying your permit?

The next step in our company X example is the consultant starting the preparation of the SIA. The project's affected area is determined, and the stakeholders are mapped based on proximity to the project area and main infrastructure—or where the probability of experiencing an impact is the highest. An analysis of alternatives for every (E)SIA is included in the final report as well. The parameters and indicators are well defined: the topics covered by the TOR. It must be noted that for the ESIA to progress, the project needs to have at least some initial design where the main project infrastructure is configured and the site is selected. The ESIA needs to know whether the project has access roads, where those are likely to be, whether there is a worker camp planned (remote projects), and any associated facility (a facility whose capacity, size, output, etc. changes due to the project).

An SIA typically includes the following steps:

1.   *Scoping.* Defining the scope and objectives of the assessment, which communities are affected, the project footprint, the area of influence, and the project-affected area. Yes, these all mean very different things! The scoping also provides for an assessment of preliminary impacts that we would anticipate based on the type of project.

2.   *Stakeholder consultation.* Engaging with affected communities and stakeholders to gather information and perspectives. This is also to provide information on the impact assessment process, the project in general, and the most likely impacts. It is essential that expectations are managed early on, especially with respect to the anticipated project benefits. Too often, people expect many.

3.   *Collection of secondary and primary data.* Statistics on the demographics, education, governance structure, local authorities, employment, and more are gathered from secondary sources to provide the context for the study. There is also primary data collection sampling directly affected people.

4.   *Analysis.* Examining the potential impacts and risks of the intervention and assessing their magnitude, their significance, their lifespan, and whether any residual impacts are expected after mitigation. This is, in my opinion, the most important section, where actual project impacts are looked at. How many jobs will be created in the short and long term? According to the baseline data, how many of those jobs could be filled by locals? Will there be a construction camp? Whose land will be expropriated or acquired? Will the project impact agricultural or pastureland

that is used as a primary source of income for the family? Are there indigenous peoples? Who is vulnerable to project impacts? Are the access roads and main transportation roads passing by sensitive social receptors (schools, hospitals, elderly care homes, remote villages, etc.)? Will houses be damaged by the vibrations of heavy goods vehicles (need for dilapidation survey for potential future claims)? Is there anything specific the locals mentioned during the consultation, such as special requests to stop work for religious holidays?

I've had several huge projects where the contractor built a whole village of workers for the duration of the construction phase. We're often talking about five to seven years or more! The largest number of workers I've seen on a project was around sixty thousand. That's right, a whole small town of people moving to a remote area for years to work on a large project. There can be cultural sensitivities and conflicts, even when workers are from the same nationality or ethnic background, let alone when people speak different languages and come from different parts of the world.

I have talked about the scope and how some impacts are not within scope. This changes for education and healthcare when workers move with families. I must admit, I've only seen this on one of my projects, but I know it can be a real thing. On this project, the contractor provided accommodation for workers who could upgrade (for a fee) to family accommodations and have their wives and children live with them. In this case, the influx of workers and people section of the (E)SIA should specifically mention that a relatively large number of people will join the project site in addition to the workers. These people will need food, education, and access to a doctor, and this will put additional stress on the local infrastructure. An experienced social specialist uses stakeholder engagement with mayors and village leaders to inquire how locals feel about this, where they think the infrastructure is insufficient for accommodating the new people, and what solution they would want to see.

Cases like this always remind me of my favorite ethnography classes at the Corvinus University of Budapest, where we talked about appropriate methods for participatory observation. The main criticism of ethnographic research was that the researcher saw the events from their point of view based on their cultural background, belief systems, and knowledge acquired over time. It is inevitable that our experiences and world view would shape what we think is best for people, but this can lead to suboptimal outcomes for locals because we have little knowledge or understanding of the ecosystem in which they are operating. The main purpose of the SIA, other than addressing real impacts, is to deal with perceived ones and consider the fears and concerns of locals.

5. *Mitigation and enhancement.* Developing strategies to minimize negative impacts and maximize positive impacts. This section of the (E)SIA is a collection of the actions that will be taken by relevant parties (developer, local government, contractors) to address the impacts identified above. This is where the discussions around cost, viability, and reality hit. The recommendations typically include an elaborate set of management plans that address various aspects of the project. There is an overarching framework document or manual called Environmental and Social Management System

(ESMS). This framework lists the impacts identified in the (E) SIA and the mitigation measures suggested. For each topic, there is a list of documents, policies, or management plans developed and implemented by the relevant party (developer, contractor, or local government). The management plans cover various areas: human resources management, local content (employing and procuring from locals), contractor management, occupational health and safety, community health and safety, construction traffic management, livelihood restoration, waste management, hazardous waste management, wastewater and water management—the list goes on. Each of these plans should be a document that lays out procedures to address risks with the assigned responsibility and timelines specific to the actual project. These plans should not be generic but should be tailored to the project site to reflect actual risks and impacts. Bigger contractors who do this type of construction work often have generic policies and plans that are then tailored to every new project. This saves time and demonstrates their commitment.

6. *Monitoring and evaluation.* Ongoing monitoring and assessment of the implementation of the management plans, mitigation measures, and other action plans in response to the identified (environmental and) social impacts. Typically, for high-risk projects and greenfield construction, significant impacts on biodiversity or social receptors require quarterly construction monitoring—biannual at minimum. In the operations phase, we monitor annually based on the agreed-upon reporting template. The monitoring includes site visits by the lender group or their independent advisors. The indicators for monitoring typically correspond to the desired outcomes of the management plans.

Now that company X has its (E)SIA, it can go back to the IFIs to discuss whether the proposed mitigation measures and management plans comply with the requirements and ultimately negotiate the contract. There is typically an Environmental and Social Action Plan (ESAP) attached to the financing agreement, making the environmental and social commitments contractually binding.

What happens to SIAs that are not undertaken for compliance? Quite frankly, I have yet to see one. The SIA by definition can be used to assess and predict development interventions' potential positive and negative impacts on social well-being, equity, human rights, and sustainability. The SIA can also be used to identify and understand a development's social and cultural dimensions and ensure that a project's benefits and costs are fairly distributed among affected communities. If this sounds like word salad to you, you're not alone. Without having a clear definition of scope and purpose, the SIA is just a broad assessment of social changes that might be connected to a policy or program.

The Purpose, the Scope, and the Timing of the SIA

Purpose

The SIA aims to identify, predict, and evaluate the potential social impacts of a proposed project on the affected communities and stakeholders. The SIA for IFI compliance works based on a TOR that is agreed upon by the lender group and the developer to respond to a set of requirements. It is very important to note that by impact, we mean the project impact—nothing less, nothing more.

The SIA's main purpose is the identification and understanding of social and cultural dimensions of development project. It also wants to ensure that these considerations are included in the decision-making, together with any potential social risk and benefit associated with a project. The SIA also sets out the plan for mitigation and compensation of adverse impacts, as well as enhancements of positive impacts. The compensation measures should be allocated fairly amongst affected communities proportionate to the anticipated adverse impacts. The SIA's stakeholder engagement component provides for community participation in decision-making while promoting transparency and accountability. The SIA also sets out the indicators and frequency for monitoring based on the identified impacts.

Scope

The scope of the SIA should be broad enough to capture all potential social impacts of the project but narrow enough to be manageable within the available resources and time. The spatial scope of the SIA should include an analysis of the project's social, economic, cultural, and environmental dimensions with the project's footprint, affected area, and area of influence. The project footprint is typically the location of the main infrastructure (e.g., the wind farm). The affected area includes any areas with close proximity to the project's associated infrastructure, such as access roads, substations, or worker accommodations. The area of influence covers the broader area around the project, including communities that might not be neighboring the project site or any of its main infrastructure but are likely going to be affected to various degrees.

The time scope of the SIA usually covers the construction and operations phases. I have seen some SIAs mentioning decommissioning. That's when the infrastructure's useful life is over, and it is basically demolished or repurposed.

The content scope of the SIA should include any project impact that corresponds to IFI requirements of compliance. These requirements are not much different from what I would look at for "SIA for fun" type work:

- *Social impacts.* The SIA may consider the potential effects on local communities, including changes in livelihood, employment, income, education, health, and social relations.

- *Economic impacts.* The SIA may assess the potential economic effects of a project, including changes in market conditions, trade, investment, and production, as well as impact on the local economy and labor markets.

- *Cultural impacts.* The SIA may evaluate the potential effects of a project on cultural heritage, traditions, and values, as well as the potential for conflicts between different cultural groups.

- *Environmental impacts.* The SIA may analyze the potential effects of a project on natural resources, ecosystems, and biodiversity, as well as the potential for pollution, waste, and climate change.

- *Gender and social equity impacts.* The SIA may identify and address the potential effects of a project on gender and social equity, including issues related to access to resources, power relations, and participation in decision-making.

- *Human rights impacts.* The SIA may consider the potential effects of a project on human rights, including issues related to access to justice, freedom of expression, and protection from discrimination and violence.

- *Indigenous peoples' impacts.* The SIA may assess the potential effects of a project on indigenous peoples' rights and interests, including issues related to land tenure, resource use, and cultural heritage.

- *Health impacts.* The SIA may evaluate the potential effects of a project on the health of local communities, including issues related to exposure to hazardous materials, water and air pollution, and disease.

- *Social resilience impacts.* The SIA may assess the potential effects of a project on the social resilience of communities, including their ability to cope with and adapt to social and environmental changes.

- *Mitigation and monitoring strategies.* The SIA may provide recommendations for mitigating adverse impacts and enhancing positive ones, as well as monitoring the implementation of these strategies over time.

It seems broad but remember that not all of these aspects are relevant to every project.

Timing

The SIA should be conducted early in the project cycle, ideally during the planning stage, to ensure the assessment findings can influence decision-making. The project site needs to be selected for the consultant to be able to start any kind of work. It is imperative that we know some rough estimates of the construction length, the number of workers needed, and a few other parameters. Early engagement of an SIA practitioner can help identify and address potential social risks associated with the project and provide for changing the project design to avoid adverse effects. The full SIA is usually prepared after the scoping for the project has taken place, when the individual project already has a preliminary design. Note that EIA and SIA (or even better ESIA) findings often have an impact on the final design of each project. This is to avoid, minimize, or mitigate any adverse environmental and/or social impact and to make sure the engagement with stakeholders is meaningful enough that their feedback and concerns are taken into account when finalizing the project design.

Limitations

My review would not be complete without mentioning a few limitations of each social impact instrument. The SIA designed for compliance purposes often has a limited scope. I have seen assessments where far-reaching conclusions were drawn. For example, a rural electrification project will bring economic benefits though reliable electricity for manufacturing, education, and healthcare. This might be true, but the project (i.e., building the overhead powerlines), will not in itself give everyone access, equal access, or affordable/subsidized access to electricity. It's simply not in the scope of the project to provide this access, or even to provide the pricing of the electricity for the residents of that area.

The following are the typical limitations and criticisms that the SIA has received:

- *Subjectivity.* The SIA relies heavily on the subjective judgments and opinions of the assessors and affected people, which can lead to inconsistencies and inaccuracies in the assessment findings. The objectivity of the assessors can be influenced by their personal biases, values, and interests. The survey questionnaires often build on perceptions and perceived impacts that can distort the mitigation measures and make us focus on the "wrong" thing.

- *Predictive uncertainty.* The SIA is often conducted before the project is implemented, based on assumptions and predictions of the potential impacts. There may be uncertainties and unpredictability in the actual effects after implementing the project.

- *Data limitations.* The SIA requires a large amount of data to establish the baseline conditions of the site and assess a project's potential social impacts accurately. However, data collection can be expensive and time consuming and may only sometimes be available or reliable. Secondary data is not always available or recent, which makes triangulation or other respectable research validation methods challenging.

- *Stakeholder bias.* The SIA may aspire to have meaningful participation and input from all relevant stakeholders, but in reality, some stakeholders might be more vocal than others, thus distorting the community feedback. Furthermore, this might lead to incomplete or inaccurate assessment of potential impacts.

- *Defined scope.* The SIA may only sometimes consider all relevant social, economic, cultural, and environmental factors that may be affected by a project. Time, resources, or expertise may limit the scope of the SIA. This typically happens when developers miss out on a joint ESIA and want to get the SIA for compliance very fast. In this case, they provide a more limited scope to gather data and just want the final product to obtain financing.

- *Implementation challenges.* The SIA recommendations for

mitigating adverse impacts and enhancing positive ones may be abstract, without providing developers with pragmatic, actionable tasks. The effectiveness of the SIA depends on the ability to translate recommendations into practical action.

As we have seen, the SIA is a study of many different subjects: archaeology in the project area, cultural heritage, ecosystem services, gender, human rights, and so on. Some projects have additional human rights impact assessments or gender impact assessments that go somewhat beyond the initial SIA scope.

How It Relates to Other Social Impact Products

In my view, the SIA should be much better utilized in the context of other social impact products. It would serve as a useful source of information on project-level risks, impacts, and measures to manage an asset in a sustainable or ESG-friendly manner. The baseline data and feedback from communities could help identify CSR activities, opportunities to invest in the community, and their activities.

In addition, the SIA is related to several other types of assessments and evaluations used to understand the potential social, economic, cultural, and environmental impacts of a project, program, policy, or action:

- *Environmental Impact Assessment (EIA).* The EIA is a process that assesses the potential environmental impacts of a project or development.

- *Health Impact Assessment (HIA).* The HIA is a process that assesses the potential health impacts of a project, policy, or program.

- *Gender Impact Assessment (GIA).* The GIA is a process that assesses the potential differential impacts of a project or policy on different genders. Note here: SIAs often mainstream gender and apply a gender lens when assessing social impacts.

- *Human Rights Impact Assessment (HRIA).* The HRIA is a process that assesses the potential impacts of a project or policy on human rights.

- *Community-Based Monitoring and Evaluation (CBM&E).* The CBM&E involves local communities in monitoring and evaluating the social impacts of a project.

CSR, ESG, impact investing, and social bonds currently don't really use any of the SIA-related terminology or approaches. I am a great believer that implementing SIA methodology would greatly benefit these social impact products. Applying this methodology would support refining the scope of the interventions, target beneficiaries, and measurement of outcomes. The SIA is a great tool that would improve the planning and reporting on these other social impact products immensely. Baseline data collection would be especially helpful to demonstrate the positive social impacts, and micro- or asset-level information on management plans and site-specific impacts would provide an additional layer of information for a full picture of opportunities and challenges.

What Is the Social Impact?

This is the exciting part of every section because these are real-life examples of social impacts. For some chapters, you will see this section be more generic, macro level with buzzword-sounding claims. This is not to say that the impact is not there, but rather to emphasize that we don't have the right framing and words to put things into context. The social impact here is largely measurable, predictable, and mitigable by experienced professionals. I have provided some examples earlier: the creation of short-term jobs for construction and long-term jobs for the operations phase of a project, impacts on productive land and livelihoods, access to natural resources, impacts on cultural heritage, and houses being damaged from construction traffic–induced vibration. The SIA can also provide frameworks to assess more intangible impacts such as changes in community cohesion or aspects of vulnerability to project impacts. The SIA for compliance works with a very specific purpose and scopes the communities, areas, and impacts within the project area of influence. There is little guesswork involved in whether an impact is there or whether someone is affected by the project. It's well described in the document.

My opinion is that the SIA provides the most tangible measurement of social impact with the relevant context well explained. Yes, I may be biased. We have baseline preproject data, and we can see the impacts manifest. We can evaluate the mitigation measures during the preconstruction, construction, and operations phases. There is little doubt whether an intervention is working or whether people are better off because it is measurable. Some indicators related to livelihoods or income levels may require triangulation because they're based on self-assessment. Nevertheless, how people feel or perceive the project's impacts on their daily lives is important. The affected population is well defined from the beginning of the project and is refined during the SIA phase. The size and composition of this defined population are unlikely to change significantly; if they do, they will be in line with local demographic trends.

The vague social impacts included in the definition translate into measurable and often visible impacts as the project nears its completion. For instance, where there was once pastureland, there is now a reservoir, and new areas have opened for grazing animals. The impacts are visible and very real. If I continue to work on the project, I see every aspect personally partly due to the biannual construction monitoring visit and partly because my job is to follow up with affected people. I often have the chance to follow families over the years throughout the different project cycles. I sometimes go to their houses. I see their kids grow up, and I see them start new jobs and businesses. I know the names of their dogs and cats. We have tea and talk about life. Seemingly, we have very little in common, but in reality, we are very similar. We want to be safe and loved, surrounded by our family and friends.

One of my most memorable projects was a solid waste project in central Asia. I remember showing up on the site and seeing hundreds of waste pickers working on the open landfill site, collecting recyclable materials. There was a group of women working together in their DIY protective equipment while their kids sat on piles of rubbish and ate lunch. I was not supposed to go on-site, according to the risk assessment of my company, but how could I not see the project for myself? There was no way I was going to just sit in the car while our consultants went and talked to the people. I wanted to talk to the people and hear their concerns in their own words. There is a saying that you should walk a mile in someone's shoes before judging them. I wanted to walk the mile and understand what life was like for them compared with how it could be after the project ended. I remember looking at the children eating, playing, and doing their homework. This further strengthened my determination to make the most of the livelihood restoration program. I understood the feelings and concerns—some tangible, some more intangible, some perceived, and some very real.

If there's one thing I've learned about working with people on the ground, it's that the way people perceive the issues matters. It can be a minor thing for us, but for them, it could be life changing. The impacts this waste project had on these people were incredible. We designed mechanisms they could use to register for official employment, social security, and even work on the new solid waste facility with a real employment contract. We needed an amazing team of social development specialists to contextualize the issues with transitioning to this new life. Previously, the people were paid daily, so a monthly salary was not desirable to them. There was a sense of shame attached to working with waste, so many turned down formal employment in the facility. There was also a sense of shame and secrecy around the actual amount of money they made—even when we tried to work with salary ranges in line with minimum wage and average wage in the region.

Yes, a social impact in the SIA context refers to the adverse and positive impacts in relation to a project, program, or policy. But it's a lot more. It's the visible changes in the quality of life, access to resources, economic opportunities, and social cohesion for the people affected by the project. When done right, the social impact can change lives. I still remember a hydropower project I had in Pakistan, where we had to physically displace four villages due to the project and its associated infrastructure. The people were living in a very rural area, in modest conditions to say the least. We did our typical census and survey of people and assets to calculate compensation and plan the relocation. I'd had limited exposure to real developing countries before, where people did not have access to basic infrastructure and facilities. One might argue what a developing country is, but let's just say a very low-income country where people in semiurban and rural areas have no access to basic sanitation and water infrastructure, and their houses are constructed of plywood, mud, or other

DIY materials. In the case of my project, when we started discussions with local village leaders about what the physical displacement meant for them, they had one request. They wanted food packages, flashlights and oil lamps, blankets, and basic medicines for the affected families. I didn't quite understand the request because every time I'd done resettlement before, people were happy to take the replacement land or the cash. I'd never faced this level of poverty before, and I was unsure whether we had the scope to address it long term within the SIA constraints. The developer agreed to draft a Community Investment Plan specific to the project-affected people to provide them with ongoing investment in local education and finance improvement of community infrastructure. This was their site-specific CSR and philanthropy program.

People don't have to be low income or vulnerable to perceive the impacts as detrimental or life changing. I had another hydro project in a low-to-middle-income country where people were not living in the kind of poverty I described before. Yet, when it came to livelihood and land impacts, they just wanted the monetary compensation so they could buy a small flat in the regional capital and get away from the mountains. They said that their land, though valuable, had no value to anyone else. No one would move to a highly seismic area of the country, far from civilization, into a small village and pay enough for their land that they could get out of this trap, as they said. This is a great example of how social development means very different things to different people.

The main principle for land impact compensation, especially agricultural land, is to offer another piece of land that is similar in size and quality so people can continue deriving income from this activity. We always say that there is no cookie-cutter solution for social impacts, and I have seen on numerous occasions that this is indeed true. That is why it's important to engage with the affected people and listen to what they have to say. It's more challenging to justify overriding our rules when we try to demonstrate compliance with the IFIs, but it's worthwhile to see the impact it makes on people's lives.

Another interesting project that involves resettlement and vulnerable groups relates to infrastructure construction in a Balkan country. This project started before I joined the bank, but I was involved in implementation monitoring for several years. I even had the chance to see the final infrastructure after it was completed while I was there for another project. This project was special for many reasons. The project involved the construction of a bridge access road in a capital city with a few hundred undocumented people living in tented villages under the bridge. These people had to be resettled and compensated for impacts, yet the social team working on the project achieved a lot more. They recognized the lack of financial literacy and the other elements of the culture of poverty that could lead to spending the compensation money in a way that risked further impoverishment. It was almost unbelievable to see people with no national IDs and children whose births were not registered. The social program included training sessions on concepts related to financial literacy, opening bank accounts, and applying for national ID cards. The team also organized a way to connect them to the employment office so they could apply for jobs and helped families enroll their kids in formal education. Many families went from living in a shed with seasonal employment and no access to education, healthcare, drinking water, or a toilet to having a house with running water, a proper bathroom, a job, kids in school, and the ability to manage a basic household budget. It was the work of a fantastic team whose members were not only experienced and knowledgeable but also caring. They cared about the people and what the opportunity to receive compensation and access to better housing meant to them. I have goosebumps just thinking of the photos I saw before and after the project. This is the true power of the SIA in action!

Some might argue that the SIA is basically common sense: you bump into someone and spill their coffee, so you offer to buy them another one. But it is so much more than that. With the data collected and the meaningful engagement with locals, there is a wealth of information on what the community needs and wants. Surely, anyone undertaking such work needs to be prepared to deliver clear messages about what is within the scope of the project and what other impacts may or may not be addressed. Luckily, there are people like me who can help companies do that. The more companies engage with the people they affect, the more they will open up to criticism. I always tell my clients that given the opportunity, we could all think of a few complaints to raise. I view grievance mechanisms as a way to start a dialogue. Initially, I expect a flood of negative feedback, but addressing them shows that the company is transparent, accountable, and responsible, which will eventually build trust with communities.

While land acquisition is not included in the book in detail, most of my examples are related to land and livelihood impacts. This is the area I specialized in during the first ten years of my career and probably something I am most passionate about. That's because this is probably one of the more complex and personal topics. I once had to do training on PS 5 Land acquisition and involuntary resettlement requirements for a Chinese contractor who was constructing a project in another country. I thought long and hard about how to bring this topic closer to a bunch of Chinese engineers. Then I reflected on my own experiences around moving houses, cities, countries, and continents and the challenges I faced despite the positive context of moving for education, opportunities, or love. The next morning, I asked the training participants to reflect on the challenges they faced in the same situation. There were several moving stories, along with some tears and heavy hearts. Everyone understood the assignment. Everyone walked a mile in the shoes of the villagers, who would be moved so the region could have a hydropower plant and access to reliable electricity.

The challenge is to conceptualize the social impact because we want to focus on the broader *good* of our intervention and fail to notice the risks and adverse impacts on the site and project levels. Some social impacts are real, while others are more of a perception. How to quantify and put a monetary value on some of the impacts I shared with you in the section? No matter how many projects I see, I always keep my white-belt mentality. The white-belt mentality means that I am open to learning, listening to the affected people, and deviating from the norm if that benefits the people most. Where possible, I aim to maximize positive impacts within the limits of the scope to ensure that companies are contractually required to turn an adverse impact into an opportunity to change lives. I don't always succeed, but I always try.

SIA Done Right

The one question that's always at the forefront of my mind is how to use SIA as a tool to identify development opportunities. When an SIA is done right, stakeholders feel empowered to participate in the process, there is a timely collection of data that feeds into the assessment, and mitigation measures are meaningful and pragmatic. Effective SIA practices consider local knowledge and experience. This can be especially valuable when working in areas where communities have unique values and perspectives. The perfect SIA acknowledges the aspects that are looked at for compliance purposes but also goes a step further to identify any proactive ways to ensure economic or community development for affected people. This really is the dream.

Here are a few examples of SIAs that were done in a not-for-compliance context that are worth mentioning:

- *The Jubilee Debt Campaign.* This is a UK-based charity that works to end poverty caused by unjust debt. The organization conducted an SIA of the Jubilee 2000 campaign, which aimed to cancel the unpayable debts of the world's poorest countries. The SIA found that the campaign had contributed to significant debt relief for these countries and had improved their social and economic conditions.

- *The London 2012 Olympic and Paralympic Games.* This event incorporated a comprehensive SIA into its planning process. The evaluation identified the games' potential social impacts, such as residents' displacement, changes to local businesses, and disruptions to transport and infrastructure. The review informed the design of the games and enabled the effective management of social impacts during the event.

- *The Citi Foundation.* This is a global philanthropic organization that supports economic empowerment and financial inclusion for low-income individuals and communities. The foundation conducted an SIA of its Pathways to Progress program, which aims to improve the economic mobility of young people in urban areas. The evaluation found that the program had contributed to improved participants' employment and education outcomes and strengthened local communities.

- *The Baha Mar Resort in The Bahamas.* The Baha Mar Resort, a luxury hotel and casino complex, conducted an SIA before its construction. The evaluation identified potential social impacts of the development, such as displacement of local residents and adverse effects on the natural environment. The assessment informed the project's design and enabled effective social impact mitigation during construction and operation.

These are just a few examples of SIAs outside my typical scope of operation that have been done properly. I could give you countless project examples, but I want to bring this experience closer to nontechnical audiences with projects that are easier to imagine. I would invite you to go on the websites of any IFI and look for the project disclosures. For every high-risk project, you will find the ESIA disclosed together with any additional resettlement and livelihood restoration plan.

Conclusion

The SIA is a great tool for assessing the potential social impacts of a project or program. It involves systematically gathering information, analyzing data, and engaging stakeholders to understand the possible social effects and inform decision-making. There is a difference between SIAs that are undertaken for compliance to obtain financing from IFIs and SIAs that are undertaken without having the thematic framework (standards) for the assessment. There is also a difference between project SIAs that result in a series of management plans with pragmatic actions to address project impacts during construction and operations phases and SIAs that aim to demonstrate the success of an initiative in more general terms by presenting a snapshot in time.

Social impacts are often subjective and difficult to measure. Perceptions and opinions greatly influence the "value" people place on an impact. The aim here is for companies to collaborate with the affected people to understand the best ways to mitigate project impacts and provide them with benefits within the scope of their engagement. The management plans are then designed to incorporate practical actions to address adverse impacts. I hope my stories brought you closer to the world of social performance management.

CHAPTER 2

ESG

ESG frameworks, ratings, scores, and investing have gained a lot of traction in recent years, as more and more investors are looking to put their money into companies that are *doing good* for the world. In this chapter, we'll dive deeper into what ESG is and what it is not. ESG stands for environmental, social, and governance, and it represents a set of factors that investors can use to evaluate companies based on their sustainability and ethical practices on a corporate level. Each of these three factors has its own set of considerations:

- Environmental factors refer to a company's impact on the environment, including its carbon footprint, energy usage, waste management practices, and efforts to conserve natural resources. Environmentally conscious companies often have a lower impact on the planet and can contribute to a more sustainable future. There is a whole subset of climate change–related indicators, topics, and emissions calculations, but I will not go into much detail on this.
- Social factors refer to a company's impact on society, including its treatment of employees, diversity and inclusion practices, and

impact on the local community. Companies that prioritize social responsibility often have a positive impact on their employees and the communities they operate in. I don't know about you, but I'm uneasy about these generic definitions.

- Governance factors refer to a company's management practices, including board diversity, executive compensation, and transparency of financial reporting. Companies with strong governance practices are often well managed and transparent, which can lead to more sustainable long-term growth.

The intention of ESG frameworks is to equip investors with a set of data to support their evaluation of how their investments line up with some common standards and values. For example, an investor who is passionate about protecting the environment may choose to invest in companies that are committed to reducing their carbon footprint and have a strong track record of environmental responsibility. How this is measured and what practical actions this translates into is another story. One of the key benefits of ESG investing is that it can help align a company's values with those of its investors. When investors put their money into companies that share their values, they can feel good about their investments while supporting a positive change in the world.

ESG frameworks and ESG investing have grown into a vast new area for businesses, investors, and rating companies. All are founded on the assumption that these requirements and frameworks will lead to better business practices and benefit the people. Everyone wants their business to have a sustainability or ESG strategy and conduct their activities in a responsible manner. I was excited to find out about initiatives to standardize measuring how businesses affected the environment and society, but I was disappointed when I found out what actually goes into the ESG report. My disappointment was partly related to the high-level indicators that did not say much to me about how the assets were managed or how the operational-level risks were mitigated. But I also found it misleading that there was no acknowledgment of the limitations of ESG reporting. Reporting on ESG grew into an art and industry of its own. Data scientists gather the input and format reports in line with the frameworks. It is the nature of this social impact product that the emphasis is more on the format rather than on the data input itself. Despite my strong view on this, I acknowledge that having a set of imperfect standards with good intentions is better than the free-for-all that was there before, but it seems like a missed opportunity when we have such a huge talent pool that can make ESG frameworks and ESG reporting meaningful. My main argument in this respect is that if we're going to spend the resources, why don't we aim for a more meaningful outcome?

I am not alone in my view that ESG as we know it is over. We have seen interesting yet not shocking news and developments. ESG assets dropped to USD 6.2 trillion in 2022 from USD 17.1 trillion in 2020 in the US. The ESG boom was cut short partly due to the poor financial performance of ESG funds and the poor ESG performance of the ESG funds. The promises of *doing good while making a profit* indeed seemed too good to be true. The Financial Times reported in March 2023 that MSCI, one of the leading ESG rating agencies will remove its ratings from hundreds of funds due to their updated methodology. All the links are in the biography for those who want to know more. This book is not about ESG fund performance, but rather about social impact and how it relates to the ESG frameworks. I would add that this chapter would be a useful contribution to any debate about the future of ESG and how to improve the concept and adapt to the new market conditions.

What Is It?

ESG is an investment strategy and framework that considers a company's environmental, social, and governance practices alongside traditional financial factors when evaluating potential investments. The goal of ESG investing is to support companies that are committed to making a positive impact on the world while also achieving financial success. ESG investing has grown in popularity as more investors seek to align their values with their investment portfolios. According to the Global Sustainable Investment Alliance, there were $35.3 trillion in assets under management using sustainable investing strategies worldwide in 2020, a 15 percent increase from 2018.

The main argument in support of ESG investing is that it can benefit both investors and companies. By considering ESG factors, investors can identify well-managed companies with sustainable business practices that are more likely to generate long-term financial returns. In turn, companies that prioritize ESG practices may be better positioned to attract socially responsible investors and build stronger relationships with their stakeholders. While this may not be true anymore, there was once a time when there was a demand for ESG investing because of these reasons.

The *S* in ESG refers to the evaluation of a company or organization's impact on society and its stakeholders. The social dimension of ESG encompasses a wide range of issues, including some that we saw in the SIA chapter:

- *Labor practices.* Evaluating a company's treatment of its employees, including payment of salaries, working hours, and health and safety conditions. Employee well-being is in this category as well. As you can see, these factors are largely compliance related. The company is legally required to meet national legislation and honor the conditions stipulated in the employment contract. The ESG score usually looks at hirings and firings, benefits provided to workers (working from home, childcare, healthcare, and other packages), engagement with employees, and employees' general perception and satisfaction with the workplace. The project-level approach might be misleading because the corporate headquarters of these companies are in a country with strong labor legislation that ratified most of the key ILO Conventions. The aspects that are in the gray area of labor include nonemployee workers, workers hired through agencies, outsourcing of high-risk business activities, and so on. ESG looks at the corporate-level HR policies, and any such outsourcing would be under the procurement team. Are we inflating the social impact related to employment, knowing that it is largely a legal requirement and not the goodwill of employers?

- *Human rights.* Assessing a company's respect for the rights of individuals and communities, including issues such as forced labor and discrimination. What is a human rights assessment, and what does it mean in practice? What is the scope? The more generic interpretations of human rights in the business context fail to define the clear purpose and scope of an assessment. Do you want to demonstrate that your supply chain is free of forced labor either by luck or because of your management system? How about we go a step further and set out the management plan incorporated into the procurement processes to ensure that social (and environmental) impacts are systematically addressed for each new supplier and audited on an annual basis? While this may be standard practice for many IFI-financed high-risk projects, it is not yet a requirement for everyone.

I have seen human rights mentioned in different contexts throughout my career. I have seen human rights due diligence reports, and I have talked to NGOs that wanted the IFI and the company to address the impacts. The terminology used to be frightening to most of my clients, so instead of using the term human rights, I incorporated the concepts into the performance standards and requirements so we could present them to clients in practical terms. For instance, instead of saying that we didn't want forced labor or child labor in their operations, we suggested they incorporate this into their HR policies and subsequent processes to verify age, provide employment contracts for every worker, pay salaries and overtime as stipulated in the contract, and monitor contractors to comply with these requirements as well.

- *Diversity, equity, nondiscrimination, equal opportunities, and inclusion.* Evaluating a company's efforts to promote diversity and inclusion in its workforce and operations. We have seen many variations of this over the past decades. It started with increasing the number of women in the workforce, which led to initiatives to increase the number of women in leadership positions and among decision-makers. There were initiatives to increase the representation of people of color or minority groups in the workforce, in leadership, and on boards. The tools to achieve this include quotas, affirmative action, ensuring that there is always a representative of such community on the shortlisting committee, and unconscious bias training.

- *Community relations.* Examining a company's impact and relationship with respect to local communities. This was the concept I struggled with the most. In my world, the community is very well defined. It means the people who live close to the project area that are directly or indirectly affected by the construction or the operation of the project. In the ESG world, the community can mean literally anyone. I have seen ESG reporting in which the community and community engagement referred to the customers of the company, which is fair and not technically incorrect. They *are* a community of service users. The general lack of a well-defined community in ESG reporting makes it challenging to define actual impacts. The lack of definition leads to missing out on people living around my operational or manufacturing facility and people affected by my operations or supply chain. I do see great stories of multinational companies financing CSR activities in developing countries around their manufacturing facilities. I support such initiatives, but we need to understand that ESG is a compliance-type tool, while CSR is voluntary and largely unregulated. So no amount of football club sponsorship makes up for the fact that nonemployee workers are exploited in the manufacturing plant. Legal compliance first, and then we can talk about *doing good.*

- *Stakeholder engagement.* Providing information about the company's environmental, social, and governance impacts to a variety of stakeholders. In the majority of ESG reporting, stakeholder engagement refers to a combination of one or more of the following: employee engagement, shareholder information package, *community* engagement, and outreach to stakeholders without a definition. You probably already know my feelings about the undefined stakeholders and the lack of specification on the information disclosure, its frequency, and its purpose. In my world, we have very well-defined stakeholders, who are mapped and analyzed according to their level of influence or interest. We also look at the best ways to engage with them, including frequency and channels, and we define the type of information that will be disclosed to each group. This means that we know whether we want to just provide information or require feedback, opinions, and input from a stakeholder group. Different groups get different types of information and levels of detail depending on their level of interest and influence. What a difference to the annual ESG investor report, right? I fully acknowledge both sides of the argument, and we should have more discussions to agree on what is meaningful information, an appropriate level of detail, topics, and frequency of disclosure and communication.

The other aspect of stakeholder engagement is the management of complaints from affected communities. Since the community impacts are loosely defined, most of the ESG frameworks focus on the existence of this mechanism. I do see this as a good first step. However, if communities don't know it exists and don't know how to use it, it remains meaningless. The purpose of this mechanism should be to facilitate the dialogue between the company and its affected communities and help sort out problems without having to go to court. The legal avenues still remain available for people who are not satisfied with the resolution of the complaint; however, the grievance mechanism is free of charge for the complainant, and it's usually faster to go directly to the company for resolution.

There are other social aspects that we've seen in the SIA that aren't as present in the ESG reporting and frameworks. This is partly due to the macro scope of ESG reporting, and partly because some information may be confidential. I do believe, though, that some information is not shared because there is no precedent for it. This typically includes the ESIA document and related studies and assessments. Every lender and IFI has disclosure policies and requirements that set out the timelines for disclosure as well as the information to be shared publicly. This enhances transparency with stakeholders (especially with NGOs who closely follow their activities) and ensures a more meaningful dialogue based on actual project impacts and mitigation measures.

Here are a few of the social aspects of my work that are missing from any ESG reporting:

- *Environmental and social management systems on the corporate and project/asset levels.* There is little to no information on systems designed to capture and manage environmental and social risks other than certification by the International Organization for Standardization (ISO). This organization was founded in 1947 to provide internationally recognized standards that cover various aspects of technology and manufacturing. It is a voluntary organization with an HQ in Geneva. The most relevant standards to our work include:
  - o ISO 14001:2015 Environmental Management Systems (ISO 14004:2016 and ISO 14005:2019 are related standards)
  - o ISO 45001:2018 Occupational Health and Safety Management Systems (used to be OHSAS 18001 before)
  - o ISO 2600:2010 Guidance on Social Responsibility
  - o ISO 9001:2015 Quality Management Systems

Obtaining these designations from ISO requires independent auditing by licensed verification experts, and the certification expires every couple of years. Recertification is strongly encouraged for companies that claim to be industry leaders in ESG and the management of environmental and social impacts. Having asset level ESMS or any of these standards is a good indication that the company takes risk management seriously.

- *Land and livelihood impacts.* Companies typically do not disclose how they obtained the project land or manage any operational impacts on the residents' livelihoods. Understanding the physical and economic displacement impacts and any impacts on access restrictions and livelihoods is an essential part of the SIA. If the project requires expropriation and other involuntary land/ livelihood impacts, it is the responsibility of the company to mitigate and compensate for them. On several of my projects, we tried to encourage the companies, especially those with operations in multiple countries, to develop a general set of guidelines for land acquisition and livelihood restoration that they can apply globally. This is because national legislation is often weak or poorly developed, and when projects require IFI financing, they will have to comply with a more stringent set of international standards and requirements. Without going into too much detail, the key differences include eligibility criteria, compensation amounts and in-kind compensation, additional assistance, engagement with affected people, and the level of asset survey and census data collected. There are great publications and guidance materials on resettlement developed by IFIs, academics, and consultants. I included some links in the references for further details.

- *Gender and vulnerable groups on the project level.* Corporate-level gender equality measures and policies are typically reported; however, these are mainly statistics on employees that have been measured for diversity and inclusion targets. I know we live in a world of many genders, but in the IFI world, gender still means assessing whether women are disproportionately affected by project impacts or whether they are more vulnerable to project impacts. It can be a simple thing: all consultation events are after work, when women have to get groceries, care for children, and cook dinner, so they can't attend. While it may not be true for everyone, it is the reality of many women in developing countries. I have personally seen this as an issue for projects. In some parts of the world, we have to organize separate meetings for women conducted by a female representative of the company or consulting team to accommodate cultural norms.

  Why is it important to talk about women and other vulnerable groups? Because companies report on diversity and inclusion targets and the number of women on their boards but do very little to address gender issues and vulnerability in other aspects of their operations.

I have to say, I don't think ESG is a bad thing, but the execution needs improvement. It is time to review and update the old practices. There is value in several additional dimensions that my work does not address—on the governance side specifically. ESG also addresses a variety of human rights and racial inequality aspects, along with many others: employee engagement, anticorruption and bribery, employee health and safety (though it overlaps with what I would typically cover), employee relations, customer welfare, management relations—the list goes on. In terms of ESG frameworks, the most notable is probably the Global

Reporting Initiative (GRI), which has created sustainability reporting standards that address materiality, management, and disclosure. I talk about this more in Chapter 9.

Selecting the appropriate ESG framework is critical and should consider an organization's industry, current regulatory environment, and stakeholder groups. For instance, investors, boards, and insurers may prefer frameworks that follow the Task Force on Climate-related Financial Disclosures (TCFD) or the Sustainability Accounting Standards Board (SASB), while other stakeholders might expect a framework following the UN Sustainable Development Goals (UN SDGs). Another essential factor to consider is which elements an organization want to include in its measurement. There are some low-hanging fruits that are easier to achieve and demonstrate, while others might take time to be achieved. Utilizing an action priority or impact effort prioritization matrix helps organizations quickly identify areas for focus and decide which ESG framework will enable them to reach their objectives.

Good ESG reporting focuses on how a company is addressing various human rights and environmental concerns, often in collaboration with industry groups or trade associations. This includes steps the company has taken to tackle larger dilemmas, its approach to engaging with stakeholders, and how well it ensures all employees are included in policies and procedures—even those not in the most senior roles. Effective reports are often written in a manner that makes their content accessible to readers. This means organizing human rights/ESG data into a structure that makes it simpler to comprehend and navigate. According to the United Nations Guiding Principles on Business and Human Rights, ESG reporting must be "comprehensive, clear, and transparent." This requires companies to demonstrate how their processes work regarding ESG issues, identifying any risks, and taking measures to avoid them. In addition to outlining human rights and ESG concerns, good reports also outline the steps a company is taking in collaboration with industry or trade groups to foster positive social change, as well as its plans for the future.

Stewardship is, to a large extent, a subheading of ESG. It is interlinked with sustainability as well, but it is best placed under ESG for a number of reasons. ESG is often associated with sustainability and social responsibility, at least in nontechnical terminology. In my experience, stewardship, sustainability, and social responsibility are closely intertwined, as they share the goal of ensuring the well-being of society and the environment. I have come across "stewardship" as a synonym for some of the social impact products, but it is also commonly used in the context of environmental conservation and general sustainability. It refers to the management of resources, particularly natural resources, to ensure their long-term viability and protect them for future generations. Stewardship can be viewed at various levels, from individual actions to organizational and governmental initiatives.

The main argument why stewardship fits into the social responsibility and ESG category is the common goal and overlapping issues: land stewardship (especially indigenous), corporate stewardship, or community stewardship. As part of social responsibility, organizations have the ethical (and often legal) obligation to minimize adverse impacts and promote sustainable practices. Stewardship is a great tool to contribute to these efforts. ESG, sustainability, and stewardship all have long-term perspectives and consider the interests of future generations. Note that social responsibility appears here as a way to refer to voluntary and nonvoluntary company actions to implement proactive positive impact creation. This is just another example of how confusing the terminology is with respect to these social impact products. Social responsibility is largely a concept, not a methodology.

Companies that take human rights seriously can set an inspiring example, likely leading to stronger shareholder support and an increased demand for sustainable goods and services. Furthermore, these firms will reduce their reputational risk, making them less vulnerable to activist intervention. There is a clear trend of the social dimension of ESG becoming increasingly important to investors. Consumers also look to invest in and support companies that have a positive impact on society and prioritize the well-being of their employees, communities, and other stakeholders. How does the ESG framework measure this? We can argue about that. A study from 2021 concluded that the US-based institutional investors who publicly committed to responsible investing had, at best, the same or often even lower ESG scores than institutional investors that did not make a public commitment. Greenwashing and the inflation of positive climate change impacts have been in the news as a few high-profile companies admitted to the misrepresentation of data. The Financial Conduct Authority also noted that it is often difficult to reconcile the portfolio holdings of approved EGS funds with the fund name or objective.

See? Nontechnical people get the point too.

Purpose, Scope, Timing

ESG, like any other tool for impact creation and measurement, is created with a specific purpose and scope. We must understand what this instrument can and cannot achieve or even demonstrate before we can decide whether it is the most appropriate for our purposes.

Purpose

The purpose of ESG is to promote sustainable business and operational practices that take into account a company's impact on the environment, society, and governance structures.

The purpose of ESG frameworks is to provide the structure for assessing and reporting on the different environmental, social, and governance topics, to standardize outcome measurement and make them comparable. Though ESG is not a contractual requirement, to obtain a good ESG rating, companies need to fulfill a set of criteria and comply with a set of standards. The purpose of ESG is to capture corporate-level impacts, policies, and initiatives and present them in a more standardized way, enabling investors and shareholders to make informed decisions if they choose to support *green* companies or companies with a *positive social impact* or *good governance structure*. ESG is designed to aggregate operational data on some topics within these three overarching areas and publicly disclose this data.

Other notable purposes include risk mitigation through screening for companies with poor environmental, social, or governance practices, reputational damage, or regulatory fines. The adoption of ESG frameworks also encourages long-term thinking and investing in sustainable business practices. These are all valid considerations, and I appreciate the big-picture approach. I believe that not all positive impacts are immediate, and if we all strive to improve operations bit by bit, we will eventually get to a place where ESG will be irrelevant because it is the operational standard for every company.

ESG is used by funds and investors for several other reasons as well:

- *Screening.* ESG metrics can be used to screen potential investments for sustainability, social responsibility, and good governance before making a final investment decision.

- *Portfolio management.* ESG considerations can be integrated into ongoing portfolio management processes, with companies being continually evaluated based on their ESG performance.

- *Engagement.* Investors can engage with companies to encourage them to adopt more sustainable and responsible practices. This can involve dialogue with company management, filing shareholder resolutions, or other forms of activism.

- *Crisis response.* During times of crisis or disruption, such as the COVID-19 pandemic, ESG considerations can become more important as investors evaluate companies' responses to the crisis.

- *Reporting.* ESG considerations can also come into play when companies report on their sustainability and social responsibility practices, allowing investors to evaluate their performance and make more informed investment decisions.

For all of this to be meaningful, we need to understand the contents, scope, and indicators of the ESG metrics we use.

Scope

The scope of ESG covers a wide range of factors that can impact a company's sustainability and responsible business practices on a corporate level.

To be specific, the environmental component of ESG focuses on a company's impact on the natural world. This includes factors such as:

- Greenhouse gas emissions

- Energy and water use

- Waste management

- Resource depletion

- Biodiversity

- Climate change resilience

The social component of ESG focuses on a company's impact on people and communities. This includes factors such as:

- Labor practices

- Human rights

- Community engagement

- Health and safety

- Diversity and inclusion

- Supply chain management

The governance component of ESG focuses on the structures and processes that govern how a company operates. This includes factors such as:

- Board composition and independence

- Executive compensation

- Risk management

- Transparency and disclosure

- Anticorruption policies

- Shareholder rights

In addition to these more defined areas, the scope of ESG also includes broader issues such as:

- Sustainability

- Responsible investment practices

- Long-term thinking and planning

- Social and environmental impact measurement

- Reporting and transparency

While some of these topics are rather generic, difficult to measure, and often subjective, others are more straightforward. It is important to add that several of the ESG factors are mainly compliance with legislation (labor, waste management, GHG emissions, health and safety, anticorruption, biodiversity), while others go beyond this compliance aspect and allow the company to opt in or out. The exact scope may vary depending on the company or industry as well as the framework that is used as a basis for reporting or rating the performance.

Timing

ESG frameworks are designed for the long run. Ratings are provided on an annual basis or even less frequently with an assessment of compliance or alignment for each indicator or criterion within the given framework. This is good news for companies that care about ESG scores because the annual checks can identify the areas for improvement. With the relevant guidance, company performance can be enhanced over time. For investors, it provides an assessment of trends in business practices and can point out the weaknesses of the business. Some investors choose to integrate ESG considerations into their investment process from the beginning, using these metrics to screen potential investments and identify companies that prioritize sustainable and responsible business practices.

Other investors may choose to take a more proactive approach, engaging with companies to encourage them to adopt more sustainable and responsible practices. In some cases, ESG considerations may also come into play during periods of crisis or disruption. For example, in the wake of the COVID-19 pandemic, many investors have become more focused on companies' responses to the crisis, including their treatment of employees and their impact on communities.

Limitations

While it may be a broad framework, there are a lot of things ESG cannot do. Without repeating what was already said, here I will focus on the main limitations I have faced while trying to assess the social impact of ESG. It is a corporate-level set of indicators that largely follow national legislation compliance with respect to the social aspects. Yes, there are additional beyond-compliance elements in employee well-being, but those are often marginal in real impact terms. A company following ESG frameworks and strategies is often inflating positive impacts on the environments and communities due to the vague indicators and attributable indirect impacts.

The other main limitation of ESG investing is the lack of standardization—though attempts have been made. ESG metrics are not standardized, and it has no clear-cut methodology for gathering data. This means that different providers may use different definitions and interpret the data differently. What is the baseline for increasing people of color in the workforce? Last year's statistics or the statistics of comparable firms? Several indicators are binary, without the option to qualitatively evaluate their meaning. For instance, companies score points if they have a flexible working policy, but the indicators don't usually clarify how these policies are implemented. In this case, indicators may include how many people have the option to work from home, how many people who apply for it get approved, and whether there are part-time working options for employees. The company offering parental leave (which is mandatory under national legislation in many countries) scores points, but the ESG rating doesn't say whether they offer more time than legally required or whether there are other returning-to-work schemes to help new parents adjust to family life. This leads to different interpretations of the data and the results that tend to exaggerate positives and hide negatives.

The truth is that the whole ESG rating methodology and system is largely based on the credit rating methodology. The ESG rating teams tried to use the credit rating systems; however, there was a mismatch in the type of data input that led to the simplification of the ESG data input. This is partly the reason, I believe, for ESG measuring what it is currently measuring and having significant limitations to provide more meaningful statistics and differentiation between corporate-level and asset-level impacts.

The disclosure requirements are somewhat standardized, yet the data availability on several of the more meaningful indicators remains limited, especially on the social side. Some of the social topics around employment and the conditions of employment might be perceived as more personal or privileged information by the company and its workers. Think of how many job adverts don't state salaries or the full benefits package. The other aspects around the disclosure of community information might also be limited and misleading. Indicators such as the number of community meetings say very little about the actual communities selected for the meetings, their relation to the company or its operations, the topics discussed, and the overall outcome of the engagement in terms of building trust with those communities. Even if we want to look at the corporate-level disclosures, I have yet to find indicators or public information on the environmental and social management frameworks used to address asset-level environmental and social risks—other than national legislation of course.

There is also an element of subjectivity when it comes to interpreting the data and the ratings. What is an appropriate level of waste to be generated by the company? How many employees should a company have? What is the acceptable cost of providing better conditions for employees than required by law? To what lengths should a company go to engage with communities? Is it a company's role to address human rights issues if those are not directly related to their operations? When we try to limit ourselves to numbers and quantify social impacts, we end up making the same mistake over and over again: we forget that we are talking about people. We forget that perceptions and the quality of the change matter.

Is ESG for every company? Probably not. Some companies might not have operations that could be or should be covered by any rating. For instance, software companies may have different ESG priorities than fashion brands with complex supply chains. That is why many frameworks are striving to converge their efforts and develop an all-inclusive framework for ESG reporting that applies to all businesses. Establishing standards that can serve as benchmarks for a company's commitment to ESG is also necessary. These could include factors like how much ESG risks and opportunities impact long-term competitiveness and whether a business has implemented a net-zero climate plan. The key difference between social enterprises and ESG-driven businesses is that social enterprises were created with the mandate to create positive *social impact* (however we define that), but ESG-driven businesses operate normally, save for measures put in place to address adverse impacts and enhance benefits for employees and *society*.

When ESG is used to make investment decisions, we must ask ourselves whether the information presented is useful for our purposes. It will not come as a surprise that funds that have, for instance, a *green* portfolio of renewable energy assets score high on ESG ratings. Companies may engage in greenwashing, or overstating their ESG credentials, to attract ESG investors. This can make it difficult for investors to accurately evaluate a company's true ESG performance and identify companies that prioritize sustainable and responsible business practices in practice, not only on paper. While ESG investing can provide valuable insights into a company's sustainability, social responsibility, and governance practices, it is important to recognize its limitations. Investors should carefully evaluate ESG metrics and consider them alongside other quantitative and qualitative data when making investment decisions. By recognizing and addressing these limitations, investors can make more informed investment decisions and promote sustainable and responsible business practices.

The risk of green or social washing is also related to the high-level overview of assets, where on the surface we see renewable assets and no fossil fuels, so we can rest assured that the emissions are low, and the operations don't significantly contribute to climate change. This argument may be valid but fails to investigate what it takes to build and operate those assets. Are these assets managed in a sustainable way? I will not go into much detail on the environmental aspects, but regarding social aspects, none of the ESG ratings of *green* funds tell us anything about labor and working conditions, supply chain management, contractor management, the health and safety of workers and communities, engagement with communities and social license to operate, how the land was obtained for the project, and whether the project took away grazing land from locals without compensation. The holistic approach I'm trying to promote here would offer us a more pronounced understanding of concepts like green investing and positive social impact.

This book is not about energy policy, and I will not go into any opinions on fossil fuels vs. renewable energy. I've worked on several types of energy-generating and transmission projects around the world and can tell you that there are social and environmental risks with all of them. We have to select a location and take land that is most likely used by locals who derive livelihoods from it. There is a set of access roads and associated infrastructure that also requires land acquisition. There are impacts on the community, which will get workers coming to the area for the construction phase of the project. We have the risk of inadequate working conditions, especially further down the chain of contractors and subcontractors. *Green* projects carry risks too, even when there are arguments for the macro-level good they bring to the country.

I don't want to sound like I am completely against ESG because that's not true. I just want to highlight that the industry of impact assessment and management has evolved, thanks in part to more widespread knowledge and public awareness. What worked for companies fifteen to twenty years ago is no longer appropriate. The increased reporting and disclosure requirements eat up a lot of the company resources without bringing much benefit at this stage. Here I would like to add an important point on the people who work at banks and funds to carry out the data collection on ESG metrics. This is not a criticism, merely an observation. Most ESG teams are made up of data scientists who collect the information and put it into the right template for each reporting requirement. This is not necessarily a bad thing, especially for environmental factors that are likely to be numeric. I have seen a trend of ESG reporting teams being separated from the ESG team that does portfolio screening. In these instances, the data scientists remain on the reporting side, and subject matter experts, including some of my colleagues, develop the technically meaningful criteria to screen investments. However, there is still the old way of doing ESG, where bankers and investment specialists with some interest in the environment and climate change take the seats of qualified subject matter experts and develop ESG indicators as a direct response to markets and shareholder preference.

There was once a strong correlation between high ESG ratings and superior financial performance. If we are honest here, we note that some of it might be due to greenwashing of otherwise profitable assets and companies that had low ESG value to add. The other aspect was the trend in the market that favored anything *green* or *high social impact* or *investing with impact*. As far as I can see, this has run its course because people are more aware of macro impacts being attributed to projects, assets, and operations that have little to do with such impacts directly or only contribute to a certain extent.

While it might have been a competitive advantage five to ten years ago to have a high ESG rating, now almost every company has a rating that is favorable. The business of rating agencies was created as a direct response to the hype of ESG frameworks. There were a few smaller companies engaged in this twenty years ago, and then all the major credit rating agencies set up a team to provide an ESG rating for companies. In my line of work, the ESG rating of a company almost doesn't matter because we work on a different level (project or asset) and because of the limited information in ESG reports that are appropriate for our assessment.

You might note that I speak very little about corporate governance. That's because it is often treated completely differently from the *E* and *S* in ESG. It requires different expertise to assess those. In my line of work, there's another department that carries out these assessments, and I only get to see the final report.

To summarize my long list of issues with ESG as it is and provide a constructive start for new discussions, I offer the following bullet points:

- ESG needs to incorporate asset-level data for a more holistic approach.
- ESG needs to comment on the company's ESMS and evaluate the

implementation of procedures, management plans, and policies.

- ESG needs to separate legal requirements and additional activities that go beyond compliance (voluntary vs. compliance based).
- There must be better definitions for what is within the scope, especially when discussing employees (corporate level vs. how they manage on the asset level), communities, and engagement.

I believe that improving the abovementioned aspects of ESG would provide a greater understanding of what is measured and would clarify several aspects of the framework. The regulatory requirements and voluntary standards can be confusing, as each framework requires different data and reporting formats. One of the most significant updates on the social aspects of ESG is the supply chain management requirements. In addition to greater emphasis on such issues on the framework level, the EU has recently adopted a new CSDDD/CSRD (Corporate Sustainability Due Diligence Directive and Corporate Sustainability Reporting Directive) that requires companies to undertake the environmental and human rights due diligence of their supply chain, even if it's outside the EU. This proposed new approach reviews asset-level social and environmental risks (exactly what the SIA could do!) and tries to incorporate this data into corporate-level reporting. This gives the momentum for a discussion on recalibrating ESG and its social elements!

How It Relates to Other Social Impact Products

When I first heard about ESG all those years ago, I thought it would somehow reflect asset-level management plans and systems, along with what

I would call tangible impacts. For me, ESG is a corporate-level reflection of regulatory compliance and some voluntary standards or mechanisms that the company is imposing on itself. The line between mandatory and voluntary is often blurry, and thus *positive social impacts* get overreported.

ESG and sustainability are used almost synonymously, but they don't mean the same thing. ESG is a reporting framework, a strategy, a macro-level reflection that allows for rating and comparison. Sustainability is more of a long-term approach to achieving change, taking into account both social and environmental elements. The original definition of sustainability was heavily tilted toward environmental sustainability and preservation. Now, it represents a more integrated approach to operations within an organization and an essential aspect of corporate governance. This is another example of having overlapping concepts and terminology that many people use in a less appropriate context.

ESG and sustainability reporting often include CSR initiatives, impact investing, and other stewardship activities. CSR is a voluntary approach to supporting communities and people. We will talk more about CSR later, but typically this would include the sponsorship of sports clubs and civil society organizations that focus on a topic that might be completely irrelevant to the operations of the company. In ESG, they would report such CSR initiatives under the community engagement bracket. One of the issues I raised before is that there is little explanation about this initiative being voluntary, and it is targeting certain beneficiaries selected by the supporting organization, not the company. We have seen how this leads to generic claims such as "supporting local communities," "providing access to education," or "providing better access to . . ." You name it. In my world, we are very specific about who is affected and what the impact is. We simply cannot claim that everyone within a community benefits or that building a hospital will lead to overall better access to healthcare.

ESG does provide a good framework for evaluating the company's overall commitment to supporting whatever communities they choose to support, as well as following current trends in diversity, inclusion, equity, equality, and the like. What I want to see is the efforts categorized as mandatory and voluntary with the most appropriate tools to achieve them. For instance, human resources policies are best used to address diversity and inclusion, but it might be CSR that responds to the needs of a selected and defined community. In the ESG world, this community investment does not have to correspond with communities that are affected by the operations of the company. For instance, there is legislation governing the prevention of public access to construction sites, general health and safety requirements for the public, or noise levels. In my world, these are included in a management plan that highlights the issue and offers practical actions to mitigate it. Let me emphasize that this is in response to adverse impacts and risks that the community is exposed to as a result of the company's operations. In the ESG world, we might have health and safety statistics on injuries and fatalities.

Other proactive and voluntary social impact products that ESG could interact with include impact investing. I've read so many books on impact investing, but I've yet to understand how the indicators that demonstrate social impacts and differentiate generic and inflated impacts from actual ones are selected. There's a whole chapter on this later on. If we use ESG factors to build our portfolio, we are most likely impact investing—or investing with a positive environmental and social impact. Reviewing ESG factors or investing in companies that use ESG frameworks is a good start, especially if one is aware of the limitations I listed in the previous section.

ESG is also closely related to responsible investing. The concept of responsible investing overlaps with impact investing and ESG in the way it tries to have financial returns while also keeping in mind the impacts on people and the environment. I don't know about you, but it seems like there's an awful lot of interest in doing wonderful things out there, but we haven't come to an agreement on what it means and how to actually do it. While I was researching responsible investing, and even just surveying friends and family members, it was clear that everyone wanted their money to be used to *do good* while having a financial return on investment. When I asked what type of businesses they think should be supported, there was often the generic answer: companies that care about their employees. Okay, so companies who follow national legislation and offer fair compensation, paid leave, and maternity leave? Is the bar so low? Next up, the recommendation was to look for companies that give back to the community. To put the question nicely: What community are we talking about exactly? The counterargument another person voiced is that it's not mandatory for companies to care about the community. Instead of arguing about the principle, I would rather focus on what this *caring* looks like in practice. In the developed world, it can be donations to charities or support for local kids' sports clubs. It's a different context when multinational companies have manufacturing facilities in developing countries and provide the only well-paid jobs to locals. Where we draw the line between caring as mandated by law and caring as going the extra mile is what should be the focus of such discussions. It would be easier to manage expectations and clarify what the company is willing and able to supply.

The positive trend that I see within the ESG sphere too is the acknowledgment of supply chain issues—from not only a business continuity perspective but a human rights perspective as well. I deal with this issue daily on my renewable projects and, to a certain extent, other projects that have large contractor workforces. To be very succinct, in the ESG context, human rights in the supply chain means the potential for child labor and forced labor. To a large degree, these are the only elements of labor violations and risks that are examined. The contextual risk analysis of the supply chain (e.g., the country of origin, reputational risks, media reports of violations, etc.) informs the company, who can then audit their supply chain to screen for this (which is now a CSDDD/CSRD requirement for EU-based companies). There are mechanisms embedded in the procurement of contractors that can stop these human rights violations. In my field, we also do more complex labor audits that look at the types of contracts (seasonal or permanent), third-party workers or workers hired through agencies (not direct employees), occupational health and safety, working hours, mandatory rest periods, payment structures, bonded labor, the conditions of employment, migrant workers, labor accommodations, and more. It is extremely thorough. I am not arguing that every company should do the same for all their suppliers, but there is merit—especially for high-risk sectors.

What Is the Social Impact?

ESG is rather demonstrating and assessing existing impacts as opposed to creating new ones—at least on the social side. ESG incorporates elements of social in the form of its impact on stakeholders such as employees, customers, suppliers, and the community at large. ESG investing promotes social responsibility by evaluating a company's ethical practices, such as labor practices, diversity, equity, inclusion policies, community engagement, and customer relations.

ESG is not a magic pill that will help companies solve all the issues in their operating environments or their *communities*. The broader social impacts of ESG include:

- Promotes ethical and responsible business practices

- Encourages companies to prioritize employee welfare and development

- Fosters a diverse and inclusive workplace culture

- Reduces social and economic inequalities

- Addresses social challenges such as labor exploitation and discrimination

- Promotes community engagement and development

- Encourages companies to adopt sustainable business practices

- Improves product safety and reduces environmental impact

- Creates incentives for companies to be transparent and accountable to stakeholders

- Contributes to the overall well-being of society.

If even half of this is true in practice, ESG is worth it! While some claims are macro level and detached from the reality of business operations, there is, of course, a benefit to changing the culture in which we do business and defining better values for humanity. By incorporating social considerations into investment decision-making,

ESG investing aims to promote positive social outcomes and address social challenges such as income inequality, labor exploitation, and discrimination. Bringing about change is never easy, and being mindful of the impacts and desired impacts is a good start. I do believe that we've now progressed into the next phase, in which we can have better definitions of our social impact products and can choose the one that's most appropriate for our purposes.

There are tangible impacts within the ESG sphere especially related to working conditions and supply chain management. These are more meaningful from my perspective than some of the other community and stakeholder engagement–type indicators. I still feel, though, that the *S* in ESG is like the little sibling that has been in the background for a long time without much attention or understanding. I do hope this book will help us start a conversation on how to better define impacts within the context of company operations in a more meaningful way, with increased transparency regarding the limitations. Corporate-level impacts and initiatives are important, but we need to differentiate between those at the macro level and those on the portfolio or asset level, especially when we use ESG to screen investments. The aspect of my job that is missing from ESG is the impacts related to land acquisition, livelihoods, and access to natural resources. Granted that most operations are not new developments, there are a number of funds that invest in project companies that do develop new infrastructure. International best practices and national legislation have significant gaps when it comes to compensating for project impacts. ESG is missing out on adding an extra layer to the assessment.

Examples of ESG Done Right

The integration of ESG factors into business decision-making was increasingly important for companies that want to be seen as responsible and sustainable. Now this seems to be changing; however, the initiatives remain in place.

One of the most prominent examples is Patagonia. The outdoor apparel company has been a leader in sustainability and social responsibility for many years. Patagonia uses organic cotton and recycled materials in its products and has implemented fair labor practices across its supply chain. The company also invests in environmental causes and has donated over $100 million to grassroots environmental organizations. The company uses multiple social impact products combined: ESG, CSR, impact investing. I think I could literally list them under every chapter—but I won't.

Another example of a company that has successfully integrated ESG considerations into its operations is Unilever. The consumer goods company set ambitious goals to reduce its environmental impact and has made significant progress toward achieving them. Unilever also prioritizes employee development, diversity, and inclusion in its workplace culture. The company has been recognized for its sustainability efforts, and its CEO has been vocal about the importance of ESG considerations in business decision-making.

Microsoft is another company that has made significant efforts to promote diversity and inclusion in its workforce and has set ambitious goals to increase the representation of underrepresented groups. The company has implemented policies to support employee well-being and development and has made significant investments in renewable energy.

Microsoft has also committed to being carbon negative by 2030.

Nestle is a food and beverage company that has prioritized sustainability and social responsibility across its operations. The company has implemented sustainable sourcing practices and has made significant progress toward reducing its environmental impact. Nestle also prioritizes employee development and diversity and inclusion in its workplace culture.

Finally, BlackRock is a global investment management firm that has made significant efforts to integrate ESG considerations into its investment decision-making. The company has developed proprietary tools to evaluate ESG risks and opportunities across its investment portfolios and has set ambitious goals to increase its investments in sustainable assets. BlackRock also engages with companies in its investment portfolios to encourage them to adopt more sustainable and responsible business practices.

There are countless other companies who have done their best to contribute to the *greater good* of environmental and social sustainability. ESG has its limitations when it comes to demonstrating actual impacts created, mitigated, or enhanced. The ratings, while being suitable to demonstrate compliance with a certain set of criteria, fall short of managing all impacts related to operations.

Conclusion

ESG is aimed at corporate-level reporting of mandatory and voluntary standards and requirements. As opposed to the SIA, the ESG is not a direct response to operations-related impact mitigation, especially on the social side. The environmental aspects could be argued otherwise.

The ESG reports on macro-level indicators, and they very rarely capture impacts on the asset or project level. This makes reporting on stakeholder engagement and community impacts somewhat vague because the context is missing.

To address some of the existing limitations, I have provided some tangible actions we should consider. I highlighted how it is probably time for these discussions to take place because people are increasingly aware of ESG and social responsibility and they want more transparency regarding the actual measurable impact on a well-defined set of stakeholders. Although we have seen many large companies successfully integrate ESG considerations to screen or manage operations and investments, there's still room to improve.

As the importance of ESG ratings fades, it is likely that more companies will try to find the next best thing for sustainability. I can only guess what that would look like, though I am hopeful that pragmaticism and common sense return and that we can forget about social washing forever. Changing the way we do business or look at practices is a huge cultural shift, and that takes time. I believe that ESG, as we know it today, is over, and it will be replaced by a better-defined set of mandatory and voluntary indicators that allow for a better overview of the management of certain business risks, social impact management being an integral part of it.

CHAPTER 3

IMPACT INVESTING

Impact investing is basically a type of investing strategy that wants to generate both financial returns and positive social or environmental impacts – or both. I'm not arguing that there could be no investment that generates financial generates both social and environmental returns, though based on my experience, where the company has significant gains on the environmental front—and this is especially true for climate adaptation and mitigation projects—there is often minimal positive social impact. The reverse is also true: where the social benefit is significant, there is likely to be less of an environmental benefit. The idea behind impact investing is to use the power of capital to drive positive change in the world through environmental or social impact. Now, you might be wondering how impact investing differs from traditional investing. Well, traditional investing is primarily focused on generating financial returns for investors, while impact investing seeks to achieve a double bottom line: financial returns and positive social or environmental impacts.

There are different delivery mechanisms to use this tool. Some impact investors invest directly in social enterprises or businesses that have a clear social or environmental mission. Other impact investors choose funds that focus on starting new ventures that have specific impact areas, such as clean energy, affordable housing, or access to healthcare. One of the key benefits of impact investing is that it allows people to align their investments with their values—similar to ESG, and choose to invest in causes they care about. The impacts can be immediate and tangible showcasing the change their investments are making in the world.

But impact investing isn't just about doing good—it can also be a smart financial decision. Many impact investments have shown strong financial returns, and some studies suggest they can even outperform traditional investments in the long run, though it might be unrelated to the impact aspect of the investment and more related to tapping into new markets.

As governments and businesses around the world grapple with pressing issues like climate change, income inequality, and gender discrimination, many investors are searching for new ways to invest their capital in a way that produces both social and financial returns. This has sparked the recent growth of impact investing, which has become an accessible source of funding for numerous socially oriented projects. Impact investing is rapidly gaining traction in the finance world.Now that ESG seems to be a standard practice, investors might be open to being more adventurous and proactively creating positive social impacts.

What Is It?

Impact investing can take many forms and delivery mechanisms. Impact investors might invest directly in businesses that have a clear social or environmental mission. These enterprises may be structured as for-profit businesses or nonprofit organizations. Others invest in funds that focus on specific impact areas, such as clean energy, affordable housing, or access to healthcare. This is a largely unregulated area from the social and environmental perspective, with mainly voluntary impact measurement frameworks and standards.

Impact investing follows the steps and principles of other social impact products and starts with defining the impact objectives. Impact investors often have several goals in mind but limit their activities to certain sectors or topics. While their objectives might overlap with traditional businesses or philanthropic investment models, there are key distinctions between them. Impact investing depends on existing frameworks to govern their approach. The most popular may be ESG because of its applicability to several sectors and businesses of different sizes. Companies that already implement ESG frameworks in their operations are typically good candidates to be added to the portfolio of impact investors. These companies have already proven they can achieve a positive impact and are conscious of the environment and communities without sacrificing financial performance.

The social outcome demonstration in the impact investing context is usually characterized by its scale and product reach. Investing in educational technology might be assessed primarily based on their reach to an underserved population that's limited in magnitude, while other secondary or indirect impacts are underreported. The other extreme of the same example is the reporting of an educational technology initiative as being universally good for students and society. We have been through the layers, scope, and demonstration of impacts before, so keep in mind that impact investors might use different lenses to demonstrate the scale and magnitude of their impacts. The pure impact investing sphere is rather small, with a limited supply of opportunities that offer large-scale impacts. Demand may also be somewhat limited—especially in the developed world, where other forms of financing are available to businesses.

The developing world provides plenty of opportunities for impact investing because traditional sources of funding are limited or allocation is reserved for a specific scope that might not overlap with the impact investing efforts. Although it might be getting easier to find investments that match both impact and financial return criteria, there are still underserved geographic areas and sectors. Impact investing was not spared from a thorough assessment of inclusivity, intentionality, and influence. Inclusivity means investing in businesses or sectors that are owned by underrepresented people. This can be businesses owned by people of color or women, but it can also mean investing in businesses that provide services to underserved communities. Investing in companies that reflect the values and beliefs of investors directed capital away from certain sectors (oil and gas) and provided opportunities in others (renewables).

Impact investors can employ a regional or a community-based approach, directing capital toward underserved regions or marginalized communities via investment in infrastructure (in addition to directly supporting businesses) and stimulating economic growth while addressing local challenges. Impact investing can take the form of shareholder advocacy and engagement where investors actively engage with portfolio companies to promote better ESG practices. Of course, this focuses efforts on a corporate level rather than on project or facility assessment. Nevertheless, shareholders can use their influence to push for changes in corporate policies, promote diversity and inclusion, or encourage transparency and accountability.

Financial inclusion is probably one of the most important aspects of impact investing. We talk about financial inclusion a lot in the IFI world, and we've developed tools and products to address the gaps in the market. Defined as the availability and accessibility of affordable financial services to all segments of society, financial inclusion has emerged as a powerful catalyst for social change. It plays a vital role in poverty alleviation by providing individuals with access to essential financial services. It enables the unbanked or underbanked population to save, borrow, and invest, fostering economic stability and resilience. Financial inclusion is often mentioned in the context of gender (only men and women in this case), as in many societies women still face a significant barrier to accessing financial services. Extending financial services to women contributes to their autonomy and economic opportunities, which promotes economic independence. Women's participation in the formal financial system enables them to invest in education, healthcare, and income-generating activities, subsequently driving positive social outcomes for themselves and their families. Moreover, as women gain control over their finances, they become active contributors to decision-making processes, fostering more equitable societies. It has been well-documented through studies that when women have access to finances, they make decisions that benefit the whole household, including their children and husbands.

Financial inclusion fosters entrepreneurship and stimulates economic development. Access to credit and savings accounts enables aspiring entrepreneurs to launch and expand businesses, creating employment opportunities and driving economic growth. By facilitating the flow of capital to small and medium-sized enterprises (SMEs), financial inclusion supports innovation, increases productivity, and encourages market competitiveness.

The other, less tangible benefits of financial inclusion are a sense of dignity, security, and control over one's life. It might seem far-fetched, but we will see later on how these small things can make a big difference in a person's life. Though the impacts might not be tangible or easy to monetize and measure, we can all agree that these impacts matter. Financially inclusive communities experience reduced income inequality, improved access to public services, and enhanced social cohesion. Financial inclusion also contributes to the formalization of the economy, increasing tax income for governments and ultimately leading to a more stable and resilient society. I know, I know; these are not my usual arguments but rather those that I am so critical of. Keep in mind that I didn't say these positive impacts are all there because of financial inclusion, only that financial inclusion can contribute to those. I am very much aware there are several other factors that contribute to macro-level changes in society. It is true, though, that financial inclusion and impact investing are transformative forces that enable individuals and businesses to access capital for their activities.

Strictly speaking, I personally haven't been involved in impact investing. This is partly because most of the impact investing teams are made up of investment professionals or people with backgrounds in economics. They use theoretical and possibly ESG frameworks to develop a set of indicators that are used to measure and demonstrate impacts. There are claims about investments with *high social impact* that provide a generic description of beneficiaries and actual impacts. The publicly available reports that I read try to capture the types of impacts, but they read like fairy tales to me simply because I'm used to a better-defined group of affected people within the scope of the project. There's also a sense of detachment from the actual outcome, with a strong focus on the output. Investing in a company that goes about its profit-generating activities that happen to benefit the *greater good* is not the same as investing in one that tailors its activities to maximize this greater good (proactive direct impact creation vs. unintended positive consequences). Since impact investing is highly dependent on ESG factors, the limitations identified within the ESG sphere apply here as well. Macro-level overviews of portfolios with limited information on the social aspects and asset level. The beneficiaries are often poorly defined, or they are people who self-select into using the services offered by the company. We are again faced with the dilemma of how to measure and define what our actual impact is. Are people better off because we are more *socially responsible* or want to *do good*? Most likely yes in general, but it's hard to single out people from the general population who will attribute their improved well-being to the company we invested in.

What Are the Advantages of Impact Investing?

I'm trying not to sound too critical, but I have to say what I said before: it takes time and a joint effort to change the culture in which we view and do business. Impact investing calls into question long-held beliefs that social and environmental concerns should be addressed solely through charity donations and that market investments should be focused on maximizing financial returns. The impact investing market provides investors with different options to advance social and environmental problems via investments that also provide financial benefits.

Impact investment may help financiers decrease risk because several environmental investments are heavily subsidized by their governments. Think of renewables, electric vehicles for your companies, or recycling facilities for electric vehicle batteries. This advantage makes these kinds of investments more attractive. The social aspects of impact investing are not subsidized like this currently, but if the trend continues, we will likely see governments support higher-risk social impact investing as well.

The assumption behind impact investing is that by making small, persistent investments in firms and initiatives that have the potential to make a large beneficial impact, investors may lower their total risk while still obtaining favorable returns.

Social enterprise investment often focuses on businesses that utilize their income to enhance the lives of the poor or those who are currently underserved in the market. See why I'm skeptical? Is finding and responding to a market gap really social entrepreneurship? Green investment focuses on businesses that adopt environmentally friendly strategies, such as recycling materials or lowering energy use. The extent of the impact depends on the business model. For some impact investors, having energy efficiency measures included in the way the business is run is enough, while others look for whole operations that are tailored to environmental sustainability. Human capital investment focuses on businesses that create employment or help underserved populations enter the labor force. Enterprise development invests in enterprises that are growing into new markets or creating new employment. Again, how much of this is pure business sense, and how much is done for the positive impact?

Impact investment may be an excellent strategy to increase both social and environmental gains in underserved sectors or areas. Impact investors, for example, may put their capital to use in combating homelessness, hunger, poverty, and inequality by backing firms that make beneficial contributions to society. Moreover, impact investors may help safeguard natural resources and enhance public health by investing in initiatives that minimize pollution or deforestation. Another great example is regenerative agriculture, where farmers are incentivized to increase harvests and work with healthier soil. There are initiatives that support small holders to collectively sell their produce to large-scale international buyers. There's clearly a social impact for farmers who participate in these initiatives, increased employment on these farms, and access to training and equipment to maintain traditional ways of farming. While these investments may not be attractive to investors in general, with the impact investing lens, there is a strong sense of purpose.

Impact investment can be used to respond to a variety of social issues as discussed above. Poverty and inequality, for instance, by increasing access to jobs for low-income communities or providing financing for education. It has been noted earlier that companies create employment that leads to improvement in the socioeconomic situation of whole communities. Impact investing can also be used to provide better access to certain services such as healthcare and education. Investing in education and healthcare is one way impact investors may achieve these objectives. Education has a wide-ranging influence on society, not just because of the information and skills it creates but also because of its potential to offer the chance for social mobility. Investing in education may assist in increasing access to high-quality education for all students, regardless of socioeconomic background. Investing in healthcare may help individuals all around the world by giving them access to basic health services and preventative initiatives. In my world, the generic phrase increasing access does not hold. I talked about this before, but it's important to understand who's actually benefiting from improved access to the new services.

Speaking of the big picture, impact investing might allow private investors to influence public-sector decision-making. Though it seems a bit far-fetched, impact investors can help enhance the quality of government decision-making by offering funding and other support to enterprises and groups striving to change public policy or accomplish social goals. Impact investment has a lot of advantages in that regard. For starters, it can assist in improving the efficiency and efficacy of government expenditure and cofinance initiatives that are typically the government's responsibility. These may include education, healthcare, homelessness, poverty, or even employment for ex-convicts. Impact investment, in addition to increasing public participation, may contribute to cost savings by encouraging businesses to make smarter decisions that eliminate excessive waste or harm caused by their operations. Ultimately, impact investment provides a fresh perspective on business, with the potential to benefit both public welfare and financial stability.

Impact investors can help strengthen public governance in a variety of ways. For example, they can assist in identifying and repairing faulty systems, increasing openness and accountability, and creating opportunities for underrepresented populations. Remember my assumption number one that people and companies want to do good! Impact investors can also help to establish networks and agreements around crucial topics. It may help to strengthen public confidence in governments and businesses by eliminating corruption, which is critical even if we look at ESG frameworks. You are not alone in thinking this sounds too good to be true. In fact, I could not find any examples of this scenario despite my best efforts. Though this might be a sentiment and aspiration for the future, I didn't want to miss out on giving people some ideas to go in the right direction.

Purpose, Scope, and Timing

Purpose

The purpose is very clear and has been explained before, however, it has to be added that impact investing has other aims as well. This includes the transformation of the market (and people's mindset) by demonstrating that creating a positive social impact might not be at the literal cost of the business. There is also a sense of longevity as these investments are created with a long term view, recognizing that changes take time. The delivery mechanism can change and evolve. It used to be direct investment in business, but now it is open to individual investors who can invest in portfolios, and thus indirectly supporting the impact investing field. The field also aims to support projects that have the potential to scale up over time and address challenges on a different scope.

Scope

We have talked about some of the topical scopes of impact investing before. These social issues could be anything from poverty alleviation, education, healthcare, affordable housing to access to clean water, gender equality of social inclusion. Community development is often a very interesting topic to explore as it might include a broader scope through a support of local businesses, infrastructure and job creation.

The investment can focus on a very specific community or settlement, however, some could be on a regional or national level as well. Typical spatial scope might include investment in rural areas, emerging markets.

In terms of the level of control impact investors have on their investment, we briefly touched upon the direct vs. indirect investment approaches. When the impact investors have direct equity or debt investments in businesses they have a very high degree of control over the design and delivery of the projects. In the case of indirect investments the level of control is limited and we might not have the leverage to change the scope or strategy.

Timing

Similarly to several other voluntary social impact products, the best time to start impact investing is now. There are some considerations related to time horizons, as some impact investing activities focus on addressing immediate needs (short-term), while others are more focused on long-term strategies. The majority of impact investments can be structured with flexibility in mind, allowing investors to adapt to changing circumstances or emerging opportunities. The impact goals will also influence the timing considerations for impact investments. Investments in renewable projects for instance may have longer pay back period compared to investments in microfinance.

Limitations

While impact investing has gained popularity, it is not without its limitations:

- *Limited investment opportunities.* This is one of the major drawbacks of impact investing. While the number of impact investment opportunities has increased in recent years, there are still relatively few options available compared to traditional investments.

- *Difficulty measuring impact and lack of standardization.* Unlike traditional investments, for which financial performance can be easily measured, impact investments require the measurement of both financial and social or environmental outcomes. The fact remains that it is a voluntary investment strategy, and thus there are no legal requirements to disclose information. This can make it difficult for investors to compare different impact investments and assess their impact in a consistent way. As I was doing my research for the book, I often felt as though companies and initiatives were trying to say, "My social impact is better than yours." This lack of standardized measurement means that we are comparing apples and pears. What is better: building a hospital or a school? Very much depends on the context. There are, however, approaches such as the social return on investment (SROI) methodology that try to provide a standardized measure, but we'll look at that in a later chapter. The fact remains that qualitative indicators are selected in a way that makes any measurement of social impact very subjective and open to criticism.

- *Potential for greenwashing and ultimately social washing.* There is a risk that some companies may use impact investing as a marketing tool without actually making a significant impact. Impact inflation has been a common criticism of macro-level ESG approaches, and greenwashing has been called out publicly. Several companies failed to prove the impact they were claiming in their sustainability reports. Social washing is a term I first started seeing in the mainstream media after 2020. The idea here is that the social impacts are presented as more significant than they actually are, thus putting the company in a better position when competing for impact investors or high ESG ratings.

- *Lower financial returns.* While impact investments have the potential to generate strong financial returns, they may not always be able to match the returns of traditional investments. This can make impact investing less attractive to some investors who prioritize financial returns over social or environmental impact. Can it be that optimizing for positive social outcomes is so costly? My hope is that the reason for lower returns is due the increased focus on creating a positive impact even if investors sacrifice financial return.

- *High risk.* Many impact investments are early-stage companies or in sectors with relatively high risk. Think of investing in developing markets, often without adequate legal structure or regulation. The customer base might also be low income or underserved for a reason. If customers can't afford your services, then profits will not be generated. Venturing into uncharted territory can make impact investing riskier than traditional investments, which can be a deterrent for some investors.

- *Limited liquidity.* Many impact investments are illiquid, meaning they cannot be easily sold or traded. Existing strategies might be problematic for many reasons, just imagine a fund pulling investments from an education or healthcare project because it is not profitable. They would be canceled immediately.

- *Potential for unintended consequences.* Outcomes such as social or environmental harm may not be apparent at the time of investment. There is no scope for a full impact assessment to see any direct, indirect, cumulative, or residual impacts associated with the project. It takes experience and insider knowledge to be prepared for unintended impacts, especially if those are negative.

The first thing that came to mind is the EBRD's requirement on additionality when financing projects. They say that since their aim is to facilitate a transition to a market economy, they will only finance projects that would otherwise not be eligible for loans or be attractive to investors in the private sector. Impact investing may carry the risk of subsidizing failing businesses because they serve the *greater good*. I do wonder whether impact investors encroaching on new markets prevent others from entering without any ulterior motive of impact creation. A typical example of this would be in a developing country where there is limited capital; foreign impact investors enter to create new markets and end up preventing local investors from participating.

I want to close this section by reiterating that I have limited exposure to impact investing and all my opinions and views are based on what I've heard and read. My background is an advantage when I try to understand annual reports, impact matrices, and indicators, but I know there's a lot more that's not disclosed in the public domain that can probably influence my opinion. I do think there is value in looking beyond the macro-level data and incorporating risks and opportunities with clearly defined beneficiary groups when we talk about social impacts or social benefits. As social impact products are evolving into mainstream financial products, investors and the public alike are more aware and knowledgeable of what each product can and cannot cover.

How It Relates to Other Social Impact Products

Impact investing as a strategy has been around in various forms, but the concept matured over recent years as the other social impact instruments developed as well. It is always useful to put impact investing into this social impact context because it is often deployed alongside other products. Which product was first? Which is better? It is only possible to provide an answer for that in the context of the scope.

Here is how impact investing relates to other investment strategies:

- *Socially responsible investing (SRI).* Like impact investing, SRI seeks to align investments with investors' values. We briefly mentioned the concept in the ESG section and highlighted how much it overlaps with sustainability and ESG. However, unlike impact investing, SRI does not necessarily require that investments generate positive social or environmental impacts. Instead, SRI aims to avoid investing in companies that have a negative impact on society or the environment or do not align with investors' values. As far as I understand, this is a combination of impact investing and other philanthropic initiatives.

- *ESG investing.* ESG frameworks and reports can inform impact investment strategies. It also provides the same high-level overview of the performance of the asset. ESG investing and impact investing are usually used synonymously since they largely cover the same areas. The difference I observed is that ESG investing does not necessarily require the creation of a positive impact;

mitigating negative ones and complying with relevant legislation is sufficient. Think of waste management, energy efficiency, emissions, or workforce management.

- *Philanthropy.* This involves donating money or resources to support charitable causes. We are looking at this more closely in the next chapters. While philanthropy and impact investing share the goal of promoting positive social or environmental outcomes, they differ in terms of the financial return on investment. Philanthropy does not always expect a financial return, whereas impact investing seeks to generate both financial returns and positive impacts.

- *Corporate social responsibility.* CSR is a business practice that involves taking responsibility for the impact of a company's operations on society and the environment. We can simply call this *being a good neighbor.* While CSR and impact investing share the goal of promoting positive social or environmental outcomes, they differ in the level of financial return. CSR may involve investing in social or environmental initiatives that don't necessarily generate a financial return, whereas impact investing seeks to generate both.

- *SIA.* The SIA methodology would serve as a good basis to measure the impacts associated with such investments. Impact investing is using a set of matrices and indicators (qualitative and quantitative) to establish some baseline and measure the impacts in accordance.

In addition to the listed areas, I would highlight the several hybrid approaches that all have the same purpose of positive impact creation.

Sometimes companies mix and merge social impact products to serve their purpose. This is especially true for the voluntary initiatives. I have seen CSR initiatives being called impact investments and vice versa. This general confusion about terms and definitions is why I thought it would be interesting to look at all these products and how they relate to each other.

Individual Impact Investing

Historically, impact investment was done through procedures geared toward institutional investors. Individuals can, however, engage in contributing early-stage or expansion capital to participate in impact investing:

- *Exchange-traded funds (ETFs).* ETFs such as State Street's SPDR Gender Diversity ETF are publicly traded and therefore accessible to anybody with a stock brokerage account. MSCI has eleven ETFs that track environmental, social, and governance indexes, including popular low-carbon and sustainability indexes. These are largely selected based on their ESG rating.

- *Syndicate or group investment.* There are also groups of angel investors that focus on impact, who all invest as a syndicate. Investors' Circle in the United States, Clearly Social Angels in the United Kingdom, and the worldwide investor network Toniic are a few examples.

- *Platforms for digital microfinance.* There are other web-based investment platforms that provide lower-cost investing options. Since stock agreements might be prohibitively expensive for small-scale transactions, microfinance loans are more common on these platforms than equity investments. MyC4, which was created in 2006, enabled retail investors to lend to small enterprises in African nations through local intermediaries; however, the service was permanently discontinued in 2019. Microplace was an early United States supplier of similar services, which stopped taking on new loans in 2014, noting that its outcomes "haven't scaled to the wider societal effect we hope to create."

- *Asia's impact investment.* Impact investing in Asia is a booming industry, with several funds now active. Private Impact Investors (PIIs) deployed US$904 million in impact capital in Southeast Asia between 2007 and 2017, while Development Finance Institutions (DFIs) spent US$11.9 million.

It is quite remarkable how the market is responding to the customers who want to gain access to impact investing. It remains a personal choice and responsibility to look at the framework for impact creation and measurement to ensure that our choices align with our values and to be aware of the risks associated with such products. A fun experiment is to see how many of these impact investing platforms reference other social impact products such as microfinance, ESG, and CSR.

What Is the Social Impact?

The impact in impact investing incorporates the potential social aspects with greater detail than any other social impact products we have seen so far. Many of the businesses from the early days of impact investing focus on solving human problems: providing services to underserved communities, addressing aspects of vulnerability through innovative solutions, and creating employment and economic prosperity for people. Some of the greatest innovative business solutions have come out of impact investing, though the indicators and frameworks to demonstrate these impacts were not well developed before. As the other investment products with environmental or social outcomes emerged, impact investing somehow remained a niche field—siloed from other fields where people like me work. Nearly all the people I've come across in impact investing have backgrounds in banking or economics. As I discussed earlier in the book, what makes someone a social specialist is a very complex topic.

Social impact can take many different forms, depending on the investment focus. The lack of a regulated framework is a blessing and a curse at the same time. We talked about the lack of ratability and comparability, but what's more interesting is the lack of limitations. This allows innovative solutions to be deployed to address a variety of social issues, especially if it means financial return. For example, impact investments may target underserved communities or promote gender equality, education, healthcare, affordable housing, clean energy, or sustainable agriculture. While these topics are part of the ESG frameworks to a certain extent, there is a duality of mandatory and voluntary requirements that are more or less standardized. Many ESG investors would not try to set up a business to provide housing for the homeless, even if it was somehow a for-profit endeavor. This is because of the lack of broad social coverage of ESG, though most of the ESG frameworks do consider supporting initiatives such as the Sustainable Development Goals (SDGs). I will talk more about this and how the social impact products try to align with the relevant goals. Even in my line of work, we mapped our performance standards and requirements in line with the SDGs—partly to see what areas we can contribute to and partly to help our clients demonstrate the impact.

In addition to generating social impact, impact investing can also have a catalytic effect on businesses to incentivize them to create innovative solutions. Impact investors can help create new markets and build the foundation for long-term sustainable development—however we define it. Impact investing can also help build the capacity of local organizations and businesses, promoting economic growth and creating jobs. Social issues are complex, so we need to work with complex solutions.

Simply put, here are some common examples of social impact areas that impact investing seeks to address:

- *Access to basic services.* This can include healthcare, education, water, sanitation, and affordable housing.

- *Job creation.* Impact investing can create jobs and promote economic development, particularly in underserved communities, for vulnerable employees or people who find it challenging to get employed due to their circumstances.

- *Gender equality.* This can be promoted by investing in businesses or organizations that prioritize women's empowerment and participation.

- *Environmental sustainability.* Impact investing can promote this by investing in clean energy, sustainable agriculture, and other green initiatives.

- *Social inclusion.* Impact investing can promote this by investing in businesses or organizations that focus on marginalized groups such as refugees, people with disabilities, or indigenous communities.

- *Community development.* Impact investing can support this by investing in local businesses, cooperatives, or social enterprises that promote economic growth and social welfare.

- *Health and wellness.* Impact investing can improve this by investing in medical research, or programs that promote healthy lifestyles and mental health.

- *Financial inclusion.* Impact investing can promote this by investing in businesses or organizations that provide financial services to underserved populations, such as microfinance institutions or community banks.

These are just a few examples of the many social impact areas that impact investing seeks to address. As we have seen, most of these have a loosely defined set of beneficiaries or target groups. In some cases, the social impact is limited to one community or one set of customers, while in other cases, the impact is high level and generic. It does not mean that the shift toward caring for positive social change is not valuable, but it's definitely hard to measure.

Examples of Impact Investing Done Right

I didn't have to look very hard to identify publicly available information on the impact investment initiatives of several large funds. My assumption that everyone wants to do good, especially if there is no financial downside, was proven true. The positive changes created by these companies might not be measurable in a standardized way, but they've certainly contributed toward improving the lives of many. I am a firm believer that being up front about our purpose and what we can and cannot achieve with our social impact products would eliminate a lot of the social washing that we see daily. The examples below clearly show that there is a positive social impact, but we are not able to measure it or even compare one initiative with another.

Here are some examples of social investing done right:

- Acumen is a nonprofit impact investment fund that invests in businesses that provide basic services such as healthcare, water, and energy to low-income communities in developing countries. Since its inception in 2001, Acumen has invested over USD$125 million in more than 130 companies that have had a positive impact on the lives of millions of people. For example, Acumen has invested in companies that provide affordable healthcare to rural communities in India, solar lighting to low-income households in Kenya, and mobile banking services to small businesses in Pakistan. These investments have created jobs, improved access to basic services, and generated economic growth in some of the world's poorest communities.

- The Calvert Impact Capital started as a foundation and is now operating as a financial institution that has invested over USD$2 billion in community development projects in the United States and around the world. Calvert Impact has invested in a variety of initiatives, including affordable housing, community facilities, and small businesses, to promote economic development and social welfare. For example, Calvert Impact has invested in a community development corporation that developed affordable housing for low-income families in Washington DC, a microfinance institution that provides financial services to small businesses in Peru, and a nonprofit organization that provides job training and support to individuals with disabilities in the

United States. These investments have created jobs, strengthened communities, and improved the lives of hundreds of thousands of people.

- The Omidyar Network is a philanthropic firm that invests in businesses and organizations that promote social and economic progress. The Omidyar Network has invested over USD$1 billion in initiatives such as microfinance, education, and civic engagement, to promote social inclusion and economic opportunity. For example, the Omidyar Network has invested in a company that provides affordable internet access to low-income households in India, a nonprofit organization that promotes civic engagement and public accountability in Africa, and a social enterprise that provides job training and support to refugees in the United States. These investments have helped empower individuals and communities, promote economic development, and drive positive social change.

- Patagonia has been mentioned before, however here we mention then in a different capacity. Patagonia has invested in a renewable energy company that produces wind and solar power in the United States, a regenerative agriculture initiative that promotes sustainable farming practices in Chile, and a sustainable fishing initiative that supports sustainable fisheries in Alaska. These investments have helped reduce greenhouse gas emissions, promote biodiversity, and protect ecosystems.

There are many more examples and several books about interesting stories related to impact investing. It is a powerful tool for promoting development and progress. There is a huge potential to learn from each other and calibrate impact investing to bring even more benefits that are measurable and demonstratable. I hope I will have the chance to be more involved in this field in the future.

Conclusion

Impact investing is a growing market that is largely unregulated from a social perspective. While there are limitations to impact investing, including challenges related to measurement and standardization, impact investors have the luxury of defining their own agenda without any limiting frameworks. Demonstrating impacts can be a real challenge, as they are either very specific to a certain community or very generic. This prevents the rating or comparison of businesses or investments, making these projects one of a kind.

The examples of social investing done right demonstrate the potential of impact investing to create meaningful social and environmental impacts while generating financial returns. From providing basic services to low-income communities to promoting economic development and environmental sustainability, impact investing has the potential to address some of the world's most pressing challenges. As it continues to evolve, it's important to ensure that it remains grounded in a commitment to positive social and environmental impact and to learn from other social impact products to refine the methodology of impact creation and measurement.

CHAPTER 4

CORPORATE SOCIAL RESPONSIBILITY

CSR has been a wonderful tool for companies to demonstrate their commitment to being good neighbors and taking care of their communities. CSR is a voluntary positive impact creation tool that benefits society. It's essentially a commitment that companies make to act in a socially responsible manner, beyond just maximizing profits. In recent years, CSR has become increasingly important for companies of all sizes, to address emerging issues and cultivate the culture of social responsibility. Consumers are becoming more conscious of the social and environmental impact of the products and services they use and are demanding that companies act responsibly. In response, many companies are embracing CSR as a way to enhance their reputation, build customer loyalty, and attract new customers.

But what exactly does CSR entail? There are many ways that companies can demonstrate their commitment to social responsibility. For example, they can adopt environmentally sustainable practices, reduce their carbon footprint, and implement fair labor practices. Companies that embrace these practices not only benefit society and the environment but often enjoy cost savings and increased efficiency.

It's similar to ESG and sustainability in a way but more voluntary and without legal obligations, strict guidelines, or limitations. They can also donate to charitable causes, sponsor community events, and support education and healthcare initiatives. One common way that companies demonstrate their commitment is through corporate philanthropy. This can take the form of cash donations, in-kind contributions, or volunteer work. Some companies even have their own charitable organizations that focus on specific social issues, such as education or healthcare. This enters the territory of philanthropy which we will look at more closely in the next chapter.

However, there are also criticisms of CSR. Some argue that companies engage in CSR only to improve their image, rather than out of a genuine desire to benefit society. Others argue that companies should focus on maximizing profits and leave social issues to governments and nonprofit organizations.

The power of CSR was also recognized by governments. Notably, India updated its Companies Act (2013) to add Schedule VII and the Companies Rules (2014), making it mandatory for larger companies to have a CSR program while also requiring them to have a CSR committee to approve and execute the CSR Policy/Program. Mauritius also introduced legislation mandating that companies implement corporate philanthropy in 2009. South Africa mandated the CSR committee to oversee corporate sustainability initiatives in 2008, while the UK Companies Act (2006) required company directors to take into consideration the interests of employees, suppliers, the environment, and the community. The legislative push has led to more and more companies setting up some form of a CSR initiative. Whether it is executed correctly or has the desired outcome remains a question in many cases. Despite the criticism, CSR remains an important concept in business today, not only because it is often mandatory, but also because businesses want to connect with their customers and communities. It allows companies to demonstrate their values and commitment to social responsibility and build trust with their stakeholders.

What Is It?

Strictly looking at the definition, CSR is a tool that allows companies to demonstrate their commitment to social responsibility and build trust with their stakeholders. By engaging in socially responsible actions, companies can create a positive social impact and contribute to the well-being of society. If you've come this far in the book, you know I have an issue with generic definitions like that. Every company is different, and CSR has different forms and mechanisms. Some companies outsource expertise and enter philanthropy while others have wonderful CSR experts on their payroll who know all its ins and outs. One example of CSR in action is a company that invests in education initiatives within the city or community where it's situated. By supporting education programs, a company can help improve the prospects of young people and contribute to the development of the community in which it operates. This not only benefits the individuals who receive the education but also the wider society, which benefits from a more educated and skilled workforce. This can also be taken one step further to introduce internships or graduate opportunities. While the conclusions drawn are macro level, attributable as opposed to direct impacts, they remain valid and very real.

As we have seen, CSR is typically a voluntary initiative started by a company to respond to the needs of the locals or to fund solutions to issues that are meaningful to the people on the leadership team. The budget for CSR is commonly allocated on an annual basis, and there is little variation in the type of financed activities. The main topics addressed through CSR tend to be community development, healthcare, education, shelters for the homeless, sports (supporting local football teams), food for vulnerable populations, services for the elderly, funding shelters for victims of domestic violence, for instance. The eligibility criteria for funding are not typically disclosed, and in most cases, it's not an open bidding for competing initiatives. I have seen companies asking for projects to bid for CSR funding and the senior leadership selected the project with the highest *social impact*—comparing apples and pears. CSR being discretionary with no requirements for reporting (other than the ESG or sustainability report), companies can decide they're no longer able to finance CSR activities. I have yet to see a complete discontinuation of a CSR initiative; more commonly, I see gradual downsizing and maintaining very small-scale support in the longest term. This is especially true for outsourced social impact creation where the company is funding another organization as opposed to a more hands-on approach.

However, it's important to note that CSR is not just about doing good for society. It's also about creating long-term value for the company itself. I have seen CSR be an add-on to livelihood restoration initiatives that responded directly to project-related impacts. The CSR imitative allowed for other people—not affected directly by the project—to participate in long-term value creation in agricultural production for instance. This is especially common for projects where the company is not only constructing but also operating a project (power plant for instance) and they want to maintain good relationships with locals in the long run.

Furthermore, CSR also means the integration of social and environmental considerations into their business operations and stakeholder interactions. It involves going beyond legal compliance and taking a proactive approach to addressing social and environmental issues that are relevant to the company's operations and stakeholders. My world of adverse impact mitigation could be neatly complemented by CSR initiatives.

Typically, CSR would encompass the following activities:

- *Environmental sustainability.* reducing the company's carbon footprint and minimizing the impact of its operations on the environment. Simple initiatives within the community to collect waste or recycle materials. Supporting communities by donating trees to parks or paying to upgrade public areas.

- *Ethical business practices.* promoting fairness, transparency, and integrity in all business dealings, anticorruption, antibribery, and governance. Sounds like ESG?

- *Community engagement.* investing in local communities and addressing the needs and concerns of stakeholders. This could be anything from healthcare and education to building shelters for the homeless or victims of domestic violence. There can also be donations to hospitals for specific purposes; for example, providing incubators for NICU units or sponsoring cancer screening initiatives.

- *Employee activism.* companies can provide paid time off for their employees to volunteer with other charities or initiatives. I think this is a good way for companies to indirectly engage with communities and support smaller-scale initiatives.

- *Philanthropy and charitable giving.* Now this is where definitions get confusing. While they overlap to a certain extent, technically there is a difference between philanthropy and CSR. CSR may also include contributing to social and environmental causes through charitable donations and community outreach programs—technically donating to philanthropic organizations. You can see the overlap, but I would argue that these two products have significant differences. Philanthropy in this instance is the executing agency, while CSR is the means to channel funds from a company.

The goal of CSR is to create long-term value for the company, its stakeholders, and society by balancing economic, social, and environmental considerations. If you are getting confused by definitions and overlaps, I don't blame you. I was in the same shoes when I decided to finally sit down, do my research, and write down my findings. Though labeling and guidelines are different for voluntary initiatives (CSR, philanthropy), the demonstration of positive social impacts remains important.

The Advantages of Corporate Social Responsibility

CSR has a strong focus on connecting with *communities*. Whether these are communities around the corporate headquarters, or around the manufacturing or production facilities, the initiatives aim to support workers and organizations to form better bonds, enhance morale, and make both employees and employers feel more connected to the world around them. Apart from the environmental benefits, here are some more reasons why firms embrace CSR:

- *Brand identification.* According to research published in the *Journal of Consumer Psychology*, consumers are more inclined to favor a firm that has a well publicized CSR initiative in line with consumer values over a corporation that produces superior products. Consumers are becoming more conscious of the effects that businesses may have on their communities, and many now base their purchase decisions on a company's CSR. When a corporation becomes more involved in CSR, it is more likely to gain a good brand reputation.

- *Relations with investors.* According to Boston Consulting Group research, firms that are thought to be leaders in relieving environmental, social, or governance issues have an 11 percent value premium over their competitors. Enacting a CSR strategy tends to favorably affect how investors feel about an organization and how they see the company's worth for organizations trying to gain an advantage and beat the market. As you can see, without a clear distinction between mandatory and voluntary activities, social impact products get mixed up.

- *Employee involvement.* Another study conducted by researchers from Texas A&M, Temple, and the University of Minnesota discovered that CSR-related values that connect businesses and workers act as nonfinancial employment perks that improve employee retention. Workers are more inclined to stay with a firm they trust. This decreases staff turnover, angry employees, and the total cost of hiring a new employee.

- *Risk reduction.* Consider negative behaviors such as employee group discrimination, disregard for natural resources, or the unethical use of firm assets. This sort of action is more likely to result in lawsuits, litigation, or legal processes in which the firm may suffer financial losses and be featured in the press. Companies that integrate CSR initiatives into their operations can reduce their risk by avoiding adverse impacts and enhancing positive ones, often in parallel with other social products.

CSR efforts can be challenging to evaluate strategically since not all advantages can be monetarily transferred back to the firm. For example, it may be difficult to determine the beneficial influence that planting one thousand trees may have on a company's brand image. Individual initiatives might be very localized so generic social impacts on the whole community are more challenging to measure and demonstrate. Initiatives often sponsor existing civil society organizations and their operations, thus contributing to existing impact-creation mechanisms as opposed to creating new impact.

On the other side, CSR is a completely voluntary social impact product that has been often misused to virtue signal, incentivize locals to tolerate harmful impacts of operations, or even to *bribe* local leaders. Though it is generally untrue for the majority of initiatives, I have seen versions of CSR initiatives used to make people accept the adverse project impacts without protesting. On the flip side, the majority of my projects are not like this, and the CSR initiatives are genuinely to support the community. Nevertheless, companies tend to sponsor activities that are in line with their values or the values of their customers. We can argue whether those values are *good* or *bad*, whether they are only important because a company doesn't want to be canceled. But I don't want to go there. From a strictly technical point of view, CSR has been proven to create a positive social impact, though clarification of the definition, mechanism, and guidelines would benefit the improvement of this product. What I would like to see is more transparency over available funds, who or what type of activities are eligible to apply for it, the mechanism to follow up on where the money is spent, who the beneficiaries are, and how the impact is materializing. Now I know this sounds a little controlling, but if we really use CSR as an extension of our values, then we should make sure that it is not misrepresenting our intentions.

Purpose, Scope, and Timing

This is by far my favorite section of each chapter because I feel like I am bringing new context to what we already know. A lack of definition is what led to the misunderstandings of the social impact products that were deployed with false promises from companies and disproportionate expectations from the public. CSR is one of the classic stories of this. CSR is often misunderstood as a company's obligation to *care* for customers and communities. The famous opinion that a CEO has the fiduciary duty to make the company profitable, not liked, comes to mind. Whether you agree with this statement or whether it is standing the test of time, we can agree that it is very rare that there are legal obligations for a company to go beyond compliance with ESG frameworks on the social aspects. Apart from India there are few examples of countries that legally requires a CSR program. Though, there is a lack of guidance on what this program should look like, there are plenty of resources that can inspire companies to develop their programs. In the meantime, speaking of *doing good,* I hope to inspire the conversation around why the interest to focus on extra-mile efforts, when many companies struggle with legal compliance. As stakeholder become more informed on social impact products, they will be able to guide companies towards deploying the right tool for the desired outcomes. The starting point for all these initiatives emerged from people caring for each other and wanting to genuinely *make a difference.* CSR is no different.

Purpose

In my view, the purpose of CSR is to support the communities around the business, build trust, and engage with them in the long-term. The goal is to be viewed not only as a good citizen (typically through ESG and compliance topics: taxes paid, legislation followed, etc.) but also as a good neighbor. One that cares about their communities, especially those who are more vulnerable. This can be children, the elderly, people with disabilities, the homeless, victims of violence or abuse, ex-inmates, or people with limited access to healthcare or education. Vulnerability is an interesting concept in the context of the CSR. In my world, we assess whether certain groups are disproportionately affected by the project or more vulnerable to certain project impacts. For CSR, the dimensions of vulnerability can encompass a variety of aspects: general vulnerability based on age, health condition, gender or self-identity, sexual orientation, and socioeconomic status.

The purpose of CSR may not be to introduce systemic changes in the city, region, or country, but to voluntarily supportongoing (or new) initiatives that that are in line with its own values to give back to the community. I feel like I'm going in circles as I explain this because of the vague definitions of *community* and *giving back* to them. Typically, CSR would look at issues outside the company as opposed to within the company. So topics related to corruption and discrimination are covered under other, legally binding tools.

Now on to the more divisive argument that CSR is a way for corporations to optimize taxes. Corporations use tax advantages whether they do CSR or not, so if they optimize, why not create a positive *social impact*, right? I'm all for that! I feel, though, that stakeholder and customer pressure often put companies in a challenging position in which they are expected to support certain global trends and social movements. I will not name any of these trends to avoid stepping on any toes. I am merely looking at CSR from a technical perspective as opposed to judging its validity. We don't have to go back in time very far to remember the movements that demanded companies to include more women in senior management and boards. It was considered to be a universal value that women should have equal opportunities. We all agreed that companies should be a place of equal opportunities (note how I don't use equal outcomes or equity) regardless of race, ethnicity, gender, nationality, or disability. Is CSR the best social impact product for this? I don't think so. ESG may be better because it focuses heavily on the employment and labor aspects. CSR might be a good way to increase women's access to education, internships, graduate programs, extracurriculars, or scholarships. The ESG approach is compliance with existing legislation while taking affirmative action, and CSR is the *good neighbor* approach. What has the higher *social value* or *better* impact? We're comparing apples and pears because the first option tries to proactively reach out to people who have already been educated to integrate them into the workforce, while the other creates a supply of more employable people for the future.

While there might be ulterior motives for supporting certain CSR initiatives, I'd prefer to focus on the better side of this. I'd like to believe that businesses are realizing they have a responsibility to go beyond just maximizing profits and instead create value for society as a whole. In this section, we will explore the different purposes of CSR and how they can benefit companies and society. Let's dive in and explore the different purposes of CSR:

- Enhance corporate reputation.

- Create positive social impact.

- Attract and retain talent.

- Build customer loyalty.

- Mitigate risks.

- Increase profitability.

- Meet stakeholder expectations.

Scope

The scope of CSR encompasses a wide range of activities and initiatives that can vary depending on the industry, location, and size of the company. Since it is not regulated by any legislation, CSR initiatives can cover almost anything, the only limit is our imagination and company budget! It is specifically for this reason that I would emphasize having a clearly defined scope when starting these initiatives. We have seen that there are external expectations to align with key social movements.

When we are looking at determining the scope of an initiative, it is important to focus on one or more of the following aspects:

- *Topical scope.* What topics or issues we want to address. This could be homelessness, access to education or healthcare, or supporting local youth to do more sports.

- *Industry or sectoral scope.* We might not have a topic in mind but maybe our business is connected to the healthcare sector. In this case, we might want to support or create initiatives relevant to the industry. This could be donations to research institutions, paying for refurbishment of hospital wings, or scholarships for medical students. Note how we are in the philanthropy territory again!

- *Funding structure and mechanisms.* Our scope might be limited to providing funding to initiatives, but CSR also has other mechanisms that we mentioned before. Many large companies have inhouse teams that implement more hands-on approaches to impact creation. The scope could be much better defined and tailored to the company's limits if the mechanism is to create an impact through a new initiative fully controlled by the company.

- *Spatial scope.* What I often see is the lack of clarity on where the initiatives are planned to take place. This is especially true for *community* support programs. It is important to add whether eligibility for support is governed by being in the vicinity of a facility or corporate offices. Often CSR initiatives are broad without a defined geographical focus.

As you can see, it is important for each company to define what is within the scope of its own CSR approach. This will ensure that expectations are managed with full transparency regarding what the company is supporting, how it aligns with its values, and whether there are opportunities for other initiatives to get some support. Since it is a voluntary type of support, there are no rules around the public disclosure of the company's activities. In any case, defining the scope of support every year will help target areas that matter to the company.

Timing

CSR activities can happen at different business stages, but one thing is certain: once you start it, there is an expectation that this is long-term support for the cause.

- Companies should consider incorporating CSR into their business practices early on in their development. This can help establish a culture of social responsibility and ensure that CSR initiatives are integrated into the company's operations from the beginning. However, it does beg the question of what differentiates a company with built-in CSR from the beginning, from a social enterprise. We will definitely see how these two products overlap and what differences they have.

- Times of crisis, such as natural disasters or pandemics, can present opportunities for companies to engage in CSR initiatives. These initiatives can provide much-needed support to affected communities and demonstrate the company's commitment to social responsibility.

- Companies should consider engaging in CSR initiatives when entering new markets, as this can help establish positive relationships with local communities and demonstrate the company's commitment to responsible business practices. I have especially seen this with companies expanding their manufacturing or operations into developing countries.

- Companies should also consider engaging in CSR initiatives in response to requests or concerns from stakeholders, such as customers, employees, or investors. This can help to build trust and demonstrate the company's commitment to responsible business practices.

There is no hard rule about when and how CSR should be started. When a business is ready to afford to provide support and has identified causes in line with the company's values, then that's the right time. The best time to start any CSR activity is now. And once you start, it's hard to stop without pushback from beneficiaries.

Limitations

When I was brainstorming this section, I couldn't help but remember a Hungarian folk tale about a very smart girl. The tale goes:

> *"There was a very smart girl in the village. She was so smart that even the king heard about her and wanted to meet her. To test her smarts, the king put the girl through a series of tests. After she passed all the initial challenging tests, the king had one final test for her. The king said to her: "Bring me something but bring me nothing. Let it be present and not be present at the same time." The girl thought long and hard about how to solve this, then had an idea. She got two sieves from the kitchen and caught a white dove in the garden. She then took the sieves with the dove inside to the king. The king opened the sieves, and the dove flew away. The girl said, "See? I brought something, but I also brought nothing. It is present and it isn't present at the same time."*

CSR as it is now—unregulated, often misunderstood, and undefined—reminds me of this tale. It has a huge potential to be something incredibly useful that many people can benefit from, but it's not used to its full potential in a transparent manner.

How do I participate or benefit?

The general idea is that the lack of well-defined eligibility criteria cuts off initiatives from being sponsored by corporations. The smaller-scale initiatives, by definition, will have a very small impact— sometimes only on a few people (think of sponsoring a school sports club in a small town). That's not to discount the importance of such social impacts though. It just means that there's often little to no room to self-select into it. It does not usually address wider social issues or contribute to wider positive social impact, yet the reporting on CSR almost always incorporates the generic community development narrative.

What is the legislation or the guidance?

One of the primary limitations of CSR is that there is no legal obligation for companies to perform socially responsible activities (apart from India). While some regulations may require companies to meet certain social and environmental standards, there is no universal requirement for companies to engage in CSR. Guidance and expertise is available on the market, but there are different delivery mechanisms and different approaches to implementing a CSR program. There is legislation around charitable giving, employee well-being, equality acts, and the like, which are aspects that might be related to CSR initiatives, yet these do not directly govern all types of CSR initiatives. Some companies might even decide that they would not engage in any CSR. It is very rare for large, international organizations though. CSR, much like impact investing, has a great potential to tap into areas that are currently outside the scope of the SIA or ESG.

What are the costs?

Another limitation of CSR is that it can be costly and resource intensive. CSR initiatives often require significant financial and human resources, which can be challenging for smaller companies or those operating in highly competitive industries. This can limit the ability of some companies to engage in CSR initiatives, which can impact their reputation and brand image. The expectations can run high and financial support is expected year after year. When times are tough and profits are low, it's rather challenging to voluntarily spend money on external initiatives.

How do I measure my impact?

CSR initiatives can also lack consistency and standardization across different industries and companies. There is no universal definition of what constitutes CSR, which can lead to inconsistencies in the types of activities that companies engage in. This can make it difficult for stakeholders to compare and evaluate the CSR performance of different companies, which can limit its effectiveness as a tool for promoting social goals. Some initiatives are rather small scale (e.g., planting trees for the local park), while others have a much broader reach. There is no formula that guarantees impact per pound spent, though SROI measures impact per pound spent.

What is my reach with the initiative?

CSR initiatives can also be limited in their ability to address structural issues that contribute to social problems. They may focus on addressing symptoms rather than the root causes of social issues, typically focusing on a subset of the population. This is especially true for CSR initiatives that overlap with certain government responsibilities such as education or healthcare, as the initiative might contribute to the cost of infrastructure construction. The question of operational responsibilities is not often discussed. Even if a company covered (or contributed to) the costs of construction, it is not responsible for the maintenance of institutions (paying the bills) or staffing (finding appropriate teachers). Staff members are not on their payroll, and the services/curriculums are not designed by them. They might claim direct impact for making the infrastructure available but they have no influence over who can access the services.

Am I inflating my contribution to impact creation?

Another limitation of CSR is the risk of social washing. Social washing in this context means that companies engage in superficial or misleading CSR activities to enhance their brand image or reputation. This can undermine the effectiveness of CSR as a tool for promoting social goals. We often see how companies attribute indirect impacts to macro level positive outcomes. Looking back at the previous example above, I bet we have all seen companies stating that they support kids' access to education by building new classrooms. While this is not technically incorrect, it is not the full picture.

On a positive note, CSR is a field with many great experts who have vast experience in designing, implementing initiatives, and measuring impacts. While it might be time to redefine our understanding of CSR as we know it, there have certainly been conversations around the limitations listed here. Several companies use CSR as a term for other tools because we do not yet have the appropriate language for the social impact products in the context that I offer in this book.

How It Relates to Other Social Impact Products

I want to address the relationship between SIA and CSR first. As I pointed out there have been occasions where project-related impacts resulted in measures to restore the livelihoods of directly affected people. In some cases, this meant activities around agriculture, animal husbandry, or other longer-term investments. Some companies decided that if they are spending the money to address these via training and the provision of products and tools for a relatively large number of affected people, they might as well expand these benefits to indirectly affected people focusing on the operations phase and long-term collaboration. This is where CSR begins, and the safeguarding of adverse social impacts ends.

A more recent example I can think of is when, during the SIA studies, the local community shared several infrastructure improvements that would require external intervention. Subsidized solar panels for households, support for the school so it can pay for electricity, scholarships for kids so they can go to university, a computer lab for the school, and financing for the specialist doctor to come a few times a week to treat patients or follow up. While these are typically not within the scope of the SIA because they are not adverse project impacts, CSR is a great way to address some of these localized issues to foster long-term engagement with the community. It would cost very little for the company to pay for these initiatives on an annual basis and would demonstrate their interest in becoming a really good neighbor to this community. They might not even know about these without the SIA being deployed. Strategic stakeholder engagement, as promoted by international best practices under the SIA, helps to establish two-way communication with the communities around the operational sites and understand their concerns related to the business activities. Sometimes these meetings can be opportunities to discuss other environment-related concerns: discharge to freshwaters, waste management, hazardous waste management, or emissions. CSR activities can also respond to such environmental needs.

ESG factors somewhat correlate and overlap with CSR-related aspects, especially on the social side. For instance, the concept of engaging with communities regardless of being affected by operations is the same for ESG and CSR. Sustainability and ESG, much like CSR, are concerned with the long-term impacts of business activities on *communities* and want to engage with them to *do good*. In terms of social impact, sustainability means the established relationship with stakeholders who matter as customers, brand reputation, and shareholders. Some might argue that ethical business practices and good governance of ESG also overlap with CSR initiatives. This means that a company reducing GHG emissions, minimizing waste, conserving the environment, paying the right taxes, and operating with a permit contributes to the long-term benefits of not only neighboring communities but the whole of society. The element of trust-building is important under CSR. ESG usually uses its reporting and rating to build trust through transparency. As CSR initiatives are related to company values, it is important to address the types of policies and written values a company has. Under ESG, almost all companies will have policies and statements on equal opportunity, nondiscrimination, human rights, whistleblowing, code of conduct, and requirements of reporting environmental and social aspects of operations to the board. Several of these topics can be addressed or enhanced with CSR, and CSR might also help to demonstrate company contributions toward addressing the SDGs, for instance. As I highlighted in the limitations, we need to be more honest and admit that while we might contribute to a positive impact, so are others. CSR is still voluntary while several aspects of ESG remain regulated by legislation.

CSR initiatives have a lot in common with philanthropy: the financing m e chanism (often n o fi na ncial re tu rn) an d th e vo lu ntary nature, though the mechanism to deliver the impact is different. These both can include financial donations to support a cause in line with the values of the business, but philanthropy also includes nonfinancial contributions. Philanthropy is typically an activity of an external organization that is set up to deliver a program. CSR on the other hand, can be in-house within a company or outsourced where a company is supporting other organizations in impact delivery.

Impact investing has an interesting intersection with CSR. Several of the books I've read on the topic cited initiatives that started off as CSR but grew into an impact investing business. Let's say a company is funding healthcare activities that are free or heavily subsidized for a part of the community, while others pay full price for the same services. This is the business model: the paying customers subsidize or cover the cost for those who have no means to access these services otherwise. While this business model might work in certain parts of the world, it also gives way to the disproportionate taxing of the middle class, as they are often the ones picking up the tab. The idea that a CSR initiative can be turned into a business, either social enterprise or impact investing, is not new. The premise of a social enterprise is that it provides services for underserved or vulnerable communities, or that the business is undertaken with the primary objective to bring social benefits. Impact investing also wants to see positive impacts related to the capital they put to work. In a way, these industries and products are not limited in what they can include in their scope. If something that benefits communities can be turned into a profit-making business, it's surely a win-win situation.

I have seen CSR deployed without careful consideration of how the values of the funded activities align with company values or community preference. I have seen CSR used to incentivize local leaders into supporting the operations of the company. While there are drawbacks to some of the other social impact products, the general lack of legal regulation on CSR definitely brings about a unique set of challenges. This includes eligibility criteria for participation in the initiative, deciding what the community needs and what is an effective mechanism for impact delivery. I certainly see how CSR initiatives could be greatly enhanced by defining the scope and purpose of the interventions with more transparency. The challenge remains, though, that impacts are tricky to demonstrate. That doesn't mean they're not there, it just means that providing generic descriptions of perceived positive impacts brings a risk of social washing. I very much want to see SIAs used to inform community development and CSR interventions as a standard practice.

What Is the Social Impact?

CSR initiatives are designed to promote positive social impacts by addressing social challenges and encouraging responsible business practices. It is, however, not a tool for responding to and compensating for adverse operations-related social impacts. This is the first social impact product in the book that is not necessarily about demonstrating an impact or creating a new impact from scratch, but more about contributing to other initiatives. Since there is no expectation of financial return, the expectation to demonstrate the impact appears differently.

Here the narrative and the framing of the argument are important from a demonstration point of view, while in the case of ESG or SIA, we need the numbers and comparison to preintervention baseline. CSR also uses numbers but targets impact demonstration very differently. CSR initiatives can vary in size and scope, so some initiatives may have very localizable positive impacts that can be measured by the number of new people using the services or gaining access to them for the first time. On some occasions, though, CSR initiatives involve funding preexisting organizations that get support from other companies and even the government. In these instances, it is incredibly challenging to demonstrate our company's social impact without social washing. If we fund a charity, how many of the beneficiaries are served because of our contribution?

The main purpose of CSR is not to score points or obtain a higher ranking, unlike ESG, but to make a difference. Reporting is essential for transparency, but impact demonstration relies heavily on framing the narrative and putting the impact into context. How do we measure the importance of trees in a park used by school kids in a small town? What is the monetary value of waste being recycled? How much is a shelter that provides a haven for victims of domestic violence worth? Quantification of such impacts sounds ridiculous and inappropriate. The beauty of CSR is that it can create an impact at a localized or macro level without having to bother about showcasing it in a way we saw with SIA or ESG.

Although in some cases the social impact might only cover a section of the community, it can be very significant to the people affected. I remember on one of my projects in an East African country, the developer agreed to use some of the findings from the SIA and community consultation as part of its CSR initiative. The project was a hydropower plant that had significant implications on the way of life and land use in this remote area. The communities were very rural, with limited access to electricity or running water. Several people had pit latrines, but there were families without any access to sanitation. The client listened to this and developed a long-term CSR initiative that paid for the infrastructure (cable and towers) to provide the local school with electricity so the kids could use the full day for learning and activities. The company also invested in a set of computers and tutors for the children.

The company recognized the need for better access to healthcare as well. Since it was a requirement for them to bring medical staff for the main operational areas of the project, they saw the opportunity to set certain times during the week when locals could have access to these medical services. This hybrid approach (safeguarding and CSR) cost them very little since the main cost of setting up and operating the medical office was included in the occupational health and safety budget. Costs only increased slightly to cover the extra time of the doctor. Still, for the pregnant lady and her baby, it meant easy access to potentially lifesaving care. Previously she would have had to travel for two days to see a doctor, and now she had access to one almost any time.

The same project also had the idea to upgrade housing for the people whom the project had physically relocated. Many of them lived in very poor conditions, as I discussed above, often without a borehole or a separate kitchen. Though it was partly compliance and social safeguarding, the client did go the extra mile to pay for much better housing, keeping the communities together in the new relocation site, and paying for extra household appliances and items they knew were valuable for the locals. This is how many families, who otherwise couldn't dream of it, got their first cows or donkeys. This is how most families got a kitchen for the very first time. This one project managed to cover access to sanitation, improved living conditions, electricity, education, and healthcare. The impact was localized to the communities living around the project, but it literally changed their lives.

Here is probably a good place to talk about the art of reporting these types of impacts. In my role and my world, we tend to step away from heart-wrenching stories and focus on factual reporting of compliance-based and extra mile–type initiatives. I am only human, so I was greatly impacted by meeting these people and exchanging stories. I remember distinctly a young woman, a mother of six kids who was the same age as me at the time. We interviewed her about the move and the housing conditions before and after the project. She said she is happy that her kids are going to school now and have the possibility to learn to use the computer too. She had a kitchen for the first time in her life together with a pit latrine and even a cow. Their house was more spacious, constructed with bricks and cement. She did not speak English, so we had to use a translator to help us communicate. Now, as I think of all the heart-wrenching commercials that are produced by various charities, I realize their power. I don't have this tool in my world, but the fact that we can zoom in on personal stories and bring the issues closer to the audience creates a more layered narrative. It makes me question whether we can really argue whose social impact is better or which project is better. I've spent enough time in the field to know that we can't solve every problem, and as someone who studied anthropology and ethnography, I am familiar with the biases, the white savior complex, and the paradox of being interested in issues removed from us as opposed to looking around in our own neighborhoods. The biases we have are filters that distort reality in line with our internalized belief systems. What is a meaningful way then to report on our impact?

CSR brings the possibility of qualitative and quantitative reporting and challenges my current practice of factual numerical impact reporting. My role is to listen and figure out what the people need. I then need to find the best tool available for the project and in that situation, in order to give them as much of what they want as possible. The limitation of the SIA for compliance is that it focuses on adverse impact mitigation related to projects and operations. This is not a limitation of the CSR. While I don't always have access to this tool, I encourage my clients to be proactive, at a minimum to support the communities around their project with a well-defined scope and timeline.

Another, more recent example from my work includes a renewable energy company that constructed a new solar power plant in the Balkans. The SIA identified the need for the community development, partly because it is a rural area with run down infrastructure, partly to further compensate for adverse project impacts that are more indirect on the communities. The company is contractually required to develop a community development plan. They have been unable to do so for the past two years. The reasons for this are diverse: they initially had limited social capacity, they struggled with drafting the management plans, then their internal process made the approval of new plans rather time consuming. As a last resort option, they suggested that their strategy would be to donate to philanthropic organizations and other charities in the project areas to support *sustainable development.* If you have come this far in the book, you can probably guess my response to this. The first issue that comes to mind is that the community development should target affected communities, reflect the needs raised by them and include a high level of control on the projects from the company. Simply outsourcing the delivery of impact creation to other organizations would mean that the company has no leverage over the strategies, target beneficiaries, project selection and design. They would not be able to report on direct impacts, but would rather have to resort to inflating indirect attributable impacts on a more general population. The other important aspect is the dialogue with the affected people, understanding their concerns and designing a plan that responds to those concerns.

Stakeholder engagement is essential for most of the social impact products, but it is especially important for CSR. The intent here is not to merely disclose information or inform certain stakeholders about what we are doing but rather to showcase our proactive contribution to *the greater good.* Several companies use the disclosure of CSR activities to increase their customer base and revenues through public relations (PR) activities. The contrast between PR-type engagements and engagement with affected people or target groups is very stark. When we talk about stakeholder engagement in my world, we're very specific about who is targeted and what kind of information is shared with this group. It's usually a longer-term frequent engagement that allows for a two-way dialogue. In the case of CSR used for PR, the information or the impact is usually disclosed annually as part of the sustainability reporting. For projects where CSR is tied to another social impact product, the core operations team responsible for the original safeguarding activities takes over the engagement with the target population and shares information. They don't only share the information about what is planned, but also collect information about what else the community wants, the feedback on the implementation of the financed activities, and whether there are any complaints or small adjustments that can be made to accommodate the needs. It actually requires someone to go to the site a couple of times a week, depending on the accessibility and types of activities. While many communication experts are employed to do PR-type roles and disclose information, it's a different type of art to be able to listen to people, build relationships, and understand that they will raise concerns and complains when they are given the chance to do so. The intent is not to maintain the company's good reputation but to engage, understand, and respond.

Examples of CSR Done Right

CSR initiatives can take many different forms, but the goal is always the same: to have a positive social impact—however big or small, macro or micro level. In this section, we will explore examples of companies that have implemented CSR initiatives that have had a positive social impact. From ice cream to home furnishings, technology to beverages, these companies have demonstrated that CSR is a powerful tool:

- Coffee giant Starbucks has implemented a range of CSR initiatives designed to promote social impact. The company has committed to hiring one hundred thousand Opportunity Youth by 2020, investing in farmer support centers to help coffee farmers improve their livelihoods, and sourcing coffee in a responsible and sustainable manner.

- Technology company Microsoft has implemented a range of CSR initiatives, such as committing to carbon neutrality, investing in renewable energy, and donating millions of dollars to charitable causes. Microsoft also supports employees who volunteer their time and expertise to help address social and environmental challenges.

- Cosmetics company The Body Shop has implemented a range of CSR initiatives designed to promote ethical and sustainable business practices. The company sources ingredients in a responsible and sustainable manner to support fair trade initiatives and promote environmental awareness. The Body Shop also donates a percentage of its profits to charitable causes.

- Ice cream company Ben & Jerry's has a long history of social and environmental activism. The company's CSR initiatives include sourcing ingredients in a responsible and sustainable manner, promoting fair trade, and supporting various social and environmental causes. Ben & Jerry's also advocates for policies that promote social and environmental justice.

- Footwear company TOMS has a unique CSR model: for every pair of shoes purchased, the company donates a pair to someone in need. TOMS has also expanded its giving model to include other products, such as eyewear and bags. The company's CSR initiatives also include supporting social entrepreneurship and advocating for policies that promote economic opportunity.

- Home furnishings company Ikea has implemented a range of CSR initiatives designed to promote sustainability and social responsibility. The company has committed to using only renewable energy, reducing its carbon footprint, and promoting sustainable materials. Ikea also invests in social programs that promote education, environmental awareness, and entrepreneurship.

- Beverage company Coca-Cola has implemented a range of CSR initiatives designed to promote environmental sustainability and social responsibility. The company has set ambitious goals, such as replenishing all the water it uses in its products and operations, promoting sustainable agriculture, and supporting community development programs.

- Technology company Salesforce has implemented a range of CSR initiatives. The company has committed to using only renewable energy, reducing its carbon footprint, and promoting environmental sustainability. Salesforce also invests in social programs that promote education, workforce development, and philanthropy.

By now you see that several of the large companies that were singled out in previous sections could be included here too. Patagonia, Unilever, and Microsoft all have various initiatives targeting environmental and social issues. Clearly, companies who were sensitive to social and environmental issues before ESG, CSR, or impact investing gained popularity—especially those with the financial means—are more open to exploring other social impact products.

Conclusion

CSR is one of the original social impact products, alongside philanthropy. The concept is very simple: companies identify initiatives that align with their values or correspond to the needs of the local communities, and they donate money to fund initiatives. CSR is not a legal requirement (in most cases), which means it can address a variety of different topics that don't fit under some of the other social impact products.

CSR is also used to connect with local communities to build trust and credibility by supporting initiatives that are important to them. In a way, it is not only the right thing to do but also the smart thing to do.

CSR has been proven to increase a company's customer base and drive profits. This has led many companies to inflate the positive social impact they create through their CSR initiatives.

CHAPTER 5

SOCIAL IMPACT BONDS

Social impact bonds (SIBs) are a relatively new form of financing for social programs. I use the term social impact bond, but it's interchangeable with social bond. They were first introduced in the UK in 2010 and have since gained popularity in other countries, including the United States, Canada, and Australia. At a high level, SIBs are a way for private investors to fund social programs by using the proceeds of the bond for projects that are selected based on a certain set of indicators. These indicators are set out based on the development framework and follow macro-level social topics such as education, healthcare, and social housing.

SIBs are structured as a contract between a government agency, a service provider, and private investors. The government agency is the one identifying the social problem, the desired outcomes, and the indicators to measure success. The service provider, designs, and implements the program, while private investors provide the up-front capital to fund the program. If the program achieves the desired outcomes, the government agency repays the investors, often with a financial return. If the program doesn't achieve the desired outcomes, the investors bear the financial risk. SIBs have the potential to address several social issues more efficiently on a larger scale by aligning the interests of government, service providers, and private-sector investors toward measurable outcomes.

One of the key benefits of SIBs is that they provide a way to leverage private capital for social programs that might otherwise be underfunded. Several IFIs, including IFC, have a program on social bonds that started in 2017. The bonds issued by governments or large institutions generally provide a safe financial product for investors. For an SIB to be successful, it needs to have a financial return and meet the social objectives. In this respect, SIBs are very similar to the now popular green bonds or blue bonds where the use of proceeds contributes to projects addressing environmental and climate change issues.

My involvement with SIBs is limited, though I have seen several of my projects funded through green bonds or other types of sustainability bonds. It seems to be common practice now for the major IFIs to have some sort of sustainability or green bond initiative. It aims at raising capital to fund more projects every year. The argument for IFI involvement in SIBs and other sustainability bonds incorporates the elements of their mandate and the fact that by definition all the projects they finance are a) safeguarding environmental and social receptors and b) contributing to development. I know for a fact that at least the safeguarding aspects are true. Every project I work on has to comply with the policy and safeguard against adverse impacts. Do I think every project is a development project? Depends on how we define *development*. Quoting my assumption about people wanting to *do good,* especially if there are no financial losses, the IFI SIBs seem to be a great way to satisfy investor demands. Most of those institutions have excellent credit ratings, so the probability of defaulting is low.

SIBs are not spared the criticism that they might divert funding away from initiatives that are not eligible to be funded. It might be true outside the IFI world, that SIBs are biased toward initiatives where the social impact is measurable easily and thus fulfilling not only the financial but the social obligations of the issuer. There have also been some concerns raised about the complexity of SIBs, which can make them difficult for governments and social service providers to implement. To set up a SIB, there needs to be a clear set of measurable indicators, as well as a way to track progress toward those outcomes. This can require a significant up-front investment in data infrastructure and evaluation capacity. I guess this is partly the reason why certain institutions, such as IFIs, are in a better position to set up SIBs and sustainability bonds as they already have some of this infrastructure set up.

Overall, SIBs are an interesting and potentially powerful tool for financing social programs. While there are certainly some concerns to be aware of, the potential benefits of leveraging private capital and encouraging data-driven decision-making make them worth considering as a complement to traditional forms of government funding.

What Is It?

A SIB is an instrument that is designed to finance social programs and initiatives through the proceeds of the bond. SIBs are also known as "pay for success" bonds, as they pay out returns to investors based on the successful outcomes of the social program being funded. In a SIB, private investors provide funding for a social program, and the government agrees to pay back the investors if the program achieves predetermined social outcomes. The payment is tied to the actual results of the program, and investors receive a financial return only if the program is successful in achieving its social goals.

SIBs are intended to help address social issues such as homelessness, poverty, and unemployment by providing a new source of financing for social programs. They also align the interests of investors and the government by ensuring that taxpayer money is only spent on programs that achieve real social outcomes. SIBs are still a relatively new and emerging form of financing, and they are being used to fund a growing number of social programs around the world. However, they also come with some risks and challenges, including the need for rigorous outcome measurements and the complexity of designing and implementing successful social programs.

Rather than relying solely on government funding, SIBs enable private investors to provide up-front capital for a social program. The success of the program is then measured against specific outcomes, and if these outcomes are achieved, the government or other social service providers will repay the investors with interest. Of course, no SIB is set up to fail, so success indicators are selected accordingly as you will see. The idea behind SIBs is that private investors are incentivized to invest in programs that have a proven track record of success or are likely to generate positive social outcomes. This helps ensure that resources are allocated more efficiently, and social programs are held accountable for their performance. SIBs can be used to fund a wide range of social programs, including early childhood education, job training programs, and recidivism reduction programs. For example, a SIB might be used to fund a job training program for disadvantaged youth. The investors would provide the initial funding for the program, and if the program is successful in helping participants find employment, the government or other social service provider would repay the investors with interest.

My personal exposure to the SIBs is limited. The most memorable experience relates to an intergovernmental development financial institution I worked for that had a social mandate. In all my previous roles I was focusing on safeguards and SIA with a very well-defined set of impacts related to the projects we financed. When I arrived at this institution and learned that every project is a *social* project I was wondering how that is defined and demonstrated. I found out about the social bond program where the institution issued this bond to raise capital to fund its main operations: loans for governments, municipalities, and private companies in order to implement social development projects. I was eager to learn more about the indicators, how the projects are selected, how often, and what is reported to investors. To my surprise, I had to go to the treasury because no one with the social or industry technical expertise was involved in the design and issuance of the bonds. It is not unusual to see a lack of social (or environmental) experts being involved in the various social impact products. This is partly due to the history of some products emerging as a sustainability add-on to other financial instruments. The SIBs were issued by the treasurer and were allocated to projects by the investment and banking teams. No industry specialist or social expert was involved in designing the framework, defining the desired outcomes, or even measuring the impacts.

The banking teams used the SDGs to identify the indicators and demonstrate our contribution to the different goals and targets through the implementation of our projects. There are excluded sectors that cannot be financed by the institution, but any IFI or commercial bank would have a so-called exclusion list, which details activities that are not eligible for funding, like gambling or the production of tobacco or alcoholic beverages. I wanted to refresh my memory, so I looked at at the 2019 social bond report. According to the report, the number one sector financed by SIBs was MSME support to create and preserve jobs. The second and third largest sectors were infrastructure reconstruction & rural modernization and education. There is certainly a social impact in getting people jobs or maintaining jobs, however, the types of projects we funded in this sector were not primarily what I would call *development* projects. This is not only because the projects were in developed countries—we will see that developed countries have social issues too, but more because of the types of businesses. While the MSME financing was targeting companies that have very little to no access to credit, including start-ups and enterprises owned by vulnerable groups, these were companies that often employed over one hundred people and had annual turnover in the tens of millions of euros. Could these companies really only get access to credit from a *social development* institution or could they go to a commercial bank? To be fair, we did have microenterprise clients and microcredit support transactions that would qualify as social development even if we wanted to be strict with definitions. I'll share my views on microfinance in chapter 9 in more detail.

From a social impact perspective, we have seen that almost all the social impact products touch on employment creation, training for employability, access to the labor market, and the like. The geographical location of the social impact in this example really challenges the outdated notion that we can only bring meaningful and impactful change in a developing country. Indeed, when we looked at examples of social impact tools and projects before, they were almost always in developing countries in South Asia, Africa, or South America. This SIB in the example brings the issue close to home—quite literally, as some of the projects financed by the SIB were in Hungary, my home country. Looking at meaningful social impact in a developed country context is an added layer to the already complex world of social impact creation and demonstration. In fact, the majority of examples I bring for the SIBs and the social outcome contracts (next chapter) are all from the USA and the UK.

Returning to our example SIB, it must also be noted that most of these new jobs are in rural economies, even if they are within the European Economic Area. The divide between urban and rural areas is significant in terms of economic opportunities even in developed countries. The main issue I want to highlight with respect to reporting on the number of jobs created or preserved through the projects supported by the SIB is that it fails to add this extra layer of assessment to look at the quality of those jobs and whether the employment terms and conditions meet national legislation of the given country. You might say that obviously any company operating in a developed country complies with national legislation, but I have news for you! Several of the companies we visited did not have all their operating permits, hired people on part-time contracts while making them work full time, hired seasonal workers without contracts, and so on. The great thing about ESG in this respect is that it looks at these basic legal compliance-related indicators on employment, though they are not as detailed as labor-related assessments in the SIA.

I'm not arguing for overregulation of businesses and instruments, as it might prevent potential entrepreneurs from entering the market. In a way, their initiative to create employment and grow as a company should be supported. However, the support should encompass more than the provision of funds, especially if a development finance institution is involved. There should be an initiative to have a follow-up program that improves the quality of the jobs—much like incubators for start-ups, where the businesses are supported via training on various aspects of business strategy, budgeting, marketing, and so on. This is not part of our example social bond program.

I am in favor of innovation and repurposing financial tools for social impact creation. While there are certainly some concerns or issues to clarify, the potential benefits of having funding available for programs have outweighed these concerns. Maybe some concerns were not raised because the technical experts in social development have had few opportunities to contribute to the creation of SIBs. I certainly hope this changes in the future.

Purpose, Scope, and Timing

Purpose

SIBs are an innovative financing mechanism that leverages private investment to fund social programs aimed at achieving specific social outcomes. The social outcomes are defined broadly but supported by a set of indicators that are used to measure the success of the initiative. There is no clear definition of what falls within the social outcome, whether they are macro-level changes or localized impacts:

- *Addressing funding shortages for social programs.* Many social programs suffer from chronic underfunding, which can result in lower-quality services and less positive outcomes for participants. SIBs can help to address this issue by leveraging private capital to supplement government funding. This can help ensure that social programs have the resources they need to be effective. The collaboration between the public and private sectors has proven to have significant impacts because of the combination of available funding, knowledge, infrastructure, and momentum. Every time I work with private-sector clients, they argue that time is money. They evaluate investments and studies differently from public sector clients. They want to understand what deliverables they need to produce for a project to move forward.

- *Encouraging innovation and experimentation.* Because SIBs are typically only available to investors who are interested in earning a return on their investment, there is a strong incentive to fund programs that have a proven track record of success or are likely to generate positive social outcomes. This can help encourage innovation and experimentation in the design of social programs, as providers seek to identify the ones that are most likely to be effective. This is by far the most exciting aspect for me. We have seen how certain CSR initiatives are turned into a business, but SIBs start from the beginning. They find a problem and try to come up with a bankable solution that brings social and financial returns.

- *Encouraging data-driven decision-making.* SIBs are typically designed to measure and evaluate specific outcomes, which can help to encourage a more rigorous evaluation of social programs. By measuring outcomes, social service providers can identify what works and what doesn't and can adjust their programs accordingly. This can help ensure that resources are allocated more efficiently and programs are held accountable for their performance. We can argue whether the indicators for success are *good enough*, but it doesn't change the fact that they measure some sort of social impact, even if this measurement isn't perfect.

- *Providing incentives for performance.* SIBs provide a financial incentive for social service providers to achieve specific outcomes. This can help ensure that social programs are held accountable for their performance and align the interests of investors, providers, and participants.

- *Complementing traditional forms of government funding.* SIBs can be a powerful complement to traditional forms of government funding for social programs. By leveraging private capital, SIBs can provide additional resources for social programs. This can give social programs the resources they need to be effective and can help ensure that resources are allocated more efficiently.

Scope

SIBs have been used to fund a wide range of programs, and their scope is only expected to grow as more governments and social service providers experiment with this innovative financing mechanism. As I argued before, it is important to be up front about the scope and limitations of each SIB, including the targeted sectors and performance indicators. The scope can include macro-level social impacts such as generic job creation though MSMEs or support for the upgrade of medical facilities, but there can also be more targeted SIBs that support localized activities such as upgrades for schools in a certain area.

Topical scope of SIBs include:

- *Early childhood education.* SIBs have been used here to great effect. By funding programs that provide high-quality early childhood education, SIBs can help to ensure that children are better prepared for school and have a better chance of success in later life. This can help reduce the achievement gap and promote social mobility. It's often not worth it for private sector players to fund early childcare facilities because of the high costs associated with the staff-to-child ratio, insurance, maintenance of kitchen facilities, and more. Providing funds to the government to fund early childcare facilities based on the knowledge and experience of running educational facilities is a great way to enhance the impact. This is not to say that everyone in the area where the SIB is targeting will benefit from this. Furthermore, as this is a for-profit and for-return type of social impact product, the services will not be free or heavily subsidized either. They will be available at a price. Once again as we *peel the onion* and go into other layers, we see that this SIB is not necessarily helping vulnerable or low-income households. Was that the goal of the SIB? No. The goal was to partner with the government and provide more facilities for small children as a paid service.

- *Job training programs.* SIBs have also been used to fund job training programs aimed at helping individuals acquire the skills they need to succeed in the workforce. Job creation seems to be a hot topic for many social impact products that aim to reduce unemployment and improve economic mobility.

- *Homelessness prevention.* Homelessness is a major social issue in many countries, and SIBs have been used to fund programs aimed at preventing it and providing support to those affected by it. By investing in programs that provide housing and support services, SIBs can help reduce the number of individuals who are homeless and improve their quality of life. I have seen social housing programs funded by SIBs. These run a business model in which the government or municipality takes a loan from the SIB and proceeds to build social housing. These are usually subsidized housing units for people in need. The loan is then repaid, and the

SIB has a return. The concerns relate to who will have access to social housing and its benefits. The eligibility criteria are not set by the issuer of the bond or the executing agency but by the client who takes the loan. This limited leverage and imperfect eligibility criteria can prevent vulnerable people from accessing the services. The reports are usually missing out on this with indicators only stating the number of units built or the number of families that have access to the housing. Key missing items in reports usually include the actual affordability of services, selection criteria of beneficiaries, security of tenure, and so on.

- *Recidivism reduction.* Recidivism, or the tendency of individuals to reoffend after being released from prison, is a major social issue that can have significant negative impacts on individuals and society. SIBs have been used to fund programs aimed at reducing recidivism rates by providing support services to people who have been released from prison. I personally don't have a lot of experience with this type of SIB, but I support helping people help themselves. People and circumstances change, so providing an opportunity for individuals to start over and do better is a net benefit for society. I have a bit more lenience for this type of SIB because people self-select into participating. I imagine if someone enrolls and goes through the hoops to fulfill the criteria, they're really committed to making the change. In this aspect, any external selection criteria or challenges to access seem less relevant than in some other cases.

- *Healthcare.* SIBs have been used to fund healthcare programs aimed at improving outcomes and reducing costs. By investing in programs that promote healthy behaviors and provide preventative healthcare services, SIBs can help reduce healthcare costs and improve overall health outcomes for some. My experience with SIBs for healthcare involves using bond proceeds to provide loans to modernize, refurbish, or expand medical facilities. I once had a project to expand a medical research lab financed through a loan from SIB proceeds. Quite fascinating what this type of investment can do for the *good* of the wider population, yet infrastructure alone will not solve structural access and affordability issues. We got data on the number of patients before and after our intervention, which shows that more people were treated post expansion due to the increased capacity of the facility. I see how this is a significant social impact on the macro level, but it would be interesting to know how it impacts people who had limited access before.

One of the main arguments of this book applies here too: the scope needs to be well defined so the impact can be measured in a meaningful way. We must step away from generic macro-level statements and provide more context to the impact we want to achieve and what we achieved based on our measurements. The broad scope allows for a variety of activities to be financed, but the nature of an SIB as a social impact product makes it challenging to define this scope with respect to defining and measuring the social outcome. There will be more on social outcome bonds or contracts in the next chapter.

Timing

A SIB can be launched any time there's the potential to use bond proceeds to create a social impact. It's not tied to the timing of the investment cycle. If an infrastructure project is financed by a bank but needs additional funding, an SIB can be mobilized, especially if it's a medical or education facility. There is often a mismatch in timing between the initiatives being available for funding and the SIBs being in place with the relevant scope. I have seen colleagues desperately trying to find projects they could refinance so the reporting on the SIB will please the investors. I really hate to be the one saying this, but an SIB is often merely an accounting procedure where certain funds are retroactively allocated to assets and projects that fit the criteria. Does it make the social impact any less significant? I don't think so. It still meets the purpose of the SIB if the social impact is demonstratable and measurable. This flexibility also allows for SIB funds to be allocated on a proactive and retroactive basis. This can be either a blessing or a challenge.

Limitations

SIBs are one of the more innovative ways to deliver social impact, yet all I see are macro-level claims of social impact that deal with high-level statistics as opposed to being able to demonstrate real change in people's lives. It is not necessarily a bad thing, because as we have seen in the previous sections, there is indeed a need for more infrastructure, for more investment in certain sectors that are not targeted by other social impact products. Building more schools and hospitals undoubtedly creates a positive social impact. With my background, when I'm looking for an impact, it's usually measurable and specific to a certain subpopulation. Not only do I examine the macro-level benefits, but I also go into the project-level impacts. I'm trying not to be too critical of SIBs because I think this is a very innovative way to mobilize capital for social impact creation, but there are still issues that need to be discussed.

Vague Scope

One of the main limitations of SIBs is their undefined scope. While SIBs have been used to fund a wide range of programs, they may not be suitable for all types of social programs. For example, SIBs may not be the best choice for programs that are difficult to measure or require a long-term investment. Additionally, SIBs may not be appropriate for programs that require a significant amount of up-front investment. The desired outcome of an SIB is often a macro-level impact that is challenging to demonstrate in real terms. The scope is often vaguely defined as "creating benefits for society via job creation or the establishment of certain medical or educational infrastructures." We have seen that there is indeed a benefit to making these services available, but in order to fully grasp the impact, we need to go much deeper and assess the qualitative elements. The best way to do it is to identify the beneficiaries more specifically. I have seen this identification done in a vague way as well, saying something like "people in the area will have better access to healthcare." In my opinion, this is a misleading statement and a misrepresentation of the actual impact. Everyone knows that some countries have a fully private healthcare system with limited free services. Even the state-provided services are dependent on health insurance paid by the employer. Furthermore, not all medical services are covered by the state, some have out-of-pocket expenses. Even with private insurance, certain procedures are not fully covered or not covered at all. Following this logic, we might have a very different interpretation of a project that expands or builds more hospital facilities. It's true that the total number of people treated there will rise due to the increased capacity, but it's also true that our project did nothing for the people who were outside of the medical system to begin with.

The other big question no one likes to talk about is the affordability of the services. And this, again, is probably outside the scope of the SIB—especially if the SIB is provided to fund activities that are typically a government responsibility. We can look at the example of education to see that the same arguments presented above remain true. By building more facilities and creating more spaces for kids, we are indeed supporting people who are willing and able to use the services. The typical generic statements of impact here include "five additional classrooms that can provide education for up to one hundred students." Wonderful on the macro level, but let's look at the issue more closely. Who will recruit and pay the salary of the additional teachers for those new students? Is there a need for extra classrooms? What are the enrollment requirements? I was supportive of making educational facilities available in my area, but the availability of infrastructure doesn't translate into accessibility of the service. The target beneficiaries could be better defined to make the social impact better demonstratable. If we say that an educational facility will benefit those X number of families in the area who have kids in the eligible age range, the demonstration of the impact will be more meaningful. It sounds so much better to say, for instance, that 89 of the 140 kids in the target population enrolled in the new facilities. This does not solve the issue of sustainability for the SIB-financed facility; but makes the reporting more transparent.

Up-Front Costs

Another limitation of SIBs is the up-front costs associated with their implementation. SIBs require a significant amount of planning and development, as well as fundraising and program implementation. This can be a time-consuming and expensive process, particularly for social service providers and government agencies that may not have experience with SIBs. This limitation is almost nonexistent for institutions that have been engaged in other types of bonds, especially if they've already gotten on the *green bond* bandwagon. Nevertheless, it takes time to launch a new product, especially if it requires additional technical expertise to set up the social impact framework used to determine success indicators.

Complex Structure

SIBs are structured in a complex way, which can make them difficult to understand and implement. SIBs typically involve multiple parties, including social service providers, government agencies, private investors, and intermediaries. This complex structure can make it difficult to align incentives and ensure that all parties are working toward the same social outcomes. The messages can get lost in translation especially when the scope is defined in a vague and broad manner. This means that investors buy these SIBs hoping to contribute to positive social impacts, and they end up with a report about activities that do not necessarily fit their agendas.

There can also be challenges with the implementation, given the large number of agencies, companies, and parties involved. These challenges could include delays with implementation or changes in the market that affect the financial returns. Sometimes companies use accounting techniques to retroactively reallocate proceeds from bonds to projects that fit the criteria. I see the reasoning on both sides for doing this. The SIB still supports a project that creates a positive social impact in line with the defined purpose, scope, and use of proceeds, but it's not the catalyst to make that project happen. It's merely a tool to finance something that was already a bankable transaction and received funding from other sources. The main purpose of the SIB as per the definition is to issue bonds whose proceeds are used to fund projects with a positive social impact. My gut feeling is that retroactively allocating SIB proceeds to existing social impact projects leads to social washing on a large scale, especially if these projects have vague scopes and very generic definitions. Creating a new positive impact with our products is not the same as contributing to existing impact creation.

Risk Assessment

SIBs involve a certain amount of risk, particularly for private investors. If the social program does not achieve the desired outcomes or is delayed or changed due to regulatory requirements, there may not be a return on the investment. Social issues are complex and require a unique methodology and subject matter expertise. Job creation and business growth have been identified as a desired outcome for SIBs, similar to microfinance. The issue here is that the small companies targeted by these interventions often operate without adequate licensing, employing people without contracts or without paying social security and taxes. I discovered this on a site visit where our client, a microfinance organization, did not do the proper due diligence on the beneficiaries and provided financing for companies that did not comply with legislation. Typical issues were around employment contracts (or lack thereof), lack of permits, and fines from authorities for noncompliance with hygienic and labor standards. We have talked about compliance vs. the extra mile, here, and SIBs, much like microfinance, tend to run before they can even walk. This means that while going the extra mile we forget to comply with national legislation.

Potential for Cherry-Picking

SIBs may incentivize social service providers to focus on the most easily achievable outcomes, rather than addressing the most pressing social issues. This is because investors are typically only interested in funding programs that have a high likelihood of success (social and financial), to maximize their return. This can lead to cherry-picking, where social service providers focus on the most easily achievable outcomes rather than the most important ones. We can argue about what is and what isn't important, but most of these social issues are pressing in some way. Based on my experience, the selection criteria are often related to the country's strategic investment priorities, as well as any special focus areas of the investors. Truth be told, this is both a financial and a social impact product, which means that it's required to comply with both the social impact framework used and the financial incentives. If the social impact cannot be adequately demonstrated on one project, proceeds are often reallocated to other projects where impact demonstration is easier.

Limited Scalability, Eligibility Criteria

SIBs are typically used to fund small-scale social programs, and it may be difficult to scale these programs up to reach a larger population. Additionally, SIBs may not be suitable for programs that require a significant amount of infrastructure or involve multiple stakeholders. Since the scope is broad, SIBs have the potential to cover a variety of areas, but these are mainly localized and rather small scale. In my experience, the SIBs would provide funding for MSME on-lending through a handful of institutions with credit lines of up to say EUR 200 million. It may seem like a large amount of money, but if we think about the size of the loans that could be provided for MSMEs and the participation criteria, we realize that several marginalized sectors do not qualify for financing. If the proceeds of the SIB are provided to a commercial bank to undertake on-lending activities, for instance, the bank's own exclusion list and policies in terms of sectors or the size of the company have a significant impact on the selection criteria. Some sectors are typically not eligible for commercial bank financing and end up with micro-finance organizations. SIBs should not be expected to revolutionize an industry or provide large-scale investments for infrastructure creation, but rather to provide additional financing to typically underfunded social impact projects.

SIBs are highly susceptible to overreporting of positive social impacts. In addition to the limitations included above, the issue is also the lack of subject matter experts involved when designing SIBs. I would advocate over and over again for social development specialists to be involved in the development and assessment of indicators.

How It Relates to Other Social Impact Products

SIBs are just one of many tools used to fund social programs aimed at achieving specific social outcomes. While SIBs have some unique features that differentiate them from other financing mechanisms, they are also closely related to several others.

One mechanism that is closely related to SIBs is pay-for-performance contracts. Pay-for-performance contracts are agreements between social service providers and government agencies that tie payment to the achievement of specific outcomes. Like SIBs, pay-for-performance contracts aim to incentivize social service providers to achieve specific outcomes and shift the risk of program failure from the government to the social service provider. However, these are typically funded entirely by the government, rather than by private investors. I have personally never come across a contract like this, but I have seen grants from philanthropic organizations that had to be repaid because the use of proceeds did not follow the agreed-upon criteria.

Another financing mechanism related to SIBs is impact investing. Like SIBs, impact investing aims to leverage private capital to fund social programs and achieve specific social outcomes. However, impact investing typically involves a wider range of investment vehicles and may not be tied to specific social programs or outcomes in the same way SIBs are. Impact investing is also a more hands-on approach, where the company has an in-house team to direct investments and measure success indicators. SIBs are more removed from the investor as there is another organization responsible for the implementation and monitoring of the financed program.

Public-private partnerships, though not a social impact product, have been used in my world to fund projects with a social impact product. Public-private partnerships involve the collaboration between governments and private sector entities to achieve a specific goal. SIBs can be seen as a type of public-private partnership, where private investors provide funding for social programs that are typically funded by the government.

This chapter would not be complete without mentioning the importance of solid mechanisms for setting up social frameworks and measuring their impact in real time. The SIA as a tool could aid other, newer social impact products such as SIBs though its robust and well-tested mechanisms to define and measure impacts. I'm not advocating for the implementation of SIA for SIBs because that would be missing the point, but I am advocating for using more standardized approaches to provide well-defined sets of desired outcomes and beneficiaries. This would greatly decrease the chances of social washing as it would be informed by the main principles of SIA.

While we're at it, I would also advocate for CSR initiatives to be connected to SIBs. CSR usually has a better defined set of beneficiaries and activities that respond to the needs of the locals. SIBs are the prime targets for this as we saw in the previous chapter. Both CSR and SIBs have the freedom to define their scopes due to the lack of regulations and the voluntary nature of the intervention. These can both address micro and macro initiatives while working with other organizations that have their own programs up and running. These can both be just another mechanism to finance existing initiatives that are then implemented by a third party—a civil society organization in the case of CSR and an implementing agency in the case of SIB.

What Is the Social Impact?

A SIB's social impact or anticipated outcome is defined in advance, as the primary purpose of the SIB is achieving this impact. In this way, we are working backward. For instance, as we create an SIB to finance social housing, we set out the minimum number of dwellings that we want it to finance. If it does not reach the defined outcome, the SIB is not considered achieved and the investment is lost. My main concern with respect to the SIBs is the potential for social washing due to the vaguely defined macro-level social impacts of each investment. It is not the fault of the SIB, as the initiatives are designed and undertaken by the implementing agency, often the government, who might lack the expertise to demonstrate social impacts in a way that would make sense to someone like me. We agreed that everyone wants to *do good*, and it is universally accepted that having access to social infrastructure (hospitals, schools, social housing) is a net benefit for society. Other initiatives that aim to prevent ex-inmates from reoffending or get addicts back on their feet are also a net benefit for society if achieved. For someone like me, who has to work with very well-defined impacts on a smaller group of people, looking at the macro-level claims is misleading. I must demonstrate the cause and effect attributable to the intervention or project. I must also look at what the different stages of the intervention would mean for the defined population in the project area. This includes looking at the construction phase, the operations phase, residual impacts, and often even decommissioning. This is vastly different from the approach of the SIBs and other social impact products. We return to our original thought process and questions: does it make a difference if an impact is not demonstratable or exclusively attributable to our product or intervention?

The SIB creates an opportunity to mobilize private sector capital and fund programs whose sole aim is social impact creation. There is obviously the financial return, but the projects and programs are structured in a way that maximizes their benefit for the defined (or not) group of beneficiaries. The outcomes are framed by the performance indicators, which are then used to determine whether the social impact was achieved or not. We have talked about the quality of these indicators in the limitations section, but it's important to add that the lack of a well-defined micro-level impact indicator might be due to the mismatch of expertise. As I pointed out before, several of the finance-based social impact products are mainly managed by non-E&S or social development specialists. There are cases where people like me are involved, but the administration is typically undertaken by finance and investment professionals. I do see the rationale for this; after all, it is as much of a financial product as any other. However, not having the expertise to define the social impact of a specific transaction leads to inflated macro-level claims that are challenging to substantiate.

The social impact of SIBs is measured by evaluating the success of the social program in achieving its intended outcomes. The idea is great and innovative, and it incentivizes investors to achieve those outcomes. This means that if the social program is successful, the investors in the SIB will receive a financial return on their investment. This type of innovation is rather beneficial, but the product itself is not developed or mature enough to reflect the increased public awareness of social impacts. This is where I hope this book can help. We're all aware of the famous studies about millennial investors who want their money invested in a socially responsible manner, and SIBs are a great way to achieve that. They highlight the opportunity to redirect private capital to typically underfunded activities and use financial expertise to structure a bankable transaction with all the social benefits.

The issue that doesn't get discussed enough is the selection bias that comes with any product that wants both financial and social returns. This might tilt the funding toward more easily achievable social impacts or rank social problems based on achievability and bankability as opposed to what is the greatest need in the country, region, or sector. One could argue that it is challenging to decide which social issue is more pressing. I tend to agree with this, and I would rather attempt to solve a problem than be stuck in discussions on ranking and selection. Especially if this leads to tackling issues sector by sector or topic by topic. For example, say the easy option is to fund education and healthcare projects. Once the market is saturated and there is no more need for SIB, the investors can work with other government agencies to set up SIBs that tackle other, unexplored sectors next. It does require some creativity to set up the SIB structure in a way that addresses the criticism and enhances the innovative features of this product.

I want to conclude this section on a positive note, reiterating that there is indeed a social impact, though it is often micro level, small scale, and not well demonstrated. The measurement indicators are often developed by people who are not subject matter experts in social impact assessment. Even so, SIBs are a fantastic and innovative way to mobilize private sector capital and facilitate public-private partnerships to tackle social impacts.

Examples of SIBs Done Right

In 2010, Peterborough Prison in the United Kingdom issued one of the world's first SIBs. The bond received £5 million from seventeen social investors to support a pilot program to minimize short-term prisoner recidivism. Over a six-year period, the relapse or reconviction rates of convicts released from Peterborough were to be compared to the relapse rates of a control group. Investors would earn a return that was directly proportionate to the difference between the two groups, limited to 13 percent yearly over eight years if Peterborough's reconviction rates were at least 7.5 percent lower than the control group's. The Peterborough Social Impact Bond was approved by the Ministry of Justice in 2017, and it decreased recurrent crimes by short-sentenced criminals by 9 percent, exceeding the bond's aim of 7.5 percent. As a result, investors obtained an annual return of around 3 percent.

The Rikers Island Social Impact Bond aimed to reduce recidivism rates among inmates at Rikers Island, a notorious prison complex in New York City. The SIB was designed to fund a social program called the Adolescent Behavioral Learning Experience (ABLE), which provided cognitive-behavioral therapy and education services to young inmates. The goal was to reduce recidivism rates by improving the inmates' social and emotional skills. It was funded by a group of private investors, who provided $7.2 million for the ABLE program. If the program achieved its intended outcomes and reduced recidivism rates by at least 10 percent, the investors would receive a financial return. After three years, the ABLE program had reduced recidivism rates by 20 percent. As a result, the program has been deemed a success in achieving its intended social outcome.

This example demonstrates how SIBs can be an effective way to fund social programs and achieve specific social outcomes. By leveraging private capital and tying payment to specific outcomes, SIBs can incentivize social service providers to achieve their intended outcomes and shift the risk of failure from the government to the private sector. Additionally, by requiring rigorous evaluation and measurement, SIBs can ensure that social programs are effective at achieving their intended outcomes.

Worcester Social Impact Bond—Massachusetts: This SIB aimed to reduce chronic homelessness among individuals with complex medical and behavioral health needs. It funded a social program called the Chronic Homelessness Intervention Program (CHIP), which provided housing and supportive services to participants. The program achieved a significant reduction in the number of days participants spent in hospitals and emergency rooms and exceeded the required threshold for investors to receive a financial return.

DC Pretrial Services Social Impact Bond—Washington DC: This SIB aimed to reduce the number of defendants who failed to appear in court for their pretrial hearings by funding a social program called the Pretrial Services Agency for the District of Columbia (PSA), which provided supervised release services to defendants. The program achieved a significant reduction in the number of defendants who failed to appear, exceeding the required threshold.

Social Finance India—Rajasthan: This SIB aimed to improve maternal and child health outcomes in Rajasthan, India, by funding a social program called the Udaan project, which provided community-based health services to pregnant women and new mothers. The program achieved a significant increase in the number of pregnant women receiving antenatal care and the number of children receiving immunizations.

Note how different these examples are from the MSME support SIB I provided earlier in this chapter. These examples showcase the sectors that are targeted by SIBs and how these might prove challenging for other financial institutions from a bankability perspective.

SIBs as a New Financing Tool for IFIs

I was interested to find out more about the SIB that was issued in 2017 by IFC. It's no secret that I worked closely with IFC as a consultant over the past few years. I have always looked at IFC as an innovative IFI, working in the private sector with a strong mandate to safeguard social and environmental impacts. The IFC Performance Standards are used globally as the gold standard for the management of project-level environmental and social risks and impacts. I have detailed these standards in previous chapters. As opposed to other IFIs, IFC also has different types of operations: mainstream, where IFC provides loans with E&S conditions; upstream, where IFC helps potential future clients prepare their projects for mainstream investment; and advisory services, where the client pays for IFC to help them review and update their E&S systems to ensure compliance with PS.

In 2017, IFC launched its Social Bond Program to provide an opportunity for investors to support the Sustainable Development Goals of the UN. The bond proceeds have financed a variety of programs, including Banking on Women and Inclusive Business programs. In 2022, USD 5.17 billion worth of IFC SIBs were issued, supporting seventy-six deals. The reason I want to talk more about the IFC SIBs is that I'm very familiar with the E&S due diligence process that's applied to each direct finance transaction. There is an SIA, and the impacts and beneficiaries are well defined and demonstrable. This does not mean that the limitations are not applicable to IFC SIBs; it just means that the measurement and demonstration of the impacts are a bit more in line with my world.

I want to emphasize that I was not involved in the IFC SIBs, and I did not interview anyone from the team that worked on it. I only used the publicly available data from the IFC website to share my observations and opinions.

Before we go into the highlights for 2022, these are the key principles used for the IFC SIBs:

- *Objective.* The program seeks to mobilize private capital to finance projects that deliver measurable social and/or environmental outcomes in areas such as education, healthcare, employment, and sustainable development.

- *Outcome-based financing.* The program utilizes an outcome-based financing model, in which private investors provide up-front capital to implement social projects. The financial returns for investors are linked to the achievement of predetermined social or environmental outcomes.

- *Collaboration.* The program encourages collaboration between governments, investors, service providers, and other stakeholders to design and implement projects. By bringing together different parties, the program promotes shared responsibility and accountability for achieving social impact.

- *Measurement and evaluation.* Robust measurement and evaluation frameworks are employed to assess the achievement of social outcomes. Clear performance indicators and monitoring systems are established to track progress and ensure transparency in the assessment process.

- *Risk allocation.* The program aims to allocate risks effectively among stakeholders. The investors bear the financial risk, while the service providers are responsible for delivering the desired outcomes. Governments may also share the risk by providing outcome-based payments or performance-based contracts.

- *Scalability and replicability.* The program emphasizes the scalability and replicability of successful projects. By demonstrating the viability and effectiveness of innovative financing models, the program seeks to attract additional investments and replicate successful initiatives in other regions and sectors.

- *Capacity building and knowledge sharing.* The program provides technical assistance, capacity building, and knowledge-sharing support to governments, investors, and service providers. This helps strengthen the ecosystem for SIBs and promotes the development of best practices.

- *Sustainability and market development.* The IFC aims to foster sustainability for SIBs in emerging markets. By engaging with local stakeholders and promoting regulatory and policy reforms, the program seeks to create an enabling environment for the growth and expansion of social impact investing.

The IFC Social Impact Bond Program serves as a catalyst to mobilize private sector capital and expertise toward addressing social and environmental challenges. By leveraging innovative finance mechanisms, the program aims to create positive social and environmental impacts while generating financial returns for investors.

In 2022, IFC SIBs reached nine sectors and forty-nine projects. The sectors are also defined in the report as COVID Response Finance, Agribusiness, Microfinance, Infrastructure, Gender Finance, Food & Beverage, Housing Finance, Health, and other Finance. This does not say a lot; however, it is in alignment with the main conclusions of the chapter, which state that infrastructure, job creation (microfinance and agriculture, most likely), housing, and healthcare are prime targets of SIBs. The anticipated outcomes are impressive:

- 2,425,631 farmers reached
- 503.9 million patients reached
- 137,441 students enrolled
- Power supplied to 7.3 million people
- 43,114,750 people reached with telecoms, media, and technology services
- 22,893,314 microloans provided
- 802,651 housing loans provided
- 7,136,999 loans to women-led MSMEs distributed

These numbers are significant, especially if we put them into the global context. IFC operates in some of the poorest countries and supports companies entering and expanding in emerging economies as well. I will not go into the green loan program because I am not a subject matter expert, and these products have been evaluated before. The social program, though, has eligibility criteria that cover a variety of desired outcomes, including things like affordable basic infrastructure, access to essential services (health and education, finance), affordable housing, employment generation, food security, and socioeconomic advancement. Notice how much better most of these outcomes are defined.

There's an emphasis on affordability for infrastructure and housing when reporting on outcomes. There are other, more vague outcomes reported, such as socioeconomic advancement and empowerment, that do require some creative thinking before we can translate them into a project with demonstrable advancement. Nevertheless, the selected investments all undergo a detailed due diligence process and the ESIA process. As I mentioned earlier, this includes compliance with IFC PSs that require a detailed assessment of project-related micro-level impacts of the construction and operations phases as well. The impact metrics for the SIB are selected based on a document titled "Harmonized Indicators for Private Sector Operations." This list of indicators is agreed upon by twenty-six finance institutions. The indicators are not general and high level as expected, similar to the list above in terms of quantitative data—as opposed to qualitative. The reason I'm less strict about criticizing IFC is because I know their due diligence process and compliance with the PSs means that the risks and impacts have been identified and addressed. They might not be reported as part of the SIB, but at least there's a commitment to avoid, mitigate, or compensate for any adverse impacts. As I stated above, if opportunities to proactively use other social impact products such as CSR to invest in the community on a long-term basis are identified, they are a welcome addition. This would be the perfect example of how the different social impact products would work together to maximize the positive social outcomes of a project: The SIB proceeds fund the loan for investments that require project-level social impact assessments. The identified adverse impacts are then mitigated via the ESMS while the company can invest in the community using a variety of tools such as CSR, impact investing, or philanthropy. This is no longer some far-fetched idea thanks to the IFC SIBs!

The IFC SIBs follow the Social Bond Principles (SBPs), which are voluntary guidelines that provide a framework for issuing and reporting on social bonds. These principles aim to promote transparency, credibility, and integrity in the social bond market by providing guidance on the use of bond proceeds for social projects and ensuring accountability to investors and stakeholders. The International Capital Market Association also promotes the use of SPBs with their latest Voluntary Process Guidelines for Issuing Social Bonds published in June 2023. They also published a pre-issuance checklist - see references.

The key aspects of SBPs include:

- *Use of proceeds.* The SBPs emphasize that social bonds should be issued to finance projects or programs that have clear social objectives, such as improving access to essential services, promoting employment, enhancing social inclusion, or addressing social inequalities. The use of bond proceeds should be clearly defined and aligned with recognized social and environmental frameworks.
- *Project evaluation and selection.* Issuers are encouraged to establish a robust process for evaluating and selecting eligible projects that align with the defined social objectives. This involves assessing

the social impact, feasibility, and effectiveness of the projects, considering input from relevant stakeholders.

- *Management of proceeds.* The SBPs provide guidelines for the management and tracking of bond proceeds to ensure their proper allocation to eligible social projects. Issuers should establish adequate systems to monitor and track the flow of funds and provide ongoing reports to investors and stakeholders.

- *Transparency and reporting.* Issuers are expected to provide transparent and comprehensive reports on the social bond's use of proceeds, including information on project selection, impact measurement methodologies, and the achievement of social outcomes. Regular reporting fosters accountability, facilitates investor decision-making, and builds trust in the social bond market.

- *External review and assurance.* Issuers are encouraged to seek external reviews or certifications from independent third-party assessors to enhance the credibility and transparency of their social bond framework. External reviews provide additional assurance to investors and stakeholders regarding the adherence to the SBPs.

- *Impact reporting.* The SBPs emphasize the importance of measuring and reporting the social outcomes and impacts achieved by the financed projects or programs. Issuers are encouraged to develop appropriate impact assessment methodologies to demonstrate the tangible social benefits resulting from the use of bond proceeds.

- *Consultation and stakeholder engagement.* The principles emphasize the importance of engaging with relevant stakeholders, including affected communities, throughout the bond issuance process. Issuers should seek input, consider local perspectives, and ensure the projects or programs address the specific needs and concerns of the communities involved.

- *Continuous improvement.* The SBPs promote a culture of continuous learning and improvement within the social bond market. Issuers and market participants are encouraged to share best practices, exchange knowledge, and collaborate to enhance the effectiveness and impact of social bonds.

By adhering to the SBPs, issuers aim to provide investors and stakeholders with confidence that social bonds are contributing to positive social outcomes and sustainable development. These principles help shape the rapidly growing social bond market and promote responsible investment practices. There is room for improvement in order to strengthen aspects of the SBPs, such as stakeholder engagement. I have never seen nor heard of stakeholders being consulted for SIBs. It is often unknown to the client that the project loan is funded by an SIB—unless it leads to a higher social rating for the overall project and makes it easier for the IFI to justify the investment. The SBPs only scratch the surface of using theoretical frameworks to guide the indicators we use. The SBPs recognize that there is a need to further refine the terms and definitions and improve this product because it has the significant potential to induce positive social change, especially in areas that are typically underserved by the other products. The reason why the IFC was so successful in issuing SIBs is the underlying assessments on the project level that capture the risk mitigation aspects as well.

Conclusion

SIBs are innovative financial products that were created to mobilize private sector capital to support social investments with a positive impact. This is a hands-off approach for investors who want to participate in the advancement of society through various programs that are often implemented by government agencies. The scope of SIBs can cover a variety of areas including healthcare, education, social housing, homelessness, access to jobs, and rehabilitation for ex-offenders. The vague nature of the scope is a blessing and a curse at the same time, as it makes the standardization of impact creation and measurement rather challenging, while also allowing the flow of capital to previously underfunded or underserved sectors and communities.

CHAPTER 6

SOCIAL OUTCOME CONTRACTS

Social Outcome Contracts (SOCs), also known as a kind of social impact bonds (SIBs), are a relatively new form of financing that has emerged in recent years to address social problems. These contracts provide a way to fund social programs with private capital and pay for the outcomes they achieve rather than the output they deliver. In this chapter, we will explore the concept of SOCs, their advantages and limitations, and how they can be used to address social issues.

An SOC is a form of performance-based financing that links social outcomes to financial returns. The contract is between a government agency, a private investor, and a service provider. The government agency identifies a social problem that needs to be addressed and sets a target outcome it wants to achieve. The private investor provides the funding to the service provider to deliver the program. If the program achieves the target outcome, the government agency pays the private investor a return on their investment. If the program fails to achieve the target outcome, the private investor loses their investment. Does this sound like the previous chapter you just read? Bear with me because we will be looking at the differences between SIBs and SOCs. This chapter will be shorter to avoid repeating the arguments that have been shared before and focus on the unique nature of SOCs.

Traditional funding for social programs often focuses on outputs such as the number of people served or the hours of service provided. However, this approach does not necessarily ensure that the program is achieving its intended goals. SOCs, on the other hand, focus on measurable outcomes that are directly linked to the social problem being addressed. This allows for a more targeted approach and greater accountability for results. I have very limited personal exposure to this type of social impact product; however, I do see the value of this outcome-oriented approach, especially as an add-on to other approaches, such as government funding, philanthropic support, and community engagement.

What Are Social Outcome Contracts?

A SOC is similar to an SIB in that the payment is tied to the actual results of the program, and investors receive a financial return only if the program is successful in achieving its social goals. However, SOCs differ from SIBs in that they do not necessarily involve private investors. Instead, they are typically structured as contracts between the government and a nonprofit organization or a private service provider. The goal of an SOC is to incentivize organizations to deliver effective and efficient social programs by tying payment to actual results, rather than to outputs or processes.

The process of implementing an SOC typically involves similar steps to SIB implementation. First, a social problem is identified, and a program is developed to address it. The identification can be done by the government agency, country, or regional strategy, but also by the investor and their priorities. Next, a performance-based contract is established between the program provider and the investor. The contract specifies the desired outcomes, the time frame for achieving them, and the amount of funding to be provided. The investor provides the up-front capital for the program, and if the program achieves the desired outcomes, the investor receives a return on their investment. If the program does not achieve the outcomes, the investor does not receive a return, and the program provider may be required to repay some or all of the investment. It may seem like a gamble from the investors' perspective; imagine providing the money and then having no oversight, control, or expertise in achieving the outcome.

One of the advantages of SOCs is that they can help address the issue of limited government funding for social programs. As many social programs are underfunded, their effectiveness can be limited. SOCs provide an opportunity to leverage private capital to supplement government funding and expand the scope of social programs. This can help address social problems that might otherwise go unaddressed due to limited resources or help use public funds more efficiently with greater accountability for outcomes. This is a very similar approach to what we saw with impact investing and SIBs.

Another advantage of SOCs is that they can foster innovation and experimentation in social programs. Since the funding is tied to outcomes rather than outputs, program providers are incentivized to find new and creative ways to achieve the desired results. This can lead to the development of more effective and efficient programs over time. I am all for innovation, especially if it leads to more positive social impact, however we define that. There are SOCs that don't involve private investors, but rather facilitate a contract between the government and a nonprofit organization, sometimes even a private service provider. This service provider is responsible for delivering the agreed-upon services or interventions and achieving the desired social outcomes. The funding usually comes from the government budget, but it could be linked to philanthropic organizations and impact investors. SOCs are typically used to address social problems that have a clear and measurable outcome.

Purpose, Scope, and Timing

Purpose

The purpose of SOCs is to address social problems that have traditionally been difficult to solve through government funding alone, by leveraging private capital (or NGO expertise) to supplement government funding. SOCs are used to incentivize program providers to use evidence-based approaches and incorporate data into decision-making. SOCs definitely are one of the newer approaches to addressing social issues and they might carry some risks. This is either an excuse to not use them or an opportunity to be more innovative when it comes to program design. SOCs can only be successful if the different stakeholders work together collaboratively, breaking down the silos for collaboration.

Another purpose of SOCs is to fill the funding gap. Many social programs are underfunded, which can limit their effectiveness. By leveraging private capital, SOCs supplement government funding and expand the scope of social programs. SOCs also have the potential to improve the accountability and transparency of social programs. The outcome-focus allows for a very straightforward way to evaluate the effectiveness of the program and ensure that the resources are spent where they are needed.

Scope

The scope of SOC is wide-ranging and covers a variety of social programs and interventions. The topical scope of the SOCs overlaps with the social programs targeted by SIBs, including education, employment, health, housing, and community development. They can be used to support preventative programs, which aim to address social problems before they become more severe, as well as more intensive interventions designed to address existing problems. The scope of SOCs is also expanding to include a wider range of outcomes beyond traditional social issues. For example, SOCs can be used to fund programs that address environmental sustainability, gender equality, or other social and environmental goals.

The geographical scope, similar to other social impact products, can encompass local, regional, national, or even international levels. I would imagine that the strong reliance on the government counterpart means that the majority of the SOCs are executed at the local, regional, or national level. The scale of the SOCs can also vary depending on the size of contracts and investments. There is no shortage of social issues, be it a small-scale local initiative or a more complex regional issue. The scope seems to be flexible enough to adapt to changing social, economic, and political circumstances. The flexibility enables funders and service providers to adjust their programs and outcomes based on the evolving conditions.

The SOC is probably one of the better examples of the scope being defined, due to the outcome-oriented purpose of the product. When we measure success, we need to know exactly what area, population, and specific issue we are looking at. This is a great advantage of this product.

Timing

SOCs can either be a catalyst for a project or a financing mechanism for an existing program. Yes, these contracts are typically structured so that funders provide up-front funding to service providers, who are then responsible for delivering services to beneficiaries. SOCs can be designed for the short and medium term depending on the expected time frames for achieving the outcomes. We need to make sure that the instrument is designed well prior to signing the contract with all parties having a common understanding about the details. The postcontract evaluation is essential to determine success. The SOCs can come in funding cycles; for instance, several government funding cycles are strongly related to the election cycles.

Limitations

We have seen the same patterns repeated for SIBs and impact investing. The key issues remain the same for SOCs because they use the same mechanism. I'm not certain how popular SOCs have been, as I have yet to come across them in my professional life. However, it is evident that there are limitations to this financing mechanism too. This chapter will bring no big surprises about what I identified as limitations related to this product:

Complex and resource intensive. These contracts require careful planning, data collection and analysis, and ongoing monitoring and evaluation to ensure that they are achieving their desired outcomes. This can require significant resources, both in terms of time and funding, which can limit the ability of some organizations to participate. It must be noted that once the infrastructure and process are set up, it gets easier to issue SOCs.

- *Wide scope leading to case-by-case assessment.* SOCs are typically designed to address specific social problems or outcomes, which makes it challenging to standardize their scope and impact – comparing apples and pears. The SOC can focus on micro-level impacts for a well-defined community, such as ex-offenders living in certain neighborhoods or cities. However, SOCs can also have a very broad scope with a macro-level impact, such as better access to healthcare nationwide through the construction of new hospital wings in different parts of the country. While SOCs can be an innovative tool to achieve positive social outcomes, they may only focus on issues that are compatible in terms of outcome measurement. This can be a limitation for organizations that are looking to address a wide range of social issues or who don't want to limit themselves to the specific outcomes stipulated in the contract.

- *The impact measuring challenge.* While SOCs are designed to achieve specific outcomes, there are often many factors that contribute to these outcomes, making it difficult to attribute success solely to the program. This can make it challenging to determine the true impact of the program and make informed decisions about program improvements and adjustments. What if the program is run jointly with a CSR initiative or there is a grant to support the operations? As we have seen, there are often overlaps with other initiatives, and large-scale social programs (housing, healthcare, education) are usually expensive, so a good mix of funding sources and stakeholders is required for implementation. This book has discussed, in detail, the issues around the indicators that are used by nonsocial specialists to determine what a social impact is and demonstrate that the impact was achieved through the intervention. While the advantage of the SOC is that the program is designed by subject matter experts, the demonstration of the social impact is often missing the point. What does "decreasing homelessness by 5 percent in the city" mean exactly? The sustainability of the outcome over time is not assessed and the indicators measure the success in a given time post-SOC implementation. The other, more micro-level qualitative indicators are missing from the reporting. We are also back to the debate on the best way to demonstrate the impact, by numbers or by adding more qualitative info for context.

- *Short-term focus.* The outcome-focused structure does not allow for gradual changes to receive continued financing, as each contract and payment is tied to demonstrating the achieved numbers. While many of these short-term outcomes are important for addressing immediate needs, they may not be sufficient for creating lasting change in communities.

- *Lack of flexibility.* The lack of flexibility referenced here is related to the outcomes measurement framework. Once the SOC is deployed, the instrument provides limited options to change targets and update outcomes. This can be a limitation if there are unforeseen challenges or changes in the social landscape that require adjustments to the program. The SOC, in my view, is the perfect tool to bridge a gap in a larger program or accelerate the delivery of a subprogram. The approach is no nonsense and goal oriented and serves as a building block.

- *Potential for unintended consequences.* We have seen this for other products as well. Here I would emphasize that the outcome oriented nature of the SOCs mean that only specific issues with easily measurable outcomes could be targeted with it. Even if we set up a program that could be targeted by a SOC, there could be far-reaching consequences that are unforeseen. In practice, a program designed to address homelessness might lead to fewer people sleeping on the street, thus making the area more attractive for investors. New apartment buildings with increased rent will push out lower income residents, leading to gentrification. London is a prime example of how *cleaning up* neighborhoods attracted real estate developers, leading to inflated house prices. While this scenario is highly contingent on the large-scale success of our initiative, we can't forget that addressing an issue might create another one, especially if we don't have the flexibility to change our project.

The SOC is an innovative way to address specific issues that are well defined and achievable in the short-term. The significant costs associated with several of the structural social issues need a combination of various types of financial and social impact products. The main idea for this book is exactly this: showcase what each product can and cannot do so we can maximize positive impact. The limitations may be there, but in combination with other products, SOCs have the potential to introduce great positive change.

How It Relates to Other Social Impact Products

This section will be very short because SOCs are like the little sister of SIBs. The conclusions of the previous chapter on how SIBs relate to other social impact products also apply to SOCs. We have seen that they can be a useful tool with a strong focus on a very specific social area. SOCs are just one of the many social impact products that organizations can add to the toolbox.

- *Grants and philanthropy.* Grants are often provided for initiatives with eligibility and outcome criteria. This is very similar to how a SOC works. Grants have some flexibility to adjust the scope with the permission of the organization or individual that provided the grant in case there are significant changes in the circumstances. This is not the case for SOCs. The metrics are selected to demonstrate the desired outcome. Grants, however, also offer a more nuanced, qualitative approach to measuring the success of their program or project. SOCs do not allow for this type of qualitative measurement.

- *Nonprofit organizations.* Nonprofit organizations may partner with private investors and service providers to implement SOCs. In this way, SOCs can provide a new source of funding and support for nonprofits that are working to address social issues.

- *Social enterprises.* Some social enterprises may partner with private investors and service providers to implement SOCs as a way to fund and scale their social impact – especially if they focus on specific outcomes.

- *SIBs.* Obviously, we can't leave SIBs off of the list, as SOCs are a specialized form of SIB. The approach, indicators, and structure are very similar between these two products.

SOCs overlap with impact investing and CSR as well. The previous chapter on the SIBs provides sufficient coverage of this overlap, so I didn't include it here separately. It is interesting how ESG is completely missing when it comes to SOCs and even SIBs. These products have a very different purpose and regulatory environment. The whole aspect of ESG and sustainability, whether it's looking at the environmental factors or the social ones, focuses on the long-term improvement of practices that will eventually mitigate risks and enhance benefits. This is a sharp contrast to social impact products that are created in the short term to address specific issues or provide an additional financing modality. To me, SOCs are an innovative way to make sure investments are utilized for the delivery of a positive social outcome. SOCs are time-bound, similar to SIA, with set deadlines to achieve the outcomes. The other similarity with the SIA is the focus on tangible results and demonstrable outcomes. Much like with several other social impact products, I would advocate for the inclusion of a qualified social development specialist to help with the definitions, targets, demonstration, and measurement of social impacts. I believe that the benefit will not only be clearer reporting and an analysis of what it means for the targeted population, but also less social washing and double accounting on achievements.

What Is the Social Impact?

The SOC is designed to generate an impact, an impact that is measurable in line with a predefined desired outcome. Like SIBs, SOCs work with high-level numeric baseline requirements. I must admit I was often getting lost in the definitions and comparisons during my research for this book. My preresearch assumption was that anything well-defined (scope, desired outcome, timelines) should be at the heart of a social impact product and that we need to define our impacts and intended impacts in the context of our operations. Over the course of my research, I remembered my previous training as a sociologist where I would look at these complex social impacts from an academic perspective. Fifteen years ago, I would have said that any social impact matters regardless of the scale, visibility, or demonstration of the impact. I would have provided an example that in the context of a CSR initiative supporting victims of domestic abuse, helping fifty or five hundred people is equally valuable because every life and every person matters. Then as I started working in compliance-oriented social performance management, my understanding was challenged and shaped. Now, the focus was impacts related to construction and operation, safeguarding adverse impacts that are within the scope of the project. As a contrast I'm facing yet again that the broader market for social impact products reintroduces the every impact matters concept as we are working with complex social structures, multidimensional challenges, and limited resources.

The social impact in the case of the SOC is defined by the outcome on a program-by-program basis. The focus on achieving this target outcome distinguishes SOCs from traditional funding mechanisms and even from other social impact products that often prioritize the delivery of a service or output. The SOCs have great potential because they define the scope better than other products. The SOCs by design focus on measurable outcomes, defining the target population, geographical location, and indicators for success. We could argue whether the outcomes are long term and sustainable without the SOC, but this is truly a mechanism that holds implementing agencies accountable for their performance. This is a significant advantage of this product in comparison with other nonmandatory types of social impact products.

SOCs were referred to as a catalyst for long-term change; however, I would argue that this might be an exaggeration. SOCs are the short-term building blocks accelerating tasks and subprograms within a more complex scheme with the potential to contribute to more interest (and more funding) in certain areas. SOCs can be repeated, thus providing continuous support to initiatives, especially if the defined outcomes are updated periodically to reflect the development of the program. This is probably the long-term change that is referenced as a benefit of the SOCs.

Examples of SOCs Done Right

I must admit it was a real challenge to find SOC examples, but this is what I found:

- *Bridges to Health and Healthcare Access Pay-for-Success Project.* This project, launched in Massachusetts in 2014, aimed to improve health outcomes and reduce healthcare costs for Medicaid beneficiaries with complex health needs. It successfully reduced hospitalizations and emergency room visits and achieved cost savings.

- *The Fair Chance Pledge.* This initiative, launched in 2016 by the Obama administration, encouraged employers to pledge to give people with criminal records a fair chance at employment. While not a traditional SOC, the initiative used a similar approach. The program successfully encouraged hundreds of employers to sign the pledge and create more job opportunities for people with criminal records.

- *London Homelessness Social Impact Bond.* This project, launched in 2010, aimed to reduce homelessness and improve housing stability for people with complex needs in London. It used an SIB model and successfully reduced homelessness and improved housing stability for participants.

- *Massachusetts Juvenile Justice Pay-for-Success Initiative.* This project, launched in 2014, aimed to reduce recidivism among youth involved in the juvenile justice system in Massachusetts. It successfully reduced recidivism and costs for the state.

- *Salt Lake County Pay-for-Success Project.* This project, launched in 2013, aimed to reduce chronic homelessness in Salt Lake County, Utah. It successfully reduced chronic homelessness by over 90 percent and achieved significant cost savings for the county.

- *The Global Fund Social Impact Investment.* The Global Fund—a global health organization that fights HIV, tuberculosis, and malaria—launched a social impact investment in 2018 to raise funds for its programs. The investment used an SIB model and successfully raised over $260 million to support the Global Fund's work.

- *DC Water Green Infrastructure Social Impact Bond.* This project, launched in 2016, aimed to reduce stormwater runoff and improve water quality in Washington, DC. It used an SIB model, successfully achieved its environmental goals, and provided investors with a return on their investment.

You may realize that these are SIBs in name, though they fall under the SOC category. Well, it's like a variation on an old saying: all SOCs are SIBs, but not all SIBs are SOCs. These examples nevertheless demonstrate that when designed and implemented effectively, SOCs can be a powerful tool for achieving positive social impact. They also highlight the importance of careful planning and evaluation to ensure that outcomes are measurable and achievable and unintended consequences are minimized.

Conclusion

SOCs, the little sister of SIBs, are innovative financing tools that aim to achieve specific social outcomes while providing a financial return to investors. They represent a shift toward a more results-oriented approach with a short-term focus on achieving specific outcomes. SOCs have been successfully applied to a wide range of social issues, including reducing recidivism rates, addressing chronic homelessness, and improving water quality.

CHAPTER 7

PHILANTHROPY

Philanthropy has been mentioned and briefly explained in previous chapters. I was quite excited to write about it, and I strongly believe that people who support such initiatives truly mean well. The execution may be questionable at times, and the sustainability of the initiatives may not be perfect, but the fact that someone cares enough about people to set up a nonprofit in their support is beautiful. Philanthropy has a long and rich history dating back to ancient times. In the Greek and Roman empires, wealthy individuals and institutions made donations to support the arts, education, and civic infrastructure. Needless to say, it was a voluntary transaction based on their personal tastes or relationships with the artists. The way I imagine the original, *old* philanthropy is exactly how it is portrayed in movies. The people with wealth and time admire the artists and support sharing the beauty of their creations with others. We have come a long way!

It was inevitable that the concept of philanthropy would evolve over time and turn into a more structurally organized way to make continuous donations. I think it's important to note that philanthropy is probably the only social impact product where there is a very strong sense of cause and social justice. Of the other non-compliance-based initiatives, CSR aims to be a *good neighbor*, while SIBs, SOCs, and impact investing aim to make money while doing good. This sense of mission manifests itself very differently for philanthropy, at least based on what I've observed. The more modern way to turn this cause into a nonprofit business is to organize it formally with staff members and committees. These organizations tend to be smaller and more agile than larger corporations, so resources can be mobilized much faster. The impact or cause is defined, but how the resources are allocated is flexible, and there are opportunities to experiment with new approaches to fund programs that may not be viable under other social impact products.

I must say, I was a bit biased toward philanthropy and was actively looking to get employed at a small organization that had a noble cause. When I was at university, I saw myself working hard to provide for people in need and support them in overcoming their challenges. I guess if you study sociology, you have a natural tendency to have more empathy toward the less fortunate. I never succeeded in getting a job in philanthropy because they didn't need my skillset. Most roles were related to fundraising, advocacy, and project management. While I could surely manage a project, I had no real experience in the type of advocacy these roles required, nor did I have any idea how to raise funds.

You probably already noticed that I have already used different terminology (philanthropy, nonprofit) without providing a clear difference in the meaning. This is because these terms, together with charity, are often used interchangeably. Philanthropy is the name of the social impact tool, but it has several delivery mechanisms, such as creating organizations (nonprofits), financial donations, charities, or even setting up a philanthropic organization run similarly to a company. Nonprofits and charities are typically funded by multiple donors, even individuals, whereas a philanthropic organization tends to have a few major donors. All these organizations have a strong sense of purpose and committed employees who believe in the cause.

I know it sounds naïve, but I find this approach very uplifting. How wonderful would it be to wake up every day with this strong sense of purpose? To know that our job makes a difference in people's lives? For most of us in my field, this is true, but we tend to forget. When I look around at the world of impact assessments and safeguarding, it's clear we've come a long way from being marginalized fighters out to save the environment and protect the people. I often wonder whether my colleagues still have the same sense of doing something wonderful that we had ten to fifteen years ago, when we were the minority and our work was marginalized. Philanthropy is also not marginalized anymore, and it has a significant impact on the economy. These organizations provide critical funding for innovative ideas, vulnerable groups, and valuable initiatives that are often not bankable and are overlooked by traditional funding sources. This can allow vulnerable people to become valuable members of society. There are of course the macro-level claims of empowering people to be employable and stimulate economic growth, improving the overall quality of life for people in a given community. While I have agreed with these generic, macro-level, and often unsubstantiated claims, I do wonder if there's a better way to frame the impact.

The truth is, whenever I was looking to work for an organization like this, my skills did not match the needs of the business. They needed funding—and by funding, I mean a reliable source of continuous support from donors. In a world of competing priorities, where social trends can shift, leaving an organization and its beneficiaries without any support, it's a tough fight. Without being political, I want to point out how support for women has changed over the past few decades. It started off by providing them access to education and jobs, along with the right to vote. Then there was a push for equal opportunities (not equal outcomes) when applying for typically male-dominated jobs, such as doctor, scientist, or engineer. The next significant advancement was support for victims of domestic violence and sexual harassment. As the mainstream trends change and shareholders push companies to focus on the next big thing, funding is directed toward philanthropic organizations that support beneficiaries in line with that next big thing. It has been a while since I heard about organizations fighting for women to have access to education or managerial jobs. These all evolved to include other aspects of vulnerability (race, ethnicity, sexual orientation, and gender identity).

The allocation of resources remains a significant challenge for philanthropic organizations who are often scrutinized due to the high administrative costs. The efficiency and effectiveness of resource allocation is the first thing to be scrutinized by donors and potential donors. The delicate balance between making a meaningful impact and maintaining financial sustainability is a challenge. We have seen this being the deal breaker for several other social impact products before, yet with innovative solutions investors managed to overcome this.

Philanthropy has been around and will remain for years to come. It is a crucial catalyst in social impact creation. It also supports my initial thesis that people just want to *do good*. Initially, philanthropy provided them with a small-scale, easy way to make a difference in the lives of the selected beneficiaries. This is very noble, and there is certainly room for this type of support despite the availability of other avenues to *make a change*. When I was writing this chapter, I did think about all the companies that were canceled or called out for supporting organizations whose work didn't align with the current mainstream trends. I do wonder why we try to enforce our own priorities on others, especially when they're supporting worthwhile causes without any legal or compliance pressure to do so.

When I think of philanthropy as a concept, I think of generosity, of dedication, of going the extra mile. Can we really judge people for having different priorities from us? It is a well-known truth that our perceptions of a situation depend on our perspectives, life experiences, and beliefs. Philanthropists have created a lasting legacy for generations to come supporting the issues that matter to them. This long-term view with a strong sense of mission is what makes philanthropy so powerful. Creating a generation of people who can feel that someone believed in them—even without personal contact—to support their work, their well-being, or their progress in life is a wonderful thing. We can argue on the margins about how to incorporate diversity, equality, and maybe even equity into the operations, but we need to view this in the context of what this tool can and should offer. This is not a compliance-based tool, not even designed for macro-level, large-scale impact, however, as the tool evolved the scale and scope evolved too. Philanthropy originates from someone making the effort to provide funding and support for a cause that's close to their heart. It evolved over time, but the core principle is still this: the cause and the mandate are what's most important, and there's no pressure to have financial returns. It's not just about giving money, it's about donating time, skills, and expertise as well. I probably sound very hopeful when writing this chapter. If you got this far in the book you know that I will not shy away from pointing out the obvious limitations and challenges of this tool either. This is the first product, other than CSR that is not designed to make a profit but is created with a strong purpose.

What Is It?

Let's start with the definition: Philanthropy refers to the act of promoting the welfare and well-being of others through charitable donations of money, resources, time, or expertise. It involves the voluntary effort of individuals or organizations to improve the lives of others, usually by addressing societal needs and supporting initiatives that aim to create positive social impacts. Philanthropy can take various forms such as providing financial support to nonprofit organizations, funding research and education, supporting community development projects, or engaging in direct humanitarian efforts. The underlying motivation behind philanthropy is often a desire to alleviate suffering, promote social justice, and contribute to the greater good of society.

There's a lot to unpack, here—even for people who are familiar with this tool. When I thought about philanthropy before, I always remembered those aristocratic or otherwise wealthy families that created foundations and financed libraries, cultural centers, and art exhibitions. The aim was to give back to the community. It was never about solving significant problems, but rather about showing support and sharing resources. The priorities very much depended on the family or individual who wanted to *do good*. Philanthropic initiatives were organized into foundations or other civil society organizations and charities that were set up to support a very specific group of people. Think of foundations that support children with cancer. These initiatives were never meant to make a profit or substitute government intervention. These were complimentary and unregulated and offered a way for organizations to channel donations in line with donor priorities. It provided a way for individuals to support causes without being actively involved—if they didn't want to get their hands dirty. They could support children in need or the homeless without having to work in the soup kitchen. But to physically be there and volunteer your time is also an option for those who are up for it.

I was fascinated by how philanthropy and philanthropic organizations went from a family opening a library to a group of international experts running a *company*. The sector was professionalized and institutionalized through the creation of trusts, foundations, nonprofit organizations with dedicated staff, mandates, boards, defined structures to collect and manage funds, set-out strategies, and programs. The scale and scope also expanded with the rise of industrialization and the accumulation of wealth by a few individuals and families. Philanthropy became ambitious and global in nature. Think of the reach of the Rockefeller Foundation and the Bill and Melinda Gates Foundation, which have gathered substantial resources to tackle complex issues on a global scale. Modern philanthropy embraces a more strategic and business-like approach that focuses on results and the demonstration of those results. See, for many donors, the impacts that can't be demonstrated are not there! Mainstream project management elements such as data-driven decision-making, monitoring, evaluation, performance indicators, and accountability are now standard aspects of any philanthropic organization. Philanthropy is often a collaborative effort to mobilize governments, companies, and civil society to leverage resources, expertise, and networks to address the issues related to the cause. While two hundred years ago philanthropy focused on micro-level, immediate remedies, it has now shifted toward addressing the root cause of the issues in a more sustainable and long-term manner. This shift manifests itself in the focus on policy dialogue, policy change, advocacy, and the broadening of the topics under coverage. Technology also played a huge role in making processes more efficient. Communication and collaboration are also a lot easier, especially when the organization works overseas. Online platforms are used to report on achievements, fundraising, and crowdfunding, while social media is used for outreach and engagement with interested stakeholders.

It's not only the organizations that evolved over time but also the donors supporting these organizations. Donors can now decide to fund multiple organizations to cover more of their priority areas. They're no longer required to set up their own foundation to focus on one specific issue. While philanthropy was typically associated with wealthy individuals and organizations, it's open to people of all means due to the professionalization of organizations and technological advancements. The donor outreach programs targeting individual donors moved to online platforms and can reach a much wider audience. We can now basically go online to any social media platform, find an organization we want to support, and donate with a click—all in less than thirty seconds.

The more business like operations of philanthropic organizations also lead to the professionalization of the industry. The level of talent, expertise, and knowledge among people who work in the philanthropy sector is impressive. There are experts with very specific technical expertise for any given topic, including some of the social aspects as well. The most fascinating studies or stories that I read on technical issues relate to poverty alleviation and homelessness. These are not issues I encounter often during my day to day work with social safeguards. I did have some intersections with organizations working on disaster relief and I found their knowledge and guidance very insightful.

The organizations can operate on the local, regional, national, or international level and cover a wide variety of topics. They can address certain groups of people such as children, the elderly, women, or people of color, but they can also look at topics such as poverty, hunger, homelessness, access to healthcare, and education. The typical social issues, if you like. It gives me a lot of hope to know that so many people want to solve the same issues and have the tools to help.

I am always excited when clients have their own charities or support them, either as part of their CSR initiative or independent of it. (We will talk more about intersections and overlaps later in the section.) I see this working very well for larger clients who have the resources to offer but don't want to deal with forming an in-house team. I have seen companies set up foundations because the need was identified during various impact assessments. This would be the best-case scenario for such initiatives, especially if the need is voiced or at least verified by the locals.

It's important to emphasize that philanthropy is not compliance based. There is legislation governing the operations of such organizations, but it provides relatively large flexibility in terms of the selection of topics, the volume of programs and projects, and the amount of funds to be raised and utilized. Compliance refers to managing an organization or charity in line with legislation, not the topics that need to be addressed. There are no limits to who can participate in philanthropy; it can be individuals, families, foundations, corporations, or other organizations. The support and cause can be more specific or rather general – e.g. an organization can focus on gender equality (general) or on providing support for victims of domestic violence (more specific). The participation options can range from more organized, company-like entities to more spontaneous causes, such as ones formed in response to a crisis or disaster. Unfortunately, we had plenty of examples of this in recent years, with the war in Ukraine, the earthquake in Turkey, and the post-COVID-19 economic recovery. You will see that the crisis response in all these cases was a mix of social impact products, including loans from development banks, impact investing, CSR, and philanthropic donations in an attempt to rebuild infrastructure, provide healthcare, and save small businesses.

In recent years, philanthropy has become an increasingly important aspect of modern society. As governments have become overstretched in their ability to provide adequate public services, philanthropic organizations have stepped in to fill the gap, providing funding for critical programs that help address societal problems and improve the lives of people in need. Overall, philanthropy is a powerful force for good in the world, allowing individuals and organizations to make a meaningful contribution to society and create a brighter future for all. One important aspect of philanthropy is the role it plays in promoting innovation and risk-taking. Philanthropic organizations have the freedom to experiment with new ideas and approaches, funding innovative programs that may not be possible under government or corporate constraints. By taking risks and investing in new approaches, philanthropy can help drive progress and create new solutions to complex problems.

We've seen some other social impact products tie funding to outcomes or achievements. This is not necessarily the case for philanthropy. There is no fine or direct consequence if the outcome is not achieved immediately. The outcome is often defined very vaguely, without the detailed performance indicators that we've seen with other products. The desired outcome follows the principle of every impact matters and often demonstrates impacts on a qualitative rather than quantitative basis. Philanthropy obviously still needs to demonstrate the impact, and this often involves reporting on the number of people supported or the number of lives saved through intervention, but there's typically no minimum number or threshold to achieve. The only repercussions of not delivering what the organization has promised is that people might decide to donate to someone else.

In general, philanthropy can create a sense of community and social responsibility. It also has the potential to create positive economic impacts. Although this is a very generic claim that is not necessarily substantiated, it's worth mentioning that several initiatives contribute to economic development, job creation, and entrepreneurship. The large positive is that philanthropy is usually created with a long-term view, developing partnerships with a sense of sustainability in the funding and delivery of services.

This section would not be complete without mentioning the different types of philanthropies that I've come across during my research for this book. This doesn't cover the full spectrum, and you will find interesting overlaps with other social impact products. I have come across the term *venture philanthropy*. This is essentially an approach that combines elements of traditional philanthropy and impact investing. It involves providing financial and nonfinancial support to nonprofit organizations and social enterprises in a strategic manner to derive social impact. These venture philanthropy organizations tend to adopt a more hands-on, proactive approach to their giving aiming for measurable and sustainable social outcomes by offering strategic guidance, management expertise, mentorship, and access to networks. This goes beyond the traditional grant-making model by being an active participant in organizations for the long term to help them with internal capacity, organizational effectiveness, and the scaling of positive impacts. Venture philanthropy organizations have a higher risk tolerance—much like venture capital investing—that allows for innovative approaches and experimentation while acknowledging the potential to fail. The goal remains the creation of social impact through a combination of financial resources, expertise, and active participation in operations. Corporate philanthropy refers to the charitable activities and initiatives undertaken by businesses and corporations, including resource allocation, employee volunteer hours, and the like. Community programs might be supported through nonprofit organizations, but the focus can also be on social causes and sustainability. The model seems very similar to CSR. Community philanthropy involves individuals or organizations directing their philanthropic efforts toward specific local communities or geographic regions. The aim is to address the specific needs of a particular group of people. Family philanthropy is probably the most ancient style of philanthropy, in which a family provides charitable donations and social impact activities. This often involves multiple generations of the same family carrying on the legacy and continuing to create positive impacts. Faith-based philanthropy is driven by religious or spiritual beliefs and values. In this case, individuals and organizations support causes and initiatives that are in alignment with their faith principles, such as assisting people in need or supporting education, healthcare, housing, and social justice. Impact investing was also listed and mentioned multiple times in relation to philanthropic initiatives. In a way, it's not surprising, as many nonprofits and grants rely on endowments that are invested to cover the basic operational costs of the business.

Philanthropy has been through a significant transformation to become an enterprise with costs associated with office space, staff salaries, advocacy, and the actual project implementation. International philanthropy used to be a separate category where efforts were directed to address global challenges such as poverty, hunger, health crises, education, and human rights. These days, many philanthropic organizations work in multiple countries to have more direct access to people in need. Philanthrocapitalism is described as the use of business principles and entrepreneurial approaches to philanthropy. It includes leveraging private sector strategies, innovation, and market-based solutions to create a social impact. This also seems to overlap with impact investing and venture philanthropy. Nevertheless, I give it extra points for the cool-sounding name that I will never attempt to pronounce.

Giving circles is a term referring to collective giving, where individuals come together to pool their financial resources and make collective donations. They often have shared interests or focus areas and engage in cooperative decision-making to support organizations, individuals, and projects. Before crowdfunding was a thing, I was working on a project in West Africa. An interesting thing was that the villagers donated part of their income to the collective pot. Every couple of months, the contents of the pot went to a family in the community to help improve their housing or sanitation situation, invest in their business, or buy livestock. These people would not qualify for commercial bank loans, and the relatively large sum of cash allowed them to make a bigger purchase. An initiative like this is only possible if the community does not undergo significant structural changes and there is a high level of trust among its members. We all have different backgrounds and come from different parts of the world, so it was interesting to see how my colleagues and I had different reactions when we found out about this initiative. For some, it was unimaginable to pay into the common pot, trust the village leadership to keep the pot intact, and trust that the investment one makes will come back someday. Others had better experiences with community cohesion and had a higher level of trust. Quite fascinating to see the world through the perspectives and experiences of others.

Social vs. Societal?

I realized that the word *societal* was used quite frequently when researching philanthropy and its aspects. Much more often than with other social impact products. I wondered whether this means something in terms of the content. *Societal* refers to anything that relates to or affects society as a whole. I do wonder, then, why it is not used in the case of other social impact products that claim to have macro-level impacts on society. *Societal* encompasses the broader aspects of the human social organization, behavior, and systems that exist at the level of a community, nation, or even globally. Societal factors can include cultural norms, economic systems, political structures, technological advancements, or environmental conditions. In everyday use, when we talk about societal issues or challenges, we are considering a larger-scale impact and consequences on society. This is very interesting, given that philanthropy originates from small-scale, targeted micro-impacts.

The word *social*, on the other hand, refers to the interactions, relationships, and activities that occur among individuals or groups within a society. It relates to the way people connect with one another, form bonds, and engage in social dynamics. Social factors include aspects such as social norms, values, customs, behaviors, relationships, and institutions. It's interesting that there's such a significant overlap in the aspects the terms cover. The difference seems to be that social issues typically address specific matters that impact individuals, groups, and communities within society, such as inequality, discrimination, poverty, education, healthcare, and human rights.

If we had to summarize, the difference would be that *societal* refers to the broader, collective, and systemic aspects of society while social focuses more on the interpersonal, interactive, and individual or group-level aspects of human behavior and relationships within society. I noticed that *societal* is used interchangeably with *social* by authors and sociologists to refer to things pertaining to society. My guess is that whenever there was a specific target beneficiary group or expected outcome, people started using *social* because they knew that they had very little impact on the actual institutional system that created and maintained the gap in the provision of the service. This also explains why *societal* is used more in relation to macro-level impacts. I'll stick to using *social* in this book, as this feels to me like the more appropriate term to describe these products that want to create a social impact.

Purpose, Scope, and Timing

We assume that since some social impact products have been around for a while and use everyday terms, we know the areas they cover and what they mean. This has led to confusion and inflated claims. The everyday people of the internet say the purpose of philanthropy is to promote the welfare of others, support initiatives that address societal problems, and improve the lives of people in need. While this is all true, I wonder if there's a way to describe this purpose with more clarity to differentiate this product from the others.

Purpose

The purpose of philanthropy is to make a positive impact on society and improve the well-being of people and communities around the world. There are many reasons why individuals and organizations engage in philanthropy, but the common goal is to create a better world for all. The priorities change from organization to organization. There is no promise of financial returns or achieved performance indicators. The purpose is to use donations and grants to *do good* regardless of the scale and magnitude.

Looking deeper we see that several initiatives aim to address social problems and provide support to causes that are meaningful to the donors. The purpose can also be to support research in science or technology; however, the financial support is traditionally put toward poverty, housing, human rights, education, and healthcare. The intended positive impact is not limited to a select group of people. It is expected that the changes will bring about systemic shifts that make the issue go away over time. There is no intention to turn this into a business or make a project bankable like we have seen for other products. Sometimes, the only purpose of a philanthropic initiative is to subsidize talented painters, writers, or other artists to create beautiful things. We have all heard of scholarships or grants that cover the cost of tuition or art studio space. Since the early days of humankind, art has undeniably played a significant role in community cohesion and in maintaining stories, myths, legends, and beauty for future generations. This type of social impact is so different from the tangible project-level assessments I have to undertake. Yet, I understand how impactful art can be in peoples' lives.

Philanthropy plays an important role in fostering a sense of community and social responsibility. By encouraging individuals and organizations to give back to their communities and support causes they are passionate about, philanthropy can help build strong and resilient communities that are better equipped to tackle social problems. Philanthropy can also help create a culture of giving and generosity, encouraging others to get involved and make positive impacts on the world around them. Is it farfetched? Maybe. But to quote *The Little Prince*: "You are responsible for what you tamed." I do believe that people take better care of a community garden if they put in the effort to set it up themselves. If they meet the people in need, they will be more driven to advocate for them and raise funds. We are emotional creatures, after all. This sense of personal fulfillment and satisfaction can lead to deeply meaningful and rewarding experiences, allowing people to feel they are making a real difference in the world, even if it's only a few people.

Philanthropy can be used to express values and principles. The areas targeted by philanthropy have the potential to mature into areas that can be supported by other social impact products that mobilize more funds. Think of healthcare, homeless shelters, education, and other social problems that are the focus of the social impact products that make financial returns. They all originated from someone donating food and offering shelter to people.

Scope

When looking at the scope of philanthropy we can distinguish the topical scope, delivery mechanism and spatial scope. The deliver mechanisms of philanthropy can be diverse, and it can include everything from individual acts of kindness to large-scale institutional giving. The sectors and areas covered (topical scope) depend on the values and priorities of the donors. We've looked at some of the typical areas and topics that can be covered. These greatly overlap with some of the other social impact tools we examined in this book. I want to explore the other aspects of the scope, as it is quite multidimensional.

The most visible and well-known mechanism of philanthropy is financial giving or donations. This can take many forms, including individual donations, corporate giving, and foundation grants.

Financial philanthropy is often focused on supporting specific causes or organizations, but it can also be used to fund research, develop new initiatives, and provide general operating support for nonprofits. Philanthropy also encompasses the time and expertise that individuals contribute toward causes they care about. Volunteerism is a powerful way to give back to the community and can take many forms, from providing direct service to nonprofits to serving on boards and committees.

Philanthropy can also include efforts to advance social and political change. Advocacy and activism involve using one's voice, resources, and influence to promote policies and initiatives that advance social justice, equity, and human rights. This can take many forms, including public education campaigns, lobbying efforts, and grassroots organizing. Philanthropic organizations can fund research and development efforts aimed at addressing social problems, as well as support initiatives that improve access to education and educational opportunities. An increasingly popular area is global philanthropy, where organizations work in different parts of the world. International philanthropy, sometimes referred to as global philanthropy, can include funding for disaster relief and humanitarian aid, as well as support for economic and social development initiatives in developing countries. Traditionally, philanthropy has supported arts and culture initiatives, which are essential components of a vibrant and healthy society. Philanthropic entities can fund arts organizations, museums, and cultural institutions, as well as support initiatives that promote cultural diversity and understanding.

This large scope and lack of compliance requirements make philanthropy a very potent tool for addressing issues that are overlooked by other social impact products. The financial return or impact investing aspect is relatively new. However, we have seen organizations that cover their costs using returns on invested donations. Even in these cases, the cause and the financial aspects were completely separate. The only reason to have the investments is to pay staff salary, admin costs, and the costs of provided services.

Timing

This section seems rather irrelevant to some of the social impact products but very relevant to others. Philanthropy is the former. It almost doesn't matter when someone begins supporting a cause (except for disaster relief of course) because the outcome is flexible. While target dates are relevant to some initiatives, others work long term without a set deadline to achieve outcomes. The grants and funding cycles matter significantly as they often sync up with the end-of-tax-year optimization for corporations or the election cycle for political organizations. The timing of philanthropy, in this context, refers to when the giving occurs and can have a significant impact on the effectiveness of philanthropic efforts. I am not a huge fan of these categorizations, but they help me get some perspective, so I'm going with them:

- Reactive philanthropy occurs in response to a crisis or an immediate need. Alternatively, this type of intervention can be called emergency philanthropy. For example, when a natural disaster strikes, people often donate money or resources to support relief efforts.

- Proactive philanthropy involves planning and strategic giving. This type of philanthropy focuses on identifying and addressing systemic problems, rather than responding to immediate needs. Proactive philanthropy can be more sustainable and impactful in the long term, as it seeks to address the root causes of social problems.

- Collaborative philanthropy involves working with others to achieve common goals. This can be reactive or proactive, but it is distinguished by its focus on partnership and cooperation. Collaborative philanthropy can bring together diverse perspectives, expertise, and resources to address complex social problems.

- Generational philanthropy involves passing on philanthropic values and practices to future generations. This type of philanthropy recognizes that giving is not just about making an immediate impact but also about building a legacy of giving and social responsibility that can be passed down through families and communities.

- Early-stage philanthropy involves giving to innovative projects or organizations that are in the beginning stages of development. This type of philanthropy often focuses on cutting-edge research, experimental programs, or emerging social movements. Early-stage philanthropy can be risky, but it can also have a significant impact by supporting new solutions to social problems.

- Long-term philanthropy involves sustained giving over an extended period. This type of philanthropy often focuses on supporting projects or initiatives that require ongoing funding. Long-term philanthropy can be essential for achieving lasting change, as it provides stability and continuity over time.

Even after the descriptions and categories, I would still argue that the best time to start donating and supporting your causes is now. It's best to provide continuous support that allows long-term planning for an organization. The beauty of old-school philanthropy is that generations of people followed in the footsteps of their ancestors to continue supporting causes that were important to their families.

Limitations

When I was writing my notes for this chapter, the first thought I had was that the narrow focus on one topic was a limitation. I would argue with myself by saying that every impact matters and philanthropy is just a very individualized type of social impact. Would I stop myself from helping one person suffering from a rare disease just because the impact is not significant to society? However we define *significant*, we need to agree that any support would be significant to that one person. The narrow focus and specialized expertise are limitations that could be turned into opportunities. Who's better to deal with a very specific group of beneficiaries than people who only deal with this group of people? Yet, how do we expect innovation and different results if we keep doing the same thing using experts with the same profile? Who would question a decision or provide an outsider's perspective? You see, I had to seriously take a step back from the day-to-day conveyor-belt job of reviewing policies, management plans, and impact assessments to really see some of the relationships and issues I talk about in this book. If you do something for a really long time and become very specialized in a niche area, you may develop a sense of arrogance—as I have seen—where you think you know everything and there is nothing left for you to learn. There may also be resistance to change and innovation. "If it's not broken why fix it," right?

The other limitation I considered is the size and *effectiveness* of some of these charities. It might only be a handful of people providing services to another handful of people. It might be a foundation that provides only five grants a year. I asked myself, does it matter? Is it not better to have five happy people attend school than to have none? I don't have to think very hard about that. It's just that in my world of impact assessments, we want to safeguard and provide benefits to as many people as possible within the scope of the project. The common ground is that the target beneficiaries are very well-defined in both cases. There are positive stories about this, where an organization started small, but due to an increasing number of donations and mainstream interest in its work, it became a business. This bigger scale allows for outreach to many, many more people who need support. And the *need* here is not necessarily financial. It can be access to services such as counseling for cancer patients and their families. This is an often-overlooked aspect of philanthropy. The donation is not always monetary. It can be pro bono work by lawyers for people who can't afford it or the hairdresser that offers free haircuts to the homeless on certain days of the week. It could be the clothing store that leaves a rack of clothes on the street with free items to take. The sky's the limit, as they say. It can also be grants to universities that do specific research for medical advancement. It may seem indirect and hit-or-miss, given the nature of scientific research. Maybe there is no breakthrough for months, years, or even decades. But once there *is* a breakthrough, it can have a very significant impact.

Other well-known issues and limitations include questions about accountability. The other social impact products tend to have more performance indicators and outcome-oriented approaches due to the push from financiers to use their investments for the *global good*. In the case of philanthropy, the push is not to achieve a quantitatively expressed number. It is often to help people stay alive—especially in the case of disaster risk recovery or emergency response. The more lives saved the better, but as we have seen before, anyone saved is a huge win! Especially in a crisis or emergency. None of the other social impact products can be a direct and immediate response to an emergency. Surely the other social impact products will catch up and aid medium and long-term recovery, but it was the charitable organizations that had the means to react immediately.

Scandals did not spare the industry as donors questioned the effectiveness and transparency around the use of donations that were seemingly spent on admin costs and expert fees as opposed to the programs in the case of some organizations. We could argue how much these people should make, but good experts are expensive. The charity should not be the generosity of the employees giving up on a living wage, work-life balance, and fair working conditions, but rather the results of programs implemented by the organization. I know several people working for nonprofits, charities, and philanthropic organizations. Many of them are overworked, lack balance in their life, and live in a constant state of emergency (due to the nature of the work). These roles are often based in developing countries where employees need to compromise on living standards as well due to the limited public infrastructure for electricity or running water. This really puts the local context into perspective for many of these employees.

We have seen that philanthropy can be a diverse set of actions driven by donor priorities. The resources are thus often allocated in an uneven fashion due to personal preferences. This is true only for certain types of philanthropic initiatives, the ones that are small scale and controlled by only one person, family, or company. There are other ways to look at this unevenness, such as by saying that low-hanging fruits tend to be prioritized for this type of product too. Initiatives that are visible, *easy* to implement, and result in positive outcomes in the short term are more likely to get support as opposed to more complex and costly programs. The short- or long-term nature of the initiatives very much depends on the type of philanthropy and the scale of the programs. Short-termism is often cited as a criticism where people or companies want a quick fix for an issue that is close to their hearts. We talked about how the approach deviates from the usual outcome- and target-oriented programs to be more flexible with what outcomes we want to measure. This means that philanthropic initiatives can go on for decades as long as the overall objective and target groups align with the values of the donors.

We often hear of limited resources when it comes to organizations that address issues of the most vulnerable. Though it seems that there is significant human kindness and generosity to provide funding, the resources fall short when trying to replace the role of government in the provision of many social services. The funding may fluctuate from one year to the next, programs might only get a few years of funding, and some initiatives might not even be interesting to donors. The resources needed are not only financial, they include the experts too. With the professionalization of social impact management, many experts who were previously available to work with philanthropic organizations at a lower wage are now moving toward more lucrative opportunities with development and commercial banks, consulting companies, or even going in-house to clients.

The financial resources are also allocated in line with donor interest. Some argue that this creates an opportunity to reinforce inequalities. My view is that any initiative that is undertaken to address a social issue on a voluntary basis is a worthwhile initiative—especially if it is done correctly. It is a completely voluntary type of initiative, driven by the causes that are important to donors and supporters. While not all donors come from privileged backgrounds, even those closer to the issue often struggle with understanding complex issues such as homelessness. These donors have the willingness to provide support and they look for philanthropy to educate them on the needs of the people and avenues to channel their support.

Philanthropic organizations often have a great deal of influence over their supported cause, which can result in an imbalance of power if the criteria to participate in the initiative is based on compliance with certain aspects. My example of this would be scholarships for Roma teenagers to cover the tuition of Hungarian universities. It's a worthwhile cause, and many of these kids need the extra support to cover their costs based on their socioeconomic status. I want to emphasize that not all the Roma in Hungary are poor, excluded, marginalized, and uneducated. There were, however, several programs over the past couple of decades—mainly through philanthropy—to support Roma children staying in education, having access to one hot meal a day, purchasing clothing and school supplies, accessing healthcare, and having better access to university education.

Continuing the subject of power imbalance and pushing agendas, I simply cannot miss out on mentioning how big an influence philanthropy can have on public policy. Wealth and power can influence political outcomes or push for policy changes that benefit the interests of certain people. This impact may be indirect and not immediate, but we have seen how advocacy work leads to policy changes—eventually. Whether it is matching the public interest or not, is a different discussion.

Overall, the limitations of philanthropy underscore the importance of recognizing its place as one tool in the toolbox for social change. Philanthropy should be used strategically in conjunction with other approaches so the benefits can complement the shortcomings of other products and address the complex social challenges of our time.

How It Relates to Other Social Impact Products

Philanthropy is a critical part of civil society that seeks to improve social welfare through strategic giving. It is an important and complex field that intersects with a wide range of other sectors and disciplines. These organizations emerge out of a need to address a particular social issue because the existing systems are inadequate. The purpose, scope, timing, and limitations of philanthropy may be varied and complex, but it has been a solid addition to the list of social impact products for centuries. It intersects with other fields such as government, business, nonprofits, and academia in complex and dynamic ways.

Philanthropy and the government often work together closely to address social problems. Philanthropy can provide the funding, expertise, and support for government programs and initiatives, and can also advocate for policy changes that benefit the public interest. This unique feature of philanthropy is a double-edged sword as we have seen in the limitations section above. Philanthropy and the private sector have a complex relationship, as many businesses engage in philanthropy to improve their reputation and gain social legitimacy. However, some critics argue that corporate philanthropy is a form of CSR that allows businesses to avoid more meaningful efforts to address social problems, such as paying fair wages and providing safe working conditions.

It is interesting to look at how CSR and charitable donations are very similar in terms of mechanism and approach. They are both voluntary and involve both monetary and nonmonetary donations to causes supported by a company or donor. They tend to be outsourced, so the actual implementation of a program is undertaken outside the company or donor. Volunteering or providing access to machinery or expertise are accepted forms of both CSR and philanthropy. The difference is that a CSR initiative is related to one company while philanthropy can have multiple donors. Philanthropy and nonprofits are closely intertwined, as philanthropy provides critical funding and support for nonprofit organizations. However, the relationship between philanthropy and nonprofits can be fraught, as nonprofits may feel pressure to tailor their programs and initiatives to the interests of donors, rather than the needs of their beneficiaries. I've been using charitable organizations, organizations, nonprofits, and philanthropy interchangeably in this book. It's not that I'm unaware of the differences, but more to facilitate the understanding of the mechanism: individuals or companies providing donations to a third party for a cause.

Philanthropy also involves individual donors, who play an important role in supporting social initiatives and causes. Individual donors may support nonprofits or engage in direct giving and may also be involved in advocacy or other forms of social work. However, individual donors also have their own biases and interests, which can influence their decisions and limit the impact of their philanthropy. Philanthropy may also intersect with academia, as many philanthropic organizations fund research and scholarships in a variety of fields. Philanthropy can support academic institutions, programs, and research that may not receive funding from traditional sources, but it can also influence the direction and focus of that research. Philanthropy also plays a significant role in international development by providing funding and support for initiatives that aim to improve the lives of people in developing countries. However, philanthropy can also perpetuate a *white savior* narrative and reinforce power imbalances between donors and recipients. Philanthropy also intersects with social movements, as philanthropic organizations often support advocacy and organizing efforts. However, philanthropy can also co-opt and depoliticize social movements and prioritize incremental change over more transformative social change.

In terms of the social impact products mentioned in this book, impact investing was named as a form of philanthropy before. It's easy to see how donations can be used to invest in businesses and ideas that might actually have financial returns. While philanthropy is primarily a not-for-profit-type initiative, it needs to have the financial sustainability to cover operational costs. While the operational investment side of philanthropy is different than the program implementation side, they use similar financial instruments. I pointed out in the impact investing chapter that the outdated idea that social programs make no profit is outdated.

I want to point out that several philanthropic organizations use SIA as a tool to assess potential areas for intervention. This is a different type of SIA than what we use for IFI policy compliance and project-level assessment because philanthropy aims to make systemic changes with a macro-level focus. There are still qualitative and often quantitative indicators that can demonstrate the impact, such as the number of people with access to certain services before and after the intervention. Philanthropy is not necessarily about the number, but rather about the narrative and the individual lives that are changed. Impact demonstration combines both approaches with aggregated numbers of beneficiaries as well as personal stories of individuals who were supported by the organization. Some of their commercials are heart wrenching and very emotional, while others are more uplifting and positive. While this demonstration method is widely available for philanthropy and even CSR, the SIA and ESG are focusing on compliance while SIBs and SOCs care about financial returns (and achieved social targets).

Understanding these connections between products, tools, and fields can help us develop more effective strategies for addressing some of the most burning social issues that seem to be the focus for so many individuals, organizations, companies, and governments. Philanthropy, though one of the most ancient forms of social impact products, has managed to evolve and still be relevant despite all the new, innovative products.

What Is the Social Impact of Philanthropy?

Disclaimer: I am a bit biased here because I have seen so many heartwarming stories of lives changing for the better. Impacts might be smaller in scale, but they are very significant. This is what makes this social impact product so powerful in my eyes. It can target the poorest of the poor, who often need to be lifted out of unimaginable poverty and given a new chance at life. If you ask me, that makes a much better story than the number of jobs created by the SIBs. Maybe this is the reason why so many people continue donating; to get a sense of purpose, to get that good feeling when they help someone, even if impacts and contributions are indirect.

We have all gone through hard phases in our lives and we know how much small things can mean: someone checking in on us, believing in us, a scholarship that gets us closer to our dreams. These are not one-stop-shop solutions that take us all the way, but they definitely provide a bridge to get there. And this is the line of thought that changed my view on how I would define the success of an initiative, especially in the philanthropy context. While the majority of philanthropic initiatives only provide a *partial* solution to a more complex issue, they empower people to take charge of their own lives.

One of my most significant achievements (with a demonstratable social impact) was a project in Asia with a few hundred informal waste pickers. I talked about this earlier in the book, but this is still one of the moments that defined my career as a social development specialist. I will never forget this project and the people working on it. I truly believe this shaped my whole career and gave me the passion to fight for social development. This open landfill site was to be redeveloped, which meant no more access for the waste pickers to collect recyclables for sale. Surely the traditional SIA and livelihood-specific mitigation and compensation measures were not enough to solve the issues this community faced. Several of these waste pickers had no registered address, so they were not eligible to access social services such as the unemployment office and healthcare. It also meant that they could not be formally employed by any company. We had to move mountains to convince everyone of the feasible solution. An NGO was set up that managed the grants that international institutions provided to implement the plan that would give these people a chance. The local homeless shelter agreed to register them and provide an official address so they could be formally employed and access social services. This was huge because many pickers were then given the chance to find a job outside of the landfill site, or even outside the new waste management facility. This was funded by a combination of grant money and client contributions (to mitigate adverse project impacts) and undertaken with the hope of long-term change. It has now been quite a while, but the program implementation is still ongoing.

Philanthropy has the potential to create significant social impacts, but the nature and extent of these impacts can vary depending on a range of factors. The positive change that results from the philanthropic initiative might be small scale or large scale, but it is free from the expectation of returns. As we stated earlier the scope often covers immediate crisis relief efforts that save lives. This is probably the biggest difference in social impact when compared to other tools. The other tools offer more medium to long-term solutions that often address less immediate issues. Philanthropy, however, is probably the most well regarded to create a social impact without having to go into a lengthy justification and demonstration of the impacts. Though the scale may be different.

The assessment of social impact is complex, which is why I wrote this book to help clarify some aspects. The debate and disagreement are often between the measurements, indicators, and demonstration of the impact. Some approaches focus on the quantitative demonstration, while others rely on qualitative outcomes. Philanthropy can do both, depending on the scale and scope of the organization. That's what makes this product so versatile. We have seen that it can take the form of just a handful of scholarships to an art school, but it can also be setting up cancer research organizations that now dominate the management of certain types of cancer in the UK. Cancer Research UK originated in 1902, when the Cancer Research Fund was established by Dr. Paul Ehrlich in London. This fund aimed to raise money for cancer research and support scientific investigations into the causes and treatments of cancer. In 1923, the Cancer Research Fund merged with another organization called the British Empire Cancer Campaign, forming the

British Empire Cancer Research Campaign. This organization went through several name changes and mergers and ultimately turned into Cancer Research UK in 2002. The organization funds a wide range of research projects, from basic science and translational research to clinical trials and population studies. It operates numerous research centers and institutes across the UK and collaborates with researchers and institutions around the world.

No one is saying that paying students to go to art school has no social impact, but the demonstration of this impact in comparison to other social impact products is rather challenging. The numbers are small—and what is the outcome exactly? What if they don't graduate or if they graduate with bad grades? When will our influence end: when they exit school or when they create a meaningful piece of art? How do we define the social impact of their art? These are typical questions we would use to define and demonstrate the social impacts of other products, but they seem completely irrelevant here.

Philanthropy is not a compliance-based approach; no one is forcing people to support initiatives that matter to them. It's a personal choice. However, looking at our other example, we see that the donations are funding research and equipment that revolutionize the treatment of certain diseases. In addition, Cancer Research UK provides services to family members of the patient that are not covered by insurance. This includes counseling and therapy to help the family unit cope emotionally. Reporting on success as the number of patients treated and cured makes a lot of sense in this instance. Reports might tell us what equipment was purchased with the donation and what research was funded. While we are only a small piece of this puzzle our contribution matters.

The issue of demonstration and evaluation of impact was mentioned in the limitations section of this chapter. This is certainly problematic, but I'm not sure whether addressing it by standardizing the reporting methods, indicators, and strategies would serve this product. Philanthropy may benefit from improvements in the definition of context, scale, scope, and delivery mechanism, yet the variety of initiatives makes this challenging. The long-term view and hope for systemic change make the timelines for impact demonstration and measurement challenging. It often takes decades for an organization to reach the demonstratable impact that investors want to see to deploy other social impact products to scale up the services. It shouldn't always be the goal, though, as every person helped and every life saved matters. The lack of defined timelines allows for smaller steps, more creativity, and taking the road less traveled. When it comes to social impacts, there is no cookie-cutter solution.

Examples of Philanthropy Done Right

There are many examples of philanthropy done right, where strategic giving and social investments have led to a significant positive impact on society. I have gathered a few well-known examples to demonstrate the points raised in this chapter:

- The Bill and Melinda Gates Foundation is one of the world's largest philanthropic organizations, with a focus on global health and development. Its efforts have been credited with making significant progress toward reducing the rates of infectious diseases such as malaria and polio and increasing access to vaccines and other health interventions in low-income countries. This is a large-scale, international organization that carries outreach and service provisions.

- The Ford Foundation is a private foundation with a focus on social justice and equity. It has funded a wide range of initiatives over the years, including the civil rights movement in the United States and global efforts to promote democracy and human rights. The foundation has also prioritized initiatives that address systemic inequalities, including racial and gender disparities.

- The Open Society Foundation, founded by philanthropist George Soros, focuses on promoting democracy, human rights, and open societies around the world. Its efforts have included funding civil society organizations, supporting media and independent journalism, and promoting the rule of law and accountable governance.

- The MacArthur Foundation is a private foundation with a focus on supporting creative and effective solutions to social problems. Its initiatives have included support for research and innovation in areas such as climate change, criminal justice reform, and affordable housing.

- The Chan Zuckerberg Initiative, founded by Mark Zuckerberg and Priscilla Chan, focuses on advancing human potential and promoting equity. Its efforts have included supporting education initiatives, funding research into diseases such as cancer and neurological disorders, and investing in affordable housing and criminal justice reform.

- The Skoll Foundation supports social entrepreneurs who are creating innovative solutions to some of the world's most pressing problems, such as poverty, climate change, and access to healthcare. Through its investment in social entrepreneurship, the Skoll Foundation has helped to scale effective solutions and create lasting social change.

- The Rockefeller Foundation has a long history of philanthropy, dating back to its founding in 1913. Its current focus is on building greater resilience and inclusive economies, with initiatives such as the 100 Resilient Cities program and the Power Initiative, which aims to provide access to reliable and affordable energy for people in low-income countries.

- The William and Flora Hewlett Foundation is a private foundation with a focus on solving social and environmental problems. Its initiatives include support for education, global development, and climate and energy solutions. The foundation also emphasizes collaboration and learning, seeking to identify and scale effective solutions through strategic partnerships and data-driven decision-making.

- The Carnegie Corporation of New York was founded in 1911 by industrialist and philanthropist Andrew Carnegie. Its current focus is on promoting education and democratic engagement with initiatives such as the Carnegie African Diaspora Fellowship Program and the Carnegie Community Engagement Classification. The foundation also supports research and funds scholarships in a wide range of fields, from science and technology to the humanities and social sciences.

These examples highlight the diverse range of initiatives that philanthropic organizations can support, from social entrepreneurship to education and research.

Conclusion

Philanthropy can be a powerful force for social development and change, providing critical resources and support for a wide range of initiatives. While the impact of philanthropy is not usually debated, there are many disputes about the way effects are demonstrated, scaling, and time-bound outcomes. The scope can range from micro-level impacts on the lives of a handful of people to impacts on millions through the provision of life-saving services and crisis relief.

However, it is important to recognize that philanthropy is not a panacea and sustainable social change requires a comprehensive approach that includes government action, civil society mobilization, and systemic reform. As stated earlier in the chapter, I am biased and do see the many benefits of this product. It also makes me reconsider my approach to the demonstration of impacts and the focus on outcomes. What makes it an easy sell for me is the personal approach it takes to prioritizing problems that may not seem significant if we use traditional units of measurement. The limitations and challenges are there just like with any other social impact product. What makes it heartwarming is the endless goodwill it takes for people to donate to a cause they believe in and is important to them.

CHAPTER 8

SOCIAL ENTREPRENEURSHIP

We've mentioned social entrepreneurship here and there, but we have yet to define it and provide the context around it. Social entrepreneurship is an innovative approach to addressing social issues that aims to create a positive social change through the application of entrepreneurial principles that may develop, fund, implement, and operate solutions to several social and cultural issues. Social entrepreneurship has a rich history that spans several decades. The concept emerged as a response to the limitations of traditional charity and nonprofit approaches, which we talked about in the previous chapter. The aim was to find ways to create positive outcomes in a more sustainable way. By sustainable I mean long-term in this context.

The history of social entrepreneurship goes way back, though the most exciting part is between the late twentieth century and today due to the fast pace of technological development and mainstream recognition. The origins can be traced back to the work of pioneers such as Florence Nightingale, who revolutionized nursing and public health practices in the nineteenth century. The term *social entrepreneurship* was only used in the late twentieth century, when a shift in philanthropic practices occurred during the 1970s and 1980s. People wanted to use private capital in a more effective manner other than donations and started coming up with innovative ideas on microfinance and loans to the poor. By the 1990s, the mainstream caught up with appreciating the innovative nature of social entrepreneurship. Several organizations emerged to play crucial roles in recognizing and supporting social entrepreneurs. Universities and other educational institutions started talking about it and offering courses. The growth did not stop in the twenty-first century, when social enterprises combined a variety of business strategies to achieve social missions in various sectors. As a response, the government recognized the potential for social entrepreneurship to support the gaps in their own service provision. Policies and programs evolved with the intention to proactively support social entrepreneurs—to the extent that Canada, the UK, and India even established dedicated institutions to support the implementation of such programs and policies.

The international community responded as well, making sure that social entrepreneurship was a global movement. Investing with impact gained traction, though lines between social entrepreneurship and impact investing were rather blurred at the time. In recent years, social entrepreneurship continued to evolve thanks to advancements in technology. Innovative solutions and the development of the social impact product market contributed to the amplification of positive impacts on a variety of topics. It's no surprise that this social impact product also tackles sustainable development, renewable energy, healthcare, education, poverty, homelessness, jobs for ex-inmates, and services for underserved communities. In addition to the small-medium enterprises, several larger corporations began adapting principles to understand how social or environmental considerations could fit into their businesses and investment strategies. This commitment to social impact creation created a significant shift that shaped the scope and measurement of impacts over the past three decades.

The most notable shifts are probably the growing recognition of these types of businesses as viable and impactful approaches to addressing social changes. It moved from a niche, peripheric activity into the heart of general business practices. The increased support also brought increased funding, resources, frameworks, and refined methodologies. Technology also enabled outreach with increased connectivity and access to online platforms, crowdfunding, and digital tools to demonstrate and create social impacts. When I started looking for good examples of social entrepreneurship, I found many apps that were created to solve a problem but they are not necessarily social enterprises—but more about this later. Another significant shift was the blurring of boundaries between the business, nonprofit, and government sectors. Social entrepreneurs embraced a kind of hybrid model that combined the elements of traditional entrepreneurship with a social mandate. The main type of social entrepreneurship evolved into other areas that include benefit corporations and impact-driven initiatives within corporations. The blending of the sectors and approaches opened new opportunities for collaboration, funding, and resource-sharing. The measurement and demonstration of impacts have been important aspects of the analysis of any social impact product in this book.

Social entrepreneurship is not immune to the critical set of investors who want comparable, demonstrable, and measurable social impacts for their investment. No surprise, then, that this product adopted rigorous metrics and evaluation frameworks to fit into the bigger market and use the same impact measurement tools, impact investing standards, and evidence-based practices that others do. Addressing issues around transparency and accountability clearly increased the credibility of any such initiatives and led to the creation of a whole new secondary market of incubators, accelerators, funding, capacity-building, and networks. This supportive environment enabled companies to focus on root causes and systemic change as opposed to shorter-term, superficial solutions. The complexity of the issues tackled by these businesses also increased over the decades thanks to technology and a capacity increase in the field. The trend is toward long-term, sustainable solutions and holistic approaches. Of course, this social impact product is influenced by new trends in sustainability, and it has pivoted toward climate change, resource efficiency, and ecological degradation in recent years. Initiatives included innovation to address clean energy, waste reduction, sustainable agriculture, and conservation. In a way, this shift shows that some social impacts are closely linked with environmental impacts.

The question often asked is how this type of business is different from the traditional business. Well, social entrepreneurs are different from traditional entrepreneurs because they focus on creating social and environmental benefits rather than just generating profits. They are driven by a desire to make a difference in the world and improve the lives of people in their communities. They combine a deep understanding of the social issues they are trying to address with innovative ideas and business models to create sustainable solutions. Social entrepreneur-ship may also involve a high degree of risk-taking and experimentation. Social entrepreneurs are willing to take on big challenges and try new approaches, even if they haven't been proven to work before. They are constantly learning from their experiences and refining their strategies to achieve better outcomes. I really appreciate this approach to life. Failing only means you've tried and the right solution has not presented itself to you. Standing up and trying again with different methods instead of giving up is inspiring to me. Even though, in this case, it means monetary loss.

One of the key benefits of social entrepreneurship is its ability to fill gaps in the market and address needs that are not being met by traditional businesses or the government. Social entrepreneurs often work in areas where there is little to no financial incentive for traditional businesses to invest, such as in developing countries or marginalized communities. By filling these gaps, social entrepreneurs create new opportunities for economic and social development. Social entrepreneurship also has the potential to drive systemic change by challenging existing power structures and creating new models of social and economic organization. For example, social entrepreneurs in the field of sustainable agriculture are challenging the dominant industrial agriculture model and promoting more environmentally and socially responsible alternatives. Another important aspect of social entrepreneurship is its ability to mobilize communities and build social capital. Social entrepreneurs often work closely with local communities, empowering them to take ownership of the solutions they create.

Social entrepreneurship is still a growing field that attracts a new generation of entrepreneurs who are passionate about creating positive change. Social entrepreneurship programs and incubators are popping up around the world, providing resources and support to aspiring entrepreneurs. It has the potential to transform the way we think about business, economics, and society.

What Is It?

Social entrepreneurship can be defined as the pursuit of innovative and sustainable approaches to social problems. It involves individuals or organizations that adopt an entrepreneurial mindset, employing business strategies and practices to create social value. Unlike traditional charities or nonprofit models, social entrepreneurship turns products that create social impacts into real businesses. These businesses make enough money to at least pay for their own operational costs, but sometimes they may even turn a profit. I'm of two minds about whether entrepreneurs are born or made. On the one hand, it requires a certain attitude and creativity to take a leap of faith and create something from nothing. On the other hand, ideas without structure, planning, and strategies go nowhere. In any case, the main objective here is to have a business with a positive social impact. Social entrepreneurs use business strategies to solve problems that are typically addressed by government or nonprofit organizations. They identify market failures or opportunities to create new markets that can benefit marginalized or underserved communities.

Social entrepreneurship can take many forms, including starting a new social enterprise, investing in or scaling an existing organization, or pursuing social change through a traditional business model. These entrepreneurs are often willing to take risks and pursue unusual approaches that traditional organizations or governments may not be able to. This willingness to develop novel and creative solutions to social problems is truly inspiring. The whole concept challenges our existing modus operandi in the business world, showing that creating positive social impacts can be profitable. The rebellious nature of the whole operation—especially in the early days of social entrepreneurship—attracted people who sought to use their skills and resources to make a change. The movement grew when a number of investors and organizations showed an interest in financing social enterprises. Universities responded to this boom by offering programs and training in social entrepreneurship.

According to the classic definitions, microfinance, fair trade, social enterprise, and impact investing fall in the same category. These blurred lines are extremely confusing, but a good way to clarify is that social entrepreneurship is a collective noun that has different mechanisms to deliver the impact through a business. Impact investing is definitely very distinct from a social enterprise, even if a social enterprise uses impact investing mechanisms and tools to carry out its operations. Microfinance institutions provide financial services to underserved communities, such as small business owners and farmers, who may not have access to traditional banking services. Fair trade organizations work to ensure that farmers and producers in developing countries receive fair prices for their products. Social enterprises are businesses that prioritize social or environmental impacts over profit. There's a clear overlap with other social impact products, but this may be because several of these products evolved in the same market at the same time. Social entrepreneurship is often associated with social innovation, which involves the creation of new ideas, products, or services that address social needs. These innovations may not always be as pioneering as they sound though. But we'll see more about that in the limitations sections. For now, the innovation aspect is still the key driver to enable companies to address complex issues in a creative way.

One of the primary benefits of social entrepreneurship is its ability to empower marginalized or underserved communities. Social entrepreneurs often work in areas where there is little to no financial incentive for traditional businesses to invest, such as in rural or low-income communities. By providing economic opportunities and encouraging inclusion, social entrepreneurship can help reduce poverty and promote social justice. It goes beyond mere charity or philanthropy, as it is dressed as a business with management structure, strategy, and products. This is what I learned about social entrepreneurship when I was at university. My understanding back then was that social enterprises tackle marginalized issues that are either not profitable or too complex for many organizations to properly address. These issues are multidimensional and often interdisciplinary and require a theoretical framework to be set up for impact creation.

Social entrepreneurship also has the potential to contribute to sustainable development by promoting good environmental practices and social equity. Social entrepreneurs often focus on creating sustainable business models that minimize environmental impact and promote social equity, such as by providing fair wages and working conditions for employees, using renewable energy sources, or reducing waste and emissions. See we're already in ESG territory with compliance on labor legislation.

The most common example of social entrepreneurship is to provide employment to people who are not attractive candidates in the labor market. This includes people who've been to jail, people living with certain disabilities, victims of human trafficking, and the like. While these types of social enterprises remain important, the spectrum of activities and social issues addressed is much broader now. According to a study by the British Council, social enterprises in the UK employ around two million people, accounting for 5 percent of the country's workforce. The growth in recent years is well documented by the Global Entrepreneurship Monitor (GEM) 2020/2021 report, which concludes that over 40 percent of entrepreneurs worldwide are involved in social entrepreneurship or have a strong social mission.

As I was doing my research, I did wonder whether I am a social entrepreneur, given that all my work is done to improve the social performance of companies and contribute to broader social development. If we examine social entrepreneurship in the context of being a good employer only, we might be disappointed to find that most large companies are good employers because they follow stringent legislation and International Labor Organization (ILO) Conventions. These Conventions are often ratified by countries and thus form part of the regulatory compliance for many companies. I'm going to be cheeky here and ask the same thing I asked in the ESG chapter: Is an employer still a good employer if it complies with the legal obligations but makes no attempts to go the extra mile? What does the *extra mile* mean? Several international tech companies are being referenced as adult daycares due to the extra amenities, services, and allowances that the workplace provides. Is this what we're striving for? Is this just another way to incentivize employees to work longer hours? My conclusion was that I am not a social enterprise but a socially focused enterprise that brings social impacts demonstrable by the number of projects I do and the narratives of stories from the field.

In the context of social entrepreneurship, the main factor we look at is the number of new jobs and the *type* of people employed. We don't go beyond these surface-level indicators to examine the quality of the new jobs created. We've seen this approach with SIBs and SOCs in relation to SME support for job creation. Labor issues and working conditions are tricky because they're based on a very binary system of compliance with legal and other requirements. A company either has HR policies, paid leave, and employment contracts in line with legislation or it doesn't.

The next point to consider is the objective of starting a business. In the books you read in business school, the main reason is always to make a profit. In real life, we see famous entrepreneurs who started their companies because they were passionate about solving a problem for others. In fact, many of the business talks and presentations I listened to simplified the reason for starting a business as "finding a problem and solving it." Sounds simple, right? Entrepreneurs who self-select into this way of life are generally visionaries and innovators with a strong ability to identify opportunities and imagine new possibilities. They are risk-takers who operate outside their comfort zones and are not fazed by uncertainty. This risk tolerance also includes facing rejections, setbacks, and failures on their journey. Entrepreneurs are often motivated by that deep sense of purpose and a high degree of belief in their product. Especially if the product or service is something they created. This genuine interest and dedication force them to take action and create opportunities for themselves. Resiliency, persistence, self-motivation, proactivity, and independence are all traits required to take on the role of an entrepreneur. An entrepreneur wears many hats; they know about all aspects of the business—not just the products but also the organizational logistics that enable operations. The learning never stops because the markets are fast paced, and innovative new ideas are needed time and time again. When I started my entrepreneurial journey, I had no idea what I was signing up for. While I did possess these basic traits—some more than others—there was a strong sense of passion for my profession that pushed me through the hard times.

Every entrepreneur wants to make a meaningful contribution to society, whether it's by innovating a solution or tackling a social problem. I had an issue explaining how a traditional entrepreneur and a social entrepreneur tackle social issues differently. There are so many apps for instance that tackle social issues, but we don't consider them social enterprises. There are apps to access education materials or help with CV formatting for jobs. The new AI technology provides solutions to so many issues that I could fill a book with a list. These are all solutions to challenges that people face and these solutions are there to make life easier. They often bridge a market gap and reach out to previously underserved communities. Think of all the online banks that provide services to people who might have challenges opening a traditional bank account. If you think it's easy to open a bank account, try moving to another country and opening one. You'll face the chicken and egg situation: you'll need a registered address to open an account, but you can't rent until you are able to pay rent from a local bank account. You can't buy a phone contract with a data plan without a registered address, and you also can't add foreign numbers to your bank account application.

The first real difference I found was that traditional entrepreneurs identify market gaps and address those with their products, while social entrepreneurs identify the problem and try to address that through their business. They prioritize tackling issues even if it means delayed or limited financial success. Though the rest of the argument goes that the innovation of the social enterprise is designed to create a positive change, which is true for more traditional enterprises as well.

And here comes the question of success. What does it mean in the traditional business sense? Financial returns and a business that can operate in the long term? In the social enterprise business, success is measured by the social impact of their operations—though for-profit social enterprises will add financial returns to this equation too. Another interesting aspect is the engagement with stakeholders. Traditional businesses consider their customers, employees, and shareholders as their stakeholders, while social enterprises tend to engage more broadly with other groups as well, such as beneficiaries or their products, communities, civil society organizations and nonprofits, government agencies, and investors. So based on this, a lot of businesses could be classified as social businesses, even if they don't self-identify as one. Their impact might not be measurable or demonstratable in the traditional sense, but they fit the definition by finding a market gap and helping underserved customer groups with technological innovation.

The main thing is the sense of social responsibility that seems to be a lot more common nowadays. Some of this social responsibility, especially when it comes to creating quality jobs and enforcing sustainable business practices (you know I'm not fond of generic terms like this, but bear with me), are heavily influenced by regulatory requirements, mandatory sustainability, and ESG frameworks. Several clothing companies only buy cotton that is certified by the Better Cotton Initiative (BCI) as being free from forced labor and child labor. Companies are also more conscious of what their suppliers are doing in terms of environmental and social risk management. This is partly because of shareholder pressure and partly to comply with new legislation.

Social entrepreneurship has undergone a very significant development over the past one hundred years, and it's still evolving and adapting to changing social, economic, and environmental conditions. As new challenges and opportunities arise, social entrepreneurs are developing new strategies to address them.

Purpose, Scope, and Timing

Purpose

In very simple terms, this is the main factor that differentiates a traditional business from a social enterprise. A social enterprise is created with the purpose of making a positive social or environmental impact through innovative business models and strategies. The purpose is to address a selected social, cultural, or environmental problem in a way that generates enough revenue to at least cover its own admin and operations costs. Its purpose also includes identifying a market gap that can help with the integration of underserved communities or groups of people. These market gaps are often overlooked because they are not profitable or require certain innovative and often risky solutions that are not within the mandate and scope of other organizations.

Another purpose of social entrepreneurship is to create sustainable solutions to social or environmental problems. Social entrepreneurs often focus on creating business models that are financially sustainable in the long term, rather than relying on philanthropic or grant funding. Social entrepreneurship also has the purpose of promoting social and environmental justice. They can serve as catalysts for systemic change.

Scope

In general, the scope of social entrepreneurship can cover many aspects of social impact creation, business models, and organizational structures. The scope on the enterprise level is very narrowly defined though. This means that the issue, though broad, is not solved in its entirety by the business, but instead, the business provides a contribution to a more macro-level solution.

The broader topics were mentioned before and include poverty alleviation, job creation for vulnerable groups, healthcare, education, gender equality, access to justice, civic engagement, cultural preservation, other environmental-related issues, and general social development. These provide the framework of operation, but they are multidisciplinary and connected to other aspects of life as well. It's hard to imagine a person sitting at home thinking, "I'll start a business that will address gender equality." I mean, where would they even begin? What aspect of gender equality should they focus on? Since this is not a philanthropic organization, it needs to have a product or a service that addresses a gap in the market for the identified subpopulation. See? We're already talking about the target customer base, the product, and the market analysis to start our business. Let's say we want to offer employment for women refugees who have a hard time finding a job. We could set up any type of business—a café, an accounting company, a dry cleaner—and offer training for these refugee women before employing them in the company. Being a social enterprise does not mean being a charity. These women would work normal hours, produce deliverables, complete their tasks, and get a salary. The reason why it is still a social enterprise is because this group of people who would have a hard time finding other employment are prioritized when looking for staff members.

Poverty alleviation and healthcare are also popular areas for social enterprises. We will see the examples later, but the main thing is that each social enterprise is tackling one issue at a time within the broader social problem. The scope of each company is narrowly defined in terms of the product, the customers, and the market gap. While it doesn't look much different from a typical business, the motivation behind the selection of customers and the market gap is to address the underlying systemic social issue.

Social entrepreneurship also encompasses a variety of business models and organizational structures, or impact delivery mechanisms. Social entrepreneurs may choose to start for-profit ventures, nonprofit organizations, or hybrid models. Some social enterprises fund part of their activities with grants and donations from private individuals or large corporations. They may also collaborate with existing organizations to create social and environmental impacts.

The scope of social entrepreneurship extends beyond individual entrepreneurs and organizations. It can also include systemic change, such as policy reform or changes in societal norms and values. Social entrepreneurs can advocate for policy changes that promote social and environmental justice and work to shift public perception and behavior toward more sustainable and equitable practices. I have yet to see this, but one thing is certain: if a business makes a profit, people become interested in it—especially if it is connected to *doing good*. While it's not a tool to solve all our issues, it's a good start that can address parts of the problem step by step. Raising awareness and providing innovative solutions go a long way, especially for the targeted beneficiary group.

Timing

The timing here, like with many of the other social impact products, is important in a different way than the timing of SIAs. Here, the sense of urgency is not related to a planned intervention but a pressing issue that has been ongoing. Several of the social aspects such as poverty, homelessness, access to employment, healthcare, and education are typically long-standing issues. The best time to start is right now.

Like other businesses, social enterprises have startup and operational costs that are often managed with grants, loans, or other subsidies provided by the government. The availability of such support may delay or speed up the formation of a new social enterprise. The structure and funding source might be a hybrid model where companies provide grants or microcredit for startup social enterprises. The political context might also be crucial, as the availability of funding fluctuates with the election cycle. The development stage of the social enterprise can also impact the timing. Some social entrepreneurs have all the plans, products, and structures ready to go and are just waiting for the last piece of the puzzle before they can launch. This might be a government subsidy or other support mechanism, while other social enterprises are in the early stages of planning the products and services.

Market demand is something that is often overlooked, yet even with the nonprofit type of social enterprise, the social enterprise needs to operate as a business that generates income that at a minimum covers the operational costs. The market demand for the products or services being offered needs to be understood. Social entrepreneurs must be able to identify and respond to it effectively, while also ensuring that their initiatives are socially and environmentally responsible. This is strongly correlated to the political landscape—the broader economic, technological, and social trends that we touched upon before. Savvy social entrepreneurs act fast to identify the changing market conditions and come up with solutions to respond to the new trends.

The readiness of the business is a significant factor in this timing, as is the availability of resources and support. The enterprise needs to be able to respond to the market demand in line with the current economic, political, and social landscape. It is almost evident that the impact of the social enterprise is immediate, as the products or services provided will be immediately available to the target beneficiaries. This concept of delayed impact within a set time frame does not seem to apply here. Even for social enterprises that provide services to marginalized communities. They might increase their outreach and customer base over time, but the impact on the initial group of beneficiaries will be immediate.

Limitations

Social entrepreneurs are a special kind of businesspeople who aim to utilize innovative solutions to solve social and environmental issues. In this instance, the definition of positive social impact is understood in more concrete terms than we have seen before. Social enterprises define their target audience either through the beneficiaries of the new product or by the type of employee they will favor.

In terms of our previous categorizations, we can see that social enterprises are created on a voluntary basis. There is no requirement for any enterprise to become a social enterprise and completely change its structure to accommodate this. Legally speaking, the legislation applicable to traditional enterprises is applicable to social enterprises as well. Furthermore, there are no reporting requirements, either, because technically the shareholders create the business with the sole aim of making a positive social impact—and enough cash to cover costs. There are no reporting frameworks that could provide guidance on what should be reported by any social enterprise in terms of the social impact they create. Social enterprises tend to opt in to report on their activities and use the social angle as a tool for marketing their products and services. These businesses also tend to be supported more by organizations and government initiatives that provide support and publicity for these businesses.

The measurement and demonstration of social impacts is another issue that is specific to a social enterprise. The social impact by definition is the main reason why the business is created. Say, for example, the business is created to employ people with disabilities. The measurement of success would be the percentage of employees employed that have disabilities. The target and the approach are different compared to the other quantitative measurements and demonstrations we have seen for other products. Here a business would succeed even with two employees—if that's all it takes to operate the business. The reporting I have seen during my research also connected the achievements of this one enterprise to the macro-level employment trends of people with disabilities. While there is a contribution from the company, the impact is indirect and attributable, especially if we are talking about a small business with a limited number of employees.

This ties in nicely with the next limitation, which is related to the financial sustainability of these businesses. I often think of the coffee shops that operate based on the honor system or under a pay-what-you-can model. In 1963, this idea seemed like it was not going to work, but now there are more and more coffee shops that operate based on this model. I do have to point out, though, that even for nonprofit social enterprises the operational costs need to be covered at a minimum. Without going into too much detail, we can see that a successful business has a good product that is demanded by customers on the market, optimized costs, branding, marketing, partnerships, and solid streams of revenue. While I think a social enterprise can absolutely achieve this, some old beliefs can't put positive social impacts and financial success in the same sentence. On the other hand, social enterprises may struggle to be largely profitable because they invest in creating more or better social impacts. Again the terminology of what is better or more is not quite developed to reflect the true meaning, but I guess you understand what I'm trying to say. Employing new people is costly and so is research and development of new products that have a higher social impact.

Growing up in Eastern Europe after the fall of the Iron Curtain, I must admit I also struggled with the idea of social entrepreneurship when I first heard about it and only recently started seeing the potential later in life. The great advantage is the lack of limiting frameworks, so theoretically, any kind of social impact that's a net benefit to people can be created. Much like the other social impact products, here we're also not talking about the social impacts of the operations or the social compliance with, for instance, labor legislation. We're simply talking about trying to find a way to address a social issue that's pressing for the entrepreneur. This approach provides a lot of freedom as to what social impact means in the context of the business.

Sticking to an earlier example, if an enterprise wants to provide employment for refugees, they only need to report on the percentage of their employees that are refugees to demonstrate that they are successfully creating their predetermined social impact. We are by no means obligated to go further and check whether each worker has an employment contract, working hours, and personal protective equipment in line with national legislation or whether they are locked into any sort of bonded labor contract. We assume that a person who wants to do good is doing it in line with applicable legislation. Hopefully, most social enterprises are like that, but I've worked with way too many clients who had labor issues to know that double-checking these aspects won't hurt.

Can a social enterprise with no ESG rating be a socially responsible enterprise? There are social and environmental factors on different levels that should influence our opinions and understanding of social impact products. It always comes down to whether it's voluntary-involuntary, if it's macro or micro level, the demonstration of the impact, the definition of the impact and beneficiaries in measurable terms, and whether it's in line with a theoretical social framework that can guide our understanding of the complex issue. The majority of these were applicable to the other social impact products because they were either linked to a legal requirement, a voluntary but structured framework (ESG), or research to provide clarity on impact measurement through data and indicators. However, ESG is not appropriate for all businesses and industries as we have seen.

Social enterprise seems to be left behind with the freedom to be whatever it wants to be. Some organizations go as far as to say that a business is a social enterprise because it donates a certain percentage of its profits to a charity or initiative. Based on the definitions in this book, that falls under philanthropy or CSR. Would that assumption be incorrect? Probably not, because of the mismatched definitions. This lack of structure and the constantly evolving landscape differentiates social enterprises from the rest of the products we looked at. Though it aims to create macro-level impacts through systemic changes, it can only impact the employees or the customer base. While there may be a relatively large number of businesses, it does not address the legal, political, and policy frameworks that perpetuate such systemic issues.

Impacts can be measured with various tools. Some are familiar in the context of other social impact products, while others are statistics demonstrating that the main objective of the business is met. The thing is that we cannot really *judge* these businesses because there was no obligation—other than moral obligation, perhaps—to create the business and the positive impact. And much like with philanthropy, there is no obligation to address a certain issue. We have also seen that there is no theoretical framework to provide anything other than guidance as to how the issue could be addressed. This leaves us with the conclusion we had for philanthropy: that it is a general net benefit for society, even if the impacts are not large scale or *significant*. It still addresses a pressing issue that would have been left unaddressed by many other social impact products. We are again far from addressing operations or project-level social impacts and entering the territory of generic social impacts.

Social enterprises have often been criticized because of the lack of scalability of the business. This means either the issue is too big to be addressed by one company or the business model does not work on a larger scale. While this might be true for several issues that fall under government responsibility and have deep roots that are out of reach for companies, stacking up resources, forming partnerships, and leveraging networks can address the issue. My personal note on replicating business models in different parts of the world is that success will depend on cultural differences and attitudes to entrepreneurship, social issues, and support from the developed world. I did point out earlier that several cultures have a type of crowdfunding that's like microfinance, using donations to solve for the lack of credit facilities. While it might work in some contexts, it would fail in others.

When I started this journey of writing about social impacts, I felt that the world was vilifying corporations for making a profit regardless of their efforts to address social issues through impact assessments of their operations, CSR, ESG frameworks and ratings, and donations to philanthropic initiatives. I understood that there is a difference between nonvoluntary and voluntary impact creation and measurement through my work, but I was not aware of just how little effort was made to fully explain the scope, scale, and magnitude. The expectations are significant: companies—especially companies who are perceived to be working in a nongreen sector (think oil, gas, energy)—should give back to the people. As a matter of fact, they do. Many of the nongreen companies carry out very detailed ESIAs on their operational sites and develop site-specific management plans. In addition, they very likely have CSR initiatives both on a corporate and site level with various community investments.

The Equator Principles is a set of environmental and social guidelines that financial Institutions adopt to assess and manage the potential environmental and social risks associated with project financing. (There's more about this in the next chapter, where I included the other tools that can frame our discourse and understanding of the broad concept of social impact.) So, if we have a company that complies with legislation, meets the voluntary and nonvoluntary standards for impact assessment and management, and has an ESG rating and a CSR program (on corporate and potentially operations level), what more do we expect from them? We spent this whole chapter looking at social enterprises, and we noticed that they have far less scrutiny and nonvoluntary standards than several other nonsocial companies. The contrast is because we think a social enterprise is, by definition, *good* and would never do anything scandalous, yet we have several examples of scandals that involve issues such as unfair wages, unsafe working conditions, labor exploitation, and lack of compliance with labor laws.

Goodwill Industries is a well-known social enterprise that operates thrift stores and provides job training and employment opportunities to individuals facing barriers to employment. Goodwill faced criticism for paying low wages to workers with disabilities to the extent that some argued that this practice may exploit the exemption provided under certain labor laws that allow for subminimum wages for individuals with disabilities. This was not the first time that Goodwill was criticized by the public, and many questioned whether it truly was a social enterprise, given the seemingly high salaries paid to management. I don't want to list everyone's wrongdoings here to avoid discouraging people from believing in social enterprises. My argument is that just because something is *good* in some context, that doesn't make that product or business *good* in all the metrics we have for social impact creation, management, and measurement.

Returning to our original topic, it was noted before that a social enterprise is set up in a way to achieve a defined social goal, such as to employ people with disabilities or former prisoners or to provide services to customers who are otherwise overlooked. While it's hard to measure the impact of the company's operations on the lives of people who belong to this general group, the company can demonstrate its impact and fulfillment of its agenda in other ways. They can report statistics about their workforce or the number of customers and the types of services that were popular. If a social enterprise is lucky then it is promoted to other people who fit the target customer base so they can have a larger impact. They are not set out with commitments to change the system, though they want to create systemic change through their actions. They don't have tools such as policy dialogue and advocacy to use for wider impact creation. They can triangulate the claims with secondary data, such as the number of disabled people employed before and after their operations in the area, yet these would be meaningless because the impact is an indirect contribution by a company.

There are several business networks and marketplaces for business services that cater to companies of various sizes. Social enterprises have different business needs because the typical tools for management—

restructuring, cost optimization, reallocation of resources—might not be appropriate for what the company wants to achieve. Even indicators and KPIs need to be reviewed to include social impact-specific measures in line with the business' profile. One thing leads to another: it's challenging to define the type of expertise we need for a social enterprise to thrive. We need to define the issue we want to address, understand the complexity, and identify a way to target some area through a service or product our business can provide. What sort of specialist expertise do we need to define the issue and identify the solution for it? Is this a social development specialist? Is this a business management expert? Should we rely on our common sense? The only good answer to this is that it very much depends on the profile of the social entrepreneur and the issue they are trying to tackle. Some, like employing people underrepresented in the labor market seem more straightforward even for nontechnical specialists, while other more complex issues might require subject matter experts.

Next up is the unpopular but unavoidable question: Can we really measure a social enterprise's diversity and inclusion index if its goal is to employ certain groups of people? I advocated holding traditional and social enterprises to the same standards, yet here I'll make an exception. I do not believe that traditional diversity, equality, and inclusion (DEI) measures and frameworks are applicable to products whose main social impact is to provide employment for a defined group of people. It's applicable to enterprises that provide services because they are not committed to employing only certain groups of people. A more outdated take on DEI in social entrepreneurship is thinking that it's mainly initiated by people who come from privileged backgrounds with limitations to understand and address the needs of marginalized communities. If the problems and issues are not well understood, the solutions cannot be tailored to meet the needs of the target population.

The next limitation links nicely with this idea of a bankable profit-making solution. Several social enterprises are heavily subsidized by the government and thus operate more like a philanthropic organization rather than a business. The subsidies, while an amazing tool to incentivize entrepreneurs to be creative, have led to a whole sector of social enterprises that rely heavily on subsidies and grants to fund their operations. The availability of such support might become volatile as the priorities and political landscapes change, causing unpredictability for the social enterprise and the beneficiaries it aims to support. While socially conscious consumers might favor a social enterprise, they will only become repeat customers if the service or the product is good.

Some of the ethical dilemmas were raised before, such as what happens if a social enterprise is not ethical when employing otherwise vulnerable people and making their situation even worse. Other types of questions related to ethics emerge when businesses operate in areas with limited resources and significant issues. The decision of which social issue is more pressing, whose social impact is better, is a tough one. Social enterprises can rely on academic research, customer surveys, or consultation with potential target beneficiaries, but ultimately it will come down to the owners and management of the social enterprise to prioritize an issue. The beauty and the challenge for both philanthropy and social enterprises is the freedom to choose whatever issue they want to address. This choice may be personal or informed by studies and community feedback, but it might just be an individual's preference based on their experience.

While this section is rather lengthy, it's more of a discussion than a flat-out criticism of social entrepreneurship. The new trends around responsible business practices, ESG being standard practice for many companies and the social responsibility narrative contributed to a different view on social enterprises. The currently available terminology can be misleading and can not fully articulate the nuanced differences. There are some wonderful examples of social enterprises later on that are worth mentioning and discussing because they do make a difference in people's lives. Also, while researching this chapter, I committed to making a better effort to seek out social enterprises I can buy from. After my research and my renewed understanding of social enterprises, I have an increased appreciation for the people who transform business ideas into social businesses.

How It Relates to Other Social Impact Products

While social entrepreneurship is distinct from other approaches, it also shares commonalities and overlaps with several other social impact products. It is in the voluntary category, just like philanthropy, SIBs, SOCs, and CSR. This means that it is not a legal requirement for a business to be a social enterprise. In terms of the contents and what it means to create such an impact, there are no frameworks or legal requirements targeting social enterprises. They are free to get inspired by research, academic literature, and other organizations when defining the issue they want to tackle. The scope is almost limitless as long as the business is creating a positive social impact with the innovation it sells or promotes.

In previous chapters, we talked about how philanthropy has a similar approach to social entrepreneurship. Both create a positive social impact around the areas that are identified as a priority by the founder of the organization. Certain types of social enterprises rely on grant money and donations similar to philanthropic initiatives. The measurement and reporting on social impacts also follow a similar approach for the two products. Philanthropy might be better defined with more subject matter experts working for the organizations with grants covering the operational costs. Philanthropy might have the opportunity to address more dimensions of the same social issue. If we look at employment, it might be able to provide targeted training for certain professions (more than one), internship placements, and other full-time placements with partner businesses. A social enterprise might provide training, internships, and employment but only in relation to the main activities of the business. Nevertheless, both approaches aim to be present on a long-term basis to continue addressing the social issue. It is not a quick fix with a fixed return period when the investment needs to be concluded.

Government interventions, policies, and programs were briefly mentioned before, but I think it's important to emphasize it here. These are complementary to social entrepreneurship in a way that we have only seen for philanthropy and some types of SOCs. The rest of the social impact products included in this book are more focused on the private sector. There is also a financial return requirement for SIBs and SOCs, while nearly all the other social impact products operate with timelines. It might be the maturity of the bond, the annual ESG and sustainability reporting, the completion of all impact assessment and mitigation prior to project start for SIA, or the operating frameworks for CSR (annual report). The social enterprise has no reporting requirements and is free to live without a set deadline to achieve the intended impacts. In a way, just by operating the goal is reached and the impact is created. The reason governments are important to social enterprises, other than providing funding, is the institutional support they can provide. Government interventions can create challenges for social enterprises, but they can also accelerate the operations of many companies.

Impact investing is an interesting intersection to examine here. There are clearly several overlaps in the way these are social impact products that use business and investment tools to create positive social or environmental outcomes. The product's success is measured by the positive impact and financial return (or break even for nonprofit social enterprises). The solutions and the deployment of private capital for social impact creation are also relevant in both instances. The option to innovate new approaches to problem-solving is not hindered or limited by frameworks and regulations, which allows for new models, products, and services to transform communities and contribute to a positive social impact. Not surprisingly, the financial feasibility is important in both cases. The time frames for impact creation are similar, though impact investing focuses on an agreed-upon timeline to exit the investment and count the returns. Social entrepreneurship takes a longer-term approach and aims to have a sustainable setup financially, strategically, and structurally. It is, after all, a company that's set up specifically to address the social issue that is chosen by the owner of the company.

While impact investing could follow a more hands-on approach, it tends to deploy the capital to another entity that manages and sets up the investments based on the agreed-upon criteria and indicators. Impact investing is driven by investors seeking to allocate their capital to organizations or projects that align with their values and generate positive impacts. They play a role in assessing the social performance of potential investments in line with their priorities. Notice how impact investing leans toward existing initiatives, while social enterprise is started in order to create an impact. This also implies that impact investing has a broader reach since it can pool funds and deploy them in a diversified way through existing companies and initiatives. Social entrepreneurship is likely to be smaller scale by nature.

It would be a mistake to not mention traditional entrepreneurship here. I will not repeat what I've already said about this relationship between the two types of entrepreneurs and business models. What is left to discuss is how social enterprises and traditional enterprises can collaborate to create more sustainable solutions to the identified social issues. A social enterprise, just like any enterprise, needs suppliers, a distribution network, and business partners that contribute to the enterprise's success in different ways. Providing an example of how a business can operate and be profitable while doing good can be an inspiration to other traditional entrepreneurs out there. Social enterprises can create a bridge to bring together actors from the private, nonprofit, and public sectors to tackle the issue from multiple angles. Tailored interventions like this will result in a more systemic improvement with a higher chance of success. Combining strengths and perspectives can facilitate solutions to complex issues.

Despite the many similarities and relationships with other social impact products, social entrepreneurship remains a distinct and important approach that innovatively combines traditional business with social impact creation. The outcome is a unique blend of business principles, innovation, and social issues designed to serve a well-defined group of target beneficiaries.

What Is the Social Impact?

I was excited to get to this point in the book, where I can talk about my take on what a social impact is for a social enterprise. This is partly because, like philanthropy, it's wildly different from the interpretation of social impact I encounter through my work. The core of social entrepreneurship is the creation of positive social change. Based on metrics I've used before, we can also conclude that it is demonstrable. The social impact is defined both as the impact the business might create within its operations and as creating positive and sustainable changes in society. The sole aim of the social enterprise is to create this positive impact through the business, especially since many of the target areas are overlooked by other players in the market. The scope of the social enterprise can be broad, yet it can only target one subsection of a larger issue at a time due to the constraints around the products and services a company can offer. Economic empowerment, social inclusion, and access to services and employment are all positive social impacts promised by these enterprises. I must admit I was a little skeptical as to how such wide-ranging, macro-level impacts could be referred to from the relatively small-scale operations I've seen in some of the examples. It seemed to me that significant impacts that are driven by larger corporations do not fit the traditional concept of a social enterprise but rather fall into the CSR, philanthropy, or impact investing category. This is exactly why I'm writing this book, to initiate a discussion on definitions and clarify boundaries and overlaps between these products.

Social entrepreneurship has created new opportunities for underserved communities, fostered the innovation of social and environmental solutions, and influenced policy and practice on all levels of society. As the social entrepreneurship movement continues to grow and evolve, it's likely to play an increasingly important role in creating a more just, equitable, and sustainable world. I do see a shift in companies trying to *do good* with the tools they already know and the tools that are supported by the shareholders. Typically, these tools are CSR, philanthropy, impact investing, and ESG frameworks and ratings. Several of these products overlap, and what is sometimes referred to as a social enterprise turns out to be a philanthropic organization. At the core of each of these initiatives, people want to make sure an issue that's important to them, their organization, their communities, their shareholders, and the general public is addressed in a way that falls within its scope. Reporting on this is challenging because we are not yet at the stage where the language and the terminology allow for the classification and categorization of impacts in a way that avoids social washing. What I've proposed in this book will hopefully help us answer the question I've been asking all along. What is a social impact?

Social enterprises can create jobs, provide training and education, and support the growth of local communities—especially those that are vulnerable or underserved. This is an important impact, despite its relatively small scale. Sustainable business practices, whatever they might mean in different contexts, are promoted and adopted by many companies, which can significantly change the perception of negative impact mitigation and positive impact creation. With small shifts, significant impacts can be made. The main motivation for social entrepreneurs is to create an impact, however we define it, whether it is improved access to services that are often not available to marginalized communities or improved products that are suited to the needs of marginalized groups. Social entrepreneurship is often associated with community development since the business serves the interest of a selected group of people within the community. This can contribute toward improving the overall well-being and quality of life for these people and thus integrating them into the local communities better. Social justice and equality are goals a social enterprise can work toward, especially if it targets affordable legal services and representation for underserved communities. The social enterprise builds on a gap in the market that prevents certain groups from accessing services or products—whether it is due to any special needs, financial constraints, or being a blind spot on the market.

Social entrepreneurship is a dynamic and ever-evolving concept that changes as the market of social impact products evolves. It's interesting to see how the flexibility, innovation, perseverance, dedication, and resourcefulness of traditional entrepreneurship translate into creating a positive social impact. The question of whether the old definition of a social enterprise is still valid given the regulatory environment and voluntary social impact frameworks that many companies follow remains. It is also a dilemma whether we can call a company a social enterprise because it found a market gap to cater to underserved customers. Without the background and the narrative on what makes the social impact meaningful, that enterprise is just another business on the block. The intention of the business also needs to be clarified: are we creating the impact intentionally or is it a byproduct of our standard operations? A good example is online banking and financial inclusion.

There are so many questions and provocative ideas in this small section that strengthen my belief that discussions on the future of social entrepreneurship are a must. Nevertheless, creating a positive social impact is a core element of social entrepreneurship. We can argue what this impact is and whether it is significant, demonstrable, or even related to the social nature of the business. One thing is certain: social enterprises are very personal, often led by a visionary entrepreneur who's willing to make changes to traditional business practices to accommodate the needs of marginalized communities and advocate for systemic change.

Example of Social Entrepreneurship Done Right

This is where all that contradiction from the previous section made my work challenging. How we define a social enterprise and its social impact determines whether certain businesses fall under that model. We've seen that the criterion is that a business is created to solve a social issue or create a positive social impact. We've seen that some social enterprises are for profit while others operate on a nonprofit basis. We have also briefly mentioned social enterprises that donate part of their profit or goods to those in need (regardless of how we establish this eligibility criteria). The examples I brought to you fall into some of these categories, but they often fall on the border of another social impact product or, dare I say, create a hybrid model. You can see that the issues addressed can be very specific and targeted at some groups, while in other cases these impacts are more implied and extended to a larger group of people. The examples provided demonstrate how a wide range of issues is also important for entrepreneurs as they target improving access to clean water and healthcare and empowering individuals and communities through education and training. I have a lot of respect and appreciation for anyone who enters these unregulated waters of social impact creation with the pure intention to make a difference in people's lives:

- TOMS is a well-known social enterprise that has become synonymous with the "one for one" model. For every pair of shoes sold, TOMS donates a pair to a child in need. Since its founding in

2006, TOMS has donated over one hundred million pairs of shoes and has expanded its giving to include eyewear, clean water, and safe birth kits. This is a privately held, for-profit social enterprise that donates products to children in need. The impacts are clear: kids have access to products. Yet the company faced criticism that the one-for-one model is another form of colonialism resulting in dependency on donations as opposed to empowering locals to figure out sustainable solutions. In this case, the business was founded with the clear intention of donating these products in line with the sales. The business naturally expanded to include different types of footwear, glasses, bags, and accessories. It's no surprise that as the business grew, so did its social impact. The target group is well defined, and the impact is demonstrable through statistics and metrics.

- Warby Parker is another social enterprise that has gained widespread recognition for its innovative business model. The company sells affordable, stylish eyewear online and in retail stores. For every pair sold, Warby Parker donates a pair of glasses to someone in need. Since its founding in 2010, Warby Parker has distributed over eight million pairs of glasses. I'm less familiar with this company, so I can't comment on the purpose of starting the business, but one thing is certain: the financial barriers to updating prescriptions are a real thing not only in the developing world but also in developed countries. The model is similar to what we have seen above with TOMS. Products are donated to a selected community in line with sales. Warby Parker partners with VisionSpring, another social enterprise that supports access to glasses for low-income people. The project grew with the addition of the Pupils Project in 2015, which aims to collaborate with government agencies to provide free eye tests and glasses to schoolchildren.

- Grameen Bank is a microfinance organization founded by Nobel Peace Prize winner Muhammad Yunus in 1976. The organization provides small loans to poor individuals who would otherwise not be eligible for commercial bank loans due to poor credit history or lack of collateral. This is a well-known issue in developing countries—particularly with women, who are less likely to own property and often need their husbands to sign off on loans as a guarantor. The barriers to starting small businesses and improving their economic status can be overcome through targeted action. This is what Grameen Bank recognized. Technically speaking, the company is microfinance with a social angle, but in my view, it fits with the social enterprise narrative. Since its founding, Grameen Bank has disbursed over $30 billion in loans and has had a significant impact on poverty reduction in Bangladesh and other countries. One way this impact is demonstrated is by citing the World Bank statistics that the poverty rate in Bangladesh decreased from 70 percent in 1976—the start of operations for Grameen Bank—to 21 percent in 2018. It is surely not only due to Grameen Bank, but their contribution to this is undeniable.

- Barefoot College is a social enterprise that provides education and training to rural communities in developing countries. The organization offers programs in solar energy, water management, and other sustainable livelihoods management, and empowers local people to become leaders in their communities. Since its founding, Barefoot College has benefited over 2.4 million people from ninety-three countries. While others might question whether Barefoot is truly a social enterprise given it operates more as a foundation and charity, getting its resources through donations, I included it here because they are trying to operate in the market and promote business strategies to help people utilize the training they provided.

- Better World Books is a social enterprise that has collected and sold used books online since 2003, with a portion of the profits going to support literacy initiatives around the world. Amongst its achievements is setting up and operating the Drop Box Program, where books are redirected from landfills, or the Book for Book Program, where they donate a book for every book bought from them. The achievements sound impressive, with a large amount of money donated to nonprofit partners for literacy programs and education, donations for libraries and thrift stores, donations of college textbooks, and many more initiatives. This company is operating a more traditional social enterprise model, with a core business strategy of collecting and selling used books.

- Embrace Innovations is a social enterprise that has developed an affordable infant warmer to help prevent infant mortality in developing countries. The product is a low-cost, portable, and reusable incubator that can maintain a stable temperature for up to six hours. This is truly a niche sector to operate in, yet the impact is undeniable. This business operates with a traditional social enterprise approach. A very inspiring story.

- d.light is a social enterprise that produces and distributes solar-powered lights and energy solutions in developing countries. The products are affordable and provide a clean, sustainable alternative to traditional kerosene lamps, which can be harmful to health and the environment. Since its founding twelve years ago, d.light has sold over 20 million products and has helped over 154 million people access clean energy. d.light is managing its social impact reporting very ambitiously. It uses GOGLA standardized impact metrics. I must admit, I was not familiar with this, but after a closer look, I found that it standardizes indicators to measure access to energy, income generation, CO_2 emission reduction, and comparable estimates among companies. I've had many renewable energy projects over the past couple of years, and I see great potential in using renewables for household-level energy supplies. Especially if there is no alternative from the grid. Educating people about energy and renewables and then providing them with the technology to supply their household can have a massive impact on their health, education, nutrition, and more.

At the time of writing this book, I am based in Marylebone, London. As I wrote, I became curious to see what the social enterprise scene was like close to home. Maybe I unknowingly already supported companies and people who are creating positive social impact. I looked at a few examples close to home. I would encourage you to google social enterprises in your area; you never know what you might find! Maybe a cool new coffee shop, access to used books in good condition, or simply a place where you can donate your old clothes. Here's what I found in my area:

- *The Social Pantry.* Located in Marylebone, The Social Pantry is a café and catering company that operates as a social enterprise. They provide employment and training opportunities for vulnerable individuals, including ex-offenders and those experiencing homelessness. The Social Pantry offers delicious food and beverages while simultaneously supporting its social mission. In addition to the social impacts, they've also committed to embracing circular economies and zero-waste initiatives with a tailored menu to support these efforts. This operational model seems typical for a classic social enterprise, where there is a for-profit business that has a social and environmental angle.

- *Connection at St. Martin's.* This organization is situated near Marylebone and works to address homelessness in London. Connection at St. Martin's offers various services to homeless people, including housing support, employment assistance, and mental health support. They operate social enterprises such as a café and a charity shop, where proceeds go toward funding their vital services. Charity shops are a good way for several philanthropic and nonprofit organizations to monetize donations. While this business model is nontraditional for a social enterprise, it is very creative and, in a way, helps people with different levels and complexities of vulnerability. Some need immediate help (somewhere to sleep and shower) while others need affordable secondhand clothing, shoes, and household items from the stores. This targets two groups of vulnerable people, providing them with an immediate solution to their issues. We briefly discussed the sustainability of the efforts provided in terms of the beneficiary truly having the ability to change their lives. It is a typical criticism of microfinance and, to some extent, of charities and philanthropic organizations as well. The truly amazing thing about some types of social enterprises is that while they provide immediate relief, they also provide tools, skills, and training so people can make a significant change in their lives.

- *The Bike Project.* While not directly located in Marylebone, The Bike Project is a social enterprise that operates across London, including nearby areas. They refurbish donated bicycles and provide them to refugees and asylum-seekers, allowing them to access education, employment, and other vital services. By promoting sustainable transportation and empowering marginalized communities, The Bike Project creates a positive social impact. While it's not quite clear to me why this initiative popped up in my search for social enterprises (it uses donated bikes and spends resources on improving them before giving them away), I was delighted to find this initiative. I think there isn't enough talk about affordability constraints when it comes to accessing services or even employment. London can be an expensive place, especially if you're a refugee or asylum-seeker. This organization (I can't call it a business) identified a barrier that makes it challenging for people with low incomes to commute in the city and provided an environmentally friendly alternative.

- *The Felix Project.* Although not exclusive to Marylebone, this program operates across London and aims to tackle food waste and food poverty. They collect surplus food from suppliers and redistribute it to charities and community organizations, ensuring that vulnerable people have access to nutritious meals. Their work helps reduce food waste and supports those facing food insecurity. Much like our previous example, this is more of a charity (they even state that on their website) that's working with businesses and restaurants to help everyone out. They take the food waste and give it to those who need it. It's very innovative, and there are several high-end restaurants that participate in the program.

- *Made in Marylebone.* This social enterprise has two business lines. The first one is a catering service and the second one is a meeting room hire. The target beneficiary group is homeless women who need support with getting employed. The business also offers workshops and training, specifically focused on the hospitality industry and catering. This business model is more in line with the traditional definition of a social enterprise, as there is a service and a product for sale.

These examples showcase the diverse range of social enterprises and quasi-social enterprises operating in and around my neighborhood. I hope to visit some of them and contribute to their success.

Conclusion

Social entrepreneurship seems distinct from other social impact products in many ways, yet it serves as a powerful tool for creating a positive social and often environmental impact. Traditional social enterprises have proven over time that a business can be financially successful while also proactively creating a positive social impact. This type of social impact product is voluntary and not limited by any legal or other frameworks in terms of its activities and indicators to use for impact measurement.

While social entrepreneurship has the potential to create a significant positive impact, it also has its limitations and challenges. Nonetheless, the success stories of social entrepreneurship initiatives provide inspiration and insight into how innovative and entrepreneurial approaches can create sustainable solutions to some of the world's most pressing problems.

CHAPTER 9

OTHER "SOCIAL" ASPECTS TO CONSIDER

We are through the main section of this book, with which I provided my overview of the current social impact products. This view is from a social performance practitioner whose focus is the identification, assessment, and management of project- and operation-specific impacts. In my daily life, I have the usual tools available to capture these impacts, with the SIA being a relatively well-defined approach. When I started this writing journey, I truly immersed myself in this fascinating world and was often surprised by my own perceptions or biases. I am not afraid of being wrong or having an understanding that is not compatible with some mainstream views, and I've been open about my lack of experience with some of the products in this book. I wanted to create this special chapter to go through some of the other aspects of social impact creation and management that are either tools to measure and demonstrate impacts, requirements or guidance notes that were created for a different purpose but ended up with a social dimension over time. This is not an exhaustive list by any means because the field of social impact products is ever changing and evolving. The definitions are being refined and redefined as the public expectations of companies shift from profit-making to impact-making.

Social Return on Investment

Social Return on Investment (SROI) is a methodology used to measure and evaluate the social, environmental, and economic impacts of a project, program, or organization. It provides a framework for understanding the value created by an initiative. It goes beyond traditional financial metrics to consider the broader outcomes, such as improved health, increased social cohesion, and reduced carbon emissions. SROI aims to quantify the social impact in terms of monetary value so it can be compared to the financial return of the investment. SROI considers not only the financial return on investment but also the social and environmental benefits and costs of a project. The SROI framework is based on the principles of social accounting, and it uses a range of methods and techniques such as stakeholder engagement, cost-benefit analysis, and scenario planning to determine the social value of a project. The SROI is calculated as the ratio of the estimated social value of a project to the total investment in the project. A high SROI indicates that the social impact of a project is high compared to the investment made, while a low SROI ratio indicates the opposite.

The SROI process involves identifying the inputs and outcomes of a project or program and assigning a value to each. This can include both tangible and intangible benefits, such as improved health outcomes, increased employment opportunities, reduced carbon emissions, and stronger social cohesion. Once these inputs and outcomes have been identified, they are analyzed to determine the overall value created by the initiative. This value is then compared to the resources invested in the project or program to determine the SROI.

One of the key benefits of SROI is that it enables organizations to communicate the impact of their work in a way that is meaningful and transparent. By providing a clear and concise picture of the value created by a project or program, SROI can help organizations build trust with stakeholders and demonstrate their commitment to creating social and environmental change. Another benefit of SROI is that it encourages organizations to take a more holistic approach to their work. By looking beyond traditional financial metrics and considering the broader impacts of their initiatives, organizations can identify areas in which they can create additional value and make a more meaningful contribution to society. SROI has been used by a wide range of organizations, from nonprofits, impact investing, philanthropy, and social enterprises to corporations and government agencies. It has been used to evaluate a variety of initiatives, including community development projects, education programs, health interventions, and environmental conservation efforts.

While SROI has many benefits, it also has some limitations. One challenge is that it can be difficult to assign a value to certain outcomes, such as improved mental health or increased social capital. The monetary representation of the social return may also be confusing especially if the impact is abstract, as mentioned above. Those who specialize in calculating SROI are probably better suited to comment, but it seems like a resource-intensive exercise that needs to be informed by academic research and theoretical frameworks. I must say that for SIAs I have only seen them mentioned in an academic context, not by practitioners.

One of the key elements of the SROI process is stakeholder engagement. This involves consulting with a range of stakeholders, including beneficiaries, funders, and community members, to understand their perspectives on the initiative and its impact. While measuring the value of a social impact might seem subjective, as we have seen, sometimes perceptions greatly distort the view on certain impacts. By engaging with stakeholders in this way, organizations can ensure their SROI analysis is grounded in the needs and priorities of those they are serving, especially when working with composite indices made up of several indicators. The perception of what constitutes a priority can truly change the input to the equation.

Accountability and transparency have been mentioned before in the context of reporting, impact measurement, demonstration of impacts, and attribution of positive impacts to certain operations. This is where SROI can be a very useful tool to demonstrate cause and effect to investors. Based on our assumption of people wanting to *do good*, SROI helps with articulating what that actually means. Instead of generic macro-level claims of an investment's social impact, this tool provides a number that is easily understandable to the investment crowd, who are used to working with numbers rather than stories and other qualitative indicators.

It's worth noting that SROI is not a one-size-fits-all approach. The specific methodology used will depend on the context and nature of the initiative being evaluated. It's just one of many tools and approaches that organizations can use to evaluate their impact. Other methods, such as cost-benefit analysis, and social accounting, can also be useful in different contexts. The key is to select the approach that best fits the needs and goals of the organization and its stakeholders.

What is the input to those equations? How do we come up with those numbers?

Roberts Enterprise Development Fund (REDF) developed the first version of SROI to measure the impacts of their projects in 2000.

SROI Network, which is called Social Value International, refined the methodology in 2012 and proposed a guideline to identify some key steps and define fundamental principles. In its early days, SROI gained traction as a tool primarily used by social enterprises, nonprofits, and impact investors. This was a new structured methodology for quantifying and communicating the social value generated by these organizations. This tool offered a new perspective on measuring the success of social initiatives by focusing on understanding the long-term effects and benefits of the intervention. The early adopters of SROI recognized its potential to improve decision-making, demonstrate accountability, and drive resource allocation toward high-impact initiatives. The methodology faced challenges in terms of standardization and subjectivity of valuation, it paved the way for a broader conversation on the importance of social impact measurement and investment.

I'm a practical person, so let's go through an example of an SROI equation for a hypothetical social program aimed at, say, reducing youth unemployment.

SROI = (Total Value of Outcomes and Impacts / Total Investment) x 100

Hah; the first criticism of how we come up with the total value of an impact is echoing in my head. But let's keep an open mind.

Total Value of Outcomes and Impacts: This represents the monetized value of the program's outcomes and impacts. It includes both the short-term outcomes, such as increased employability skills and job placements, and the long-term impacts, such as increased lifetime earnings and reduced social welfare costs. This reminds me of my economics class. Maybe I could write a follow-up book on the price of a social impact?! These values are assigned through techniques such as estimating the economic value of skills gained or calculating the cost savings that resulted from reduced unemployment. So we're using estimates to determine the value of our social impact. I do wonder if this underestimates or overestimates it; maybe some people won't stay employed or have great skills that enable them to access higher-paid jobs in the future. In any case, this real-life example beautifully demonstrates the challenge of the SROI model.

Total Investment: This is the total number of resources invested in the program, which could include financial contributions, staff time, infrastructure costs, and any in-kind support. It encompasses all the resources necessary for the program's implementation and maintenance. This can be based on estimates informed by previous programs that are similar in scale, but these can also be actual costs if the SROI analysis is undertaken after the intervention.

SROI: This is calculated by dividing the total value created by the total investment, then multiplying the result by one hundred to express it as a percentage. The resulting figure represents the ratio of social value generated per unit of investment.

In practical terms, if the program's total value of outcomes and impacts is estimated to be 2,500,000 of any currency unit while the total investment is 500,000 of the same currency unit, then the SROI would be 500 percent. The way we would report it is to say that for every unit of currency invested in the program, a social value is created that's equivalent to five times the initial investment. The interpretation of the results involves understanding the magnitude and context of the calculated ratio. The magnitude typically refers to how effectively an investment generates social value. A ratio greater than one indicates that the program is generating more social value than the initial investment, suggesting a positive return. Here's another example: an SROI of three means that for every unit of currency invested, a social value worth three times the original investment is created. In my mind, it's hard to compute how we can measure certain impacts this way. The other aspect to consider when interpreting results is the context of the program and the objectives of the stakeholders involved. A high SROI may be seen as successful in generating social value, but it is important to assess whether it is due to our intervention or whether other factors play a role. Comparing the SROI of similar initiatives or programs can provide insights into the program's relative performance. One last example, and then I promise we don't do more math. An SROI ratio can be reported as 6:1, which means that every dollar allocated will generate or has generated social value worth six points.

Another great thing about SROI is the fact that it provides a common language for discussing social impacts. The SROI methodology enables organizations to communicate the value of their work in a way that is easily understood by stakeholders. We are no longer comparing apples and pears. While the SROI can support prioritization through the identification of activities with the highest social impact, it doesn't solve the issue completely. This can also mean that organizations target the lowest-hanging fruits (with high SROI) and other important initiatives don't get attention because of a low SROI. Innovation is an interesting aspect of SROI. We have seen what goes in the equation and how slight changes in a project design or determined outcomes can help us increase SROI.

Returning to our original example, let's say our goal isn't just to decrease youth unemployment but to keep them employed for a minimum of five years. This guarantees that the estimates for public administration savings on welfare are high for five years, so our SROI will be high too. Using this common language may also be helpful in advocating for policy change. Public administration can do their own assessment of programs and policies they implement and see where the impact is the highest. This may lead to a changed prioritization for better or worse. What I mean by this is certain initiatives might get the spotlight because of the high SROI but those might not be the immediate priorities of their communities. Hence the emphasis on stakeholder engagement and the incorporation of the community's perceived values of the desired outcomes.

SROI is not a replacement for financial metrics or other evaluation methods. Rather, it is a complementary tool that provides a more comprehensive understanding of the value created by an initiative.

Limitations

I wanted to deviate in terms of the structure of this chapter, but the deeper I got into the SROI methodology the more I felt the need to use this opportunity and discuss some of the obvious limitations. The literature and experts are open about these limitations. There is a refreshing level of honesty about what this tool can and cannot measure. Let's see what these are:

- *Subjectivity.* One of the main limitations of SROI is that it involves subjective judgments and assumptions on the value of social impact and outcomes. SROI requires a range of inputs and estimates, including estimates of social and environmental impact, financial costs and benefits, and discount rates. These inputs are often based on subjective judgments, which can vary widely depending on the individual or group making them. This subjective judgment, on the other hand, is a useful tool for identifying priority areas with lower SROI so those initiatives can get resources as well. The valuation methodology, while sound and grounded in empirical sciences, may lead to the over or underestimation of impact values.

- *Data availability.* Another limitation of SROI is the availability of data. Conducting an SROI analysis requires access to a wide range of data, including data on social and environmental impact. This data is not always available and can vary on a case-by-case basis. In our previous example, we saw how savings on welfare costs are integrated into the equation. In some countries, there are more standardized amounts, but in other places, factors such as marital status, number of children, and capital city vs. countryside can result in significant differences in the amounts paid to job seekers. Data that is available may be incomplete, inconsistent, or outdated, which can make it difficult to conduct an accurate SROI analysis. Data collection was not part of the SROI scope, as it is usually conducted using desktop research and not based on primary data collection.

- *Time frame.* SROI requires a long-term perspective, which can be a limitation for organizations with short-term objectives or that operate in rapidly changing environments. Conducting an SROI analysis over a long time frame requires significant resources and may be difficult to sustain. This long-term view might also further distort our calculations because it's hard to estimate how prices and values will change over a longer period of time.

- *Stakeholder perspectives.* SROI requires an understanding of stakeholder perspectives, which can be challenging to achieve. Stakeholders may have different views on the outcomes that are important to measure, which can lead to differing interpretations of the results. Who's to say which member of the community is right or wrong about what's important? How many people need to agree on the priorities so the organization can tailor its program? Managing the collection of opinions from locals is challenging and requires careful planning to ensure that all members of the target group have a chance to express their views. In my experience working with communities, there are always opinion leaders and people who are more open to talking, while others remain silent even during consultation events. We work with different tools to ensure everyone has the chance to share their views through various channels, including the option to share them anonymously.

- *Cultural context.* SROI is based on Western economic principles, which may not align with the cultural context of the communities being impacted by the initiative. For example, concepts such as cost-benefit analysis and discounting future outcomes may not resonate with cultures that prioritize noneconomic values. This is a very important point to emphasize, especially now that diversity initiatives have accelerated the understanding of cultural differences worldwide. What works in one part of the world might not work in another part.

- *Overemphasis on quantitative data.* SROI can place a heavy emphasis on quantitative data, which may overlook important qualitative data and perspectives. Qualitative data can be important for understanding the nuances of social and environmental impact but may be more difficult to quantify and compare. This short paragraph could easily be the summary of this book. We're trying to use quantitative data and return-on-investment approaches to measure something subjective and hard to quantify.

- *Difficult to communicate results.* SROI results can be complex and difficult to communicate to stakeholders. The methodology involves a range of inputs and assumptions, which can make it challenging to present concisely in a way that's understandable for nonexperts. Even I struggled with grasping the interpretation of the results initially. I kept asking what it actually meant. Did it mean that for every dollar spent, someone's mental health got three times better? Of course not, but when we try to quantify abstract concepts, we end up with thoughts like this.

- *Limited scope.* SROI measures the impact of a specific initiative or program but may not capture the broader systemic changes that are necessary to achieve sustainable social and environmental outcomes. For example, an SROI analysis of a community development program may not capture the underlying structural issues that contribute to poverty and inequality.

Nothing is without its limitations, but this doesn't mean that SROI has no value or no place in our social impact product market. It's a calculation methodology that has been with us for the last twenty-three years and evolved over time, just as we grew more aware of new ways to use and improve it.

How does it relate to other methodologies for impact measurement?

While SROI has its own unique approach and methodology, it is closely related to other impact measurement frameworks and methods. Note how SROI is not a product for impact creation but a methodology to demonstrate and measure the created impact. Let's explore the relationship between SROI and other impact measurement approaches, including cost-benefit analysis, Triple Bottom Line, and the United Nations Sustainable Development Goals.

Cost-benefit analysis (CBA) is a widely used methodology for evaluating the economic impact of a particular initiative or program. Like SROI, CBA seeks to measure the social and economic value created by a particular intervention. However, unlike SROI, CBA focuses primarily on economic outcomes and seeks to monetize all impacts and outcomes. This means that CBA may overlook important social and environmental impacts that cannot be easily monetized and may place too much emphasis on short-term economic gains. I experimented with CBA for social impact assessment purposes, but they proved unfruitful due to the limitations of valuation methodology and available data to monetize impacts. It is a useful tool, however, for other purposes.

The Triple Bottom Line (TBL) is a sustainability framework that considers three interconnected dimensions: social, environmental, and economic. It goes beyond the traditional focus on the financial performance of organizations and emphasizes the importance of considering their broader impacts and responsibilities. The TBL framework suggests that organizations should strive for positive outcomes in all three dimensions simultaneously. Like SROI, TBL seeks to measure the impact of an intervention across multiple dimensions. However, unlike SROI, TBL does not seek to monetize all impacts and outcomes. Instead, TBL recognizes that social and environmental impacts are often difficult to quantify and places a greater emphasis on qualitative data and stakeholder perspectives. An example of a social output within the TBL framework could be a company implementing a community outreach program that provides job training and employment opportunities to disadvantaged individuals. By focusing on the social impact, the company aims to improve the well-being and livelihood of marginalized communities. This initiative would generate positive outcomes such as increased employability, reduced poverty rates, and enhanced social inclusion. The social output in this case aligns with the TBL principle of addressing social concerns and creating social value alongside economic and environmental considerations. I must admit that the TBL approach is a lot more familiar to me than the other monetization-based approaches.

The United Nations Sustainable Development Goals (SDGs) provide a framework for measuring and achieving sustainable development outcomes. Like SROI, the SDGs seek to measure social, environmental, and economic value. However, the SDGs are a more comprehensive and holistic framework and seek to address the underlying systemic issues that contribute to social and environmental challenges. I wrote about this in more detail further in this chapter.

In terms of the social impact products, we have seen SROI used as a methodology for impact demonstration in impact investing, social enterprises, and philanthropy. We could argue what the best way to measure and demonstrate the impacts is, but SROI is in a unique position to be more understandable to people with a finance background. The issue remains that social impacts are challenging to quantify in a meaningful way because the underlying qualitative aspects provide a depth of understanding. Creating a job means different things for the different social impact products. In an SIA context, it means mitigating adverse impacts while exploring the quality of the created job. In the context of ESG, impact investing, SIBs, SOCs, and social enterprise, creating a job is a statistic that demonstrates a positive social impact. Now that we understand the different approaches and viewpoints between macro- and micro-level impacts and qualitative and quantitative reporting styles, we have a better chance of using the tools appropriately.

Asking what the social impact is did not seem relevant, as SROI is merely a tool to measure and demonstrate an impact, not something that creates one. Nevertheless, social impact is the key component that needs to be added to the equation to calculate the SROI. Converting social impact into monetary value requires a lot of estimates and creativity. SROI emphasizes the engagement of stakeholders so they can provide their views on what the most important aspect of the planned program is. SROI could be calculated during project design and used as guidance to estimate social returns, but I have mainly seen calculations done after the implementation of programs to demonstrate their impacts to investors, shareholders, and stakeholders.

SROI can also be used in more abstract ways, such as by measuring the outcomes that would have happened without the program. This is called the "counterfactual." For example, if a nonprofit organization provides job training to unemployed individuals, the social impact would be measured by the number of individuals who obtain employment because of the program, the increase in their income, the welfare savings, savings of individuals, and the improvement in their quality of life. The social impact would then be compared to the cost of the program to determine the SROI. While I understand both aspects of such a calculation, I still struggle with the use of these numbers to demonstrate the social impact. But that's just my opinion.

My master's is in social research methods, and I specialized in quantitative research because I already had really strong basics in mathematics, statistics, calculus, probability theory, and research methodology from my bachelor's in Hungary. I did my master's part-time, as I was already working for EBRD on the implementation of social safeguards. I saw a lot of value in using numbers and statistics as a persuasive tool to demonstrate impacts. My view on this has not changed. What has changed is that I am a lot more open to adding the qualitative element to impact reporting. I gained a lot of insight into the real-life implications of our projects through fieldwork, meeting people affected by projects, and understanding their points of view and the significant impacts they will encounter due to the interventions. I guess this is what philanthropic organizations do when they create those commercials focusing on one person's story. I totally get it now: every person helped counts, even if the overall impact of the project is not significant statistically speaking.

The other thing I realized over the years is that using numbers and statistics doesn't allow for explaining the additional layers of the impact we create. With numbers, something is either statistically significant or not, there is either cause and effect or not. Real life, however, is a bit different. Even if an initiative fails to achieve the desired outcome, it may nevertheless provide tools, access, and the hope that people can get further through other means. We talked about this effect of compounding in the philanthropy chapter. Maybe even if we only help someone get a six-month internship rather than long-term employment, they would qualify for jobs outside our program. I have seen people take their livelihood compensation, invest it in education, and start a whole new career in a whole new sector. You can argue that the livelihood restoration program was not successful because they did not replicate their previous life in a different location, but you could also argue that it was successful because they are better off than before the project. People have an incredible instinct to survive and thrive even under extremely challenging conditions. Sometimes all it takes is a little help. How we quantify that potential is a real challenge, here, and that's why I'm careful to only use numbers and statistics for social impact demonstrations.

Examples of SROI Done Right

There are many examples of organizations that have successfully used SROI to measure and demonstrate the social, environmental, and economic value created by their programs. Here are a few examples:

- Acumen is a global nonprofit organization that invests in social enterprises to tackle poverty and create sustainable solutions. Acumen utilizes SROI as a key tool to assess the social impact of its investments. By applying SROI analysis, Acumen measures the value created by the improved access to essential services, enhanced livelihoods, and reduced poverty levels, enabling them to make informed investment decisions and demonstrate accountability. This is an interesting organization because its founder, Jacqueline Novogratz, started Rwanda's first microfinance institution, Duterimbere in 1986. She started Acumen in 2001 when impact investing was young and relatively unexplored. She inspired me so much that I went onto the Better World Books website (a social enterprise, if you remember) and bought her book! Practice what you preach, I guess.

- REDF is a US-based nonprofit organization that provides funding and support to social enterprises that employ people who face barriers to employment. REDF used SROI to measure the impact of its programs and found that for every dollar invested, there was a social return of $2.23, including increased income and reduced reliance on social services. We mentioned them before as they were the ones who started using SROI in 2000.

- The Halifax Food Policy Alliance published a full study in August 2016 on the SROI of their activities. This company is a collaboration between several other organizations, including the Our Food Project of the Ecology Action Centre, NEF Consulting, and the Halifax Food Policy Alliance (HFPA). The HFPA aims to build access to a "healthy, just, and sustainable food system in the Halifax region." They use public awareness campaigns, targeted programs, and advocacy for policy change to achieve this. In 2016, the SROI for their operation was USD 5.53: USD 1. This means that for every dollar invested in the HFPA, USD 5.53 is gained in benefits for the target beneficiary group.

- Food for Life is a UK charity that undertook its assessment of its social impact using the SROI tool. FFL is led by the Soil Association, and it seeks to promote the culture of good food through practical programs and the advocacy of public policy change. The study details that the period for evaluation was set at twenty-four months, and there was a strong emphasis on consultation with a wide variety of affected and interested stakeholders. The overall SROI ratio for the programs in the study is GBP 4.41 of social value created for every GBP 1 of investment. Its outcome is very similar to the other food programs in the previous example.

- Shaping Impact Group is a group of driven and dedicated investment managers who strive for more: "more sustainability, more solidarity, more justice." This group uses the SROI methodology to demonstrate the positive social impact of the start-ups and social enterprises that they support through their investments. The initiatives cover private equity, venture capital, impact investing, and philanthropy. Inzet, Shaping Impact Group's Dutch healthcare impact fund, focuses on healthcare innovations in the Netherlands. The aim here is illness prevention or making a real difference in the lives of people living with long-term illness or disability. In order to qualify for investment, the target groups of your company have to match at least two of the participating funds and foundations with a concrete and measurably high impact to enhance the quality of life of people who need chronic care. Some of the participating companies are engaged in making clinical trials accessible for all stakeholders and accelerating drug studies, developing software for mental health therapies to make treatments more efficient and accessible, and finding AI-driven solutions to manage capacity and scheduling issues in the long-term care sector.

SI2 Fund is Shaping Impact's European impact fund with a strong focus on social businesses that address current social challenges. I was curious to find out what projects are being funded and how they report on the social impact, as this was the only fund that had an annual sustainability report available at the time of writing this book. Their portfolio included socially responsible debt collection, an agency that helps employers stimulate the vitality of their employees, activities for people with dementia, and digital and financial inclusion of poor and vulnerable people—to name a few. I can certainly see that these businesses tackle important issues in society. SI2 Fund had two annual reports so far, the first one covering their activities in 2019 and the second one focusing on 2020–2021. The latter report cites five indicators to understand the impact: who (stakeholders experiencing effects and how they were underserved before), what (positive and negative effects and outcomes of the business), how much (the number of stakeholders affected), contribution (outcomes of the business activities), and the risk (the likelihood that the impact is different from expected). Based on their report, the SROI for the business that connected people looking for nonmedical home assistance with a trusted neighbor was 3.1, which means that every EUR 1 input creates a EUR 3.1 social return.

The Equator Principles

The Equator Principles (EP) are a set of environmental and social guidelines that financial institutions adopt to assess and manage the potential environmental and social risks associated with project financing. The principles are primarily applied to large infrastructure projects, such as power plants, mines, pipelines, and other significant developments. The EP were first introduced in 2003 and have been updated over time to reflect the evolving international standards and best practices. They were designed to ensure that the projects financed by the signatory financial institutions were developed in a socially responsible and environmentally sustainable manner. By adhering to these principles, financial institutions aim to promote sustainable development and mitigate potential negative impacts on communities and the environment.

Key features and use of the EP include:

- *Applicability.* The EP apply to projects with a total capital cost above a certain threshold, typically set at $10 million, although this threshold may vary among financial institutions. The principles are implemented by banks, financial institutions, and project sponsors.

- *Assessment process.* Financial institutions that adopt the EP are required to conduct an environmental and social risk assessment of proposed projects before providing financing. This assessment involves evaluating potential environmental and social impacts, stakeholder engagement, and compliance with applicable laws, regulations, and international standards.

- *Social and environmental standards.* The EP incorporate internationally recognized standards such as the International Finance Corporation (IFC) Performance Standards and the World Bank Group Environmental, Health, and Safety Guidelines. These provide guidance on various topics, including biodiversity conservation, climate change, labor and working conditions, Indigenous peoples' rights, and community health and safety.

- *Due diligence and risk management.* Financial institutions must apply appropriate due diligence and risk management processes to identify, assess, and mitigate environmental and social risks associated with projects. This includes engaging with project sponsors and stakeholders to address potential impacts, develop mitigation measures, and monitor project implementation.

- *Transparency and reporting.* EP signatories are required to publicly disclose their adoption of the principles and provide annual reports on their implementation. This promotes transparency and accountability and facilitates the sharing of best practices within the financial industry.

- *Stakeholder engagement.* The EP emphasize the importance of engaging with affected stakeholders, including local communities, Indigenous peoples, and other potentially impacted groups. This helps ensure that the concerns, perspectives, and rights of these groups are considered during project development and implementation.

- *Compliance and independent review.* Financial institutions are expected to monitor and enforce compliance with the EP throughout the project's life cycle. Additionally, independent external reviews may be conducted to verify compliance with the principles and provide assurance to stakeholders.

The EP were updated in 2019, then the new EP IV were adopted. The EP IV introduced several key changes and enhancements to strengthen the framework for environmental and social risk management in project finance. The most significant changes for this iteration include the following key aspects:

- *Applicability.* EP IV expanded the scope of the principles beyond project finance to include some project-related corporate loans and bridge loans, increasing the coverage of environmental and social risk assessment. The scope was also extended to some project-related refinancing and acquisition financing if certain criteria were met. The new preamble to the EP IV contains a note of acknowledgment from EP Financial Institutions—that is, the banks that are signatories to the EP—with respect to the management of social, human rights, and environmental impacts for all their operations, even those that are outside the EP scope at the moment.

- *Designated vs. nondesignated countries.* The EP were mainly used in nondesignated countries, which were deemed to have a weaker legal system, to manage environmental and social risks effectively. The new update requires signatories to assess whether these principles could improve project performance in designated countries as well, especially for projects with high-risk categorization (Category A and B) where EP compliance due diligence is a requirement.

- *Human rights.* The new version introduced a specific requirement to assess and manage human rights impacts in line with internally recognized standards, such as the UN Guiding Principles on Business and Human Rights.

- *Stakeholder engagement.* The main update is the full adoption of the IFC Performance Standard 7, which requires free, prior, and informed consent (FPIC) regarding the impacts on indigenous people. I've had the chance to apply IFC PS 7 to some of my projects and go through the steps of this enhanced stakeholder engagement process. It really is a significant achievement for the EP to adopt this standard.

- *Climate change.* The consideration of climate change impacts in project financing has been a hot topic for many years, now, with several initiatives requiring thorough measurement and reporting on the climate adaptation and mitigation aspects of their projects. In this instance, a climate risk assessment—including greenhouse gas emission calculations and alignment with relevant climate-related standards and targets—is added as a requirement for the updated EP. Moreover, for high-risk projects (Category A and B), the client is required to provide annual reports on GHG emission levels. This is all based on the recommendations of the Task Force on Climate-related Financial Disclosures.

The EP are applied globally by commercial banks and other financial institutions that fund large infrastructure projects. In a previous role, I was implementing the EP for several of my African projects. It is no secret that I have been working with IFC for the past couple of years, so I am familiar with their standards for environmental and social risk management. To me, the most significant impact of the EP (and IFC PS) is the protection of community health and safety and the stringent requirements on compensation for involuntary resettlement—covering physical and economic displacement, land acquisition, impacts on access to natural resources, or other impacts on livelihoods. These are very rarely covered in national legislation to the extent that is required by the EP or IFC.

ISO 26000

ISO 26000 is a set of guidelines developed by the International Organization for Standardization (ISO) to help organizations operate in a socially responsible and sustainable manner. The standard was first published in 2010 and provides guidance on a range of social responsibility issues, including human rights, labor practices, environmental sustainability, fair operating practices, consumer issues, and community involvement.

ISO 26000 is a voluntary standard, which means that companies and organizations are not required to sign up for it. However, many businesses choose to adopt it as a framework to improve their social and environmental performance and demonstrate their commitment to sustainable practices. ISO requires an independent audit to verify the implementation of the standards before awarding the standard to a company. These are undertaken by ISO-certified auditors. The certification of the company is valid for a few years, after which another independent audit is needed. This ensures that it is not a tick-box exercise and that companies continue to implement the elements of the standard.

The guidance provided by ISO 26000 is intended for all types of organizations, regardless of their size, sector, or geographic location. It encourages organizations to engage with stakeholders, identify and address their social impacts, and contribute to sustainable development. ISO 26000 promotes a holistic approach to social responsibility, recognizing that organizations should consider not only the social dimensions of their activities but also the environmental and economic aspects.

The standard provides guidance on seven core principles of social responsibility:

1. *Accountability.* Organizations should hold themselves accountable for the impacts of their decisions and activities on society, the environment, and their stakeholders.

2. *Transparency.* This involves the open and honest disclosure of information regarding an organization's social, environmental, and economic performance.

3. *Ethical behavior.* This requires organizations to uphold the fundamental values of integrity, fairness, and respect for human rights.

4. *Respect for stakeholder interests.* Organizations should consider and address the interests and expectations of their stakeholders, including employees, customers, communities, and other affected parties.

5. *Respect for the rule of law.* Organizations should respect and

comply with the applicable laws, regulations, and international norms.

6. *Respect for international norms of behavior.* Organizations should respect and promote human rights, labor standards, environmental protection, and anticorruption measures.

ISO 26000 provides practical guidance on implementing these principles, including how to identify and engage with stakeholders, how to assess social and environmental risks, and how to establish policies and procedures to ensure compliance with social responsibility standards.

Implementing ISO 26000 can have several benefits for organizations. It can enhance their reputation, credibility, and brand value by demonstrating a commitment to responsible business practices. It can help with the management of risks and improve relationships with stakeholders through enhanced engagement. ISO 26000 can also support organizations in identifying opportunities for innovation and creating positive social and environmental impacts. It is a valuable guide for any company that is looking to embed social responsibility into its core operations and contribute to sustainable development.

In addition, ISO 26000 also emphasizes the importance of continuous improvement, meaning that businesses should strive to enhance their social and environmental performance over time. This involves setting measurable goals and regularly monitoring progress toward those goals. The standard encourages collaboration and partnerships with stakeholders, including local communities, NGOs, and government agencies. By working with these groups, businesses can better understand the social and environmental issues that affect their operations and develop more effective solutions to address these issues.

ISO 26000 is applicable to businesses of all sizes and sectors and can be particularly valuable for small and medium-sized enterprises (SMEs) that may not have the resources to develop their own social responsibility policies and practices. ISO 26000 is also closely aligned with other internationally recognized standards, such as the UN Global Compact and the SDGs. ISO 26000 recognizes that social responsibility is a complex and evolving concept and encourages businesses to proactively address emerging social and environmental issues.

Microfinance and Microcredit

Microfinance, also known as microcredit, is a financial service that provides small loans to individuals who lack access to traditional banking services. The concept of microfinance was pioneered by Muhammad Yunus, a Bangladeshi economist who founded the Grameen Bank. The Grameen Bank adopted a unique lending approach, extending small loans to impoverished individuals, especially women—typically without collateral. The loans were primarily intended for income-generating activities, such as small businesses or farming ventures. This approach, often referred to as group lending or crowdfunding, emphasized collective responsibility and social capital within communities. These beneficiaries were not eligible for commercial bank loans due to the lack of collateral, so providing them with access to credit and financial services enabled their entrepreneurial aspirations to potentially lift them out of the cycle of poverty. We talked about this in the social enterprise section. Since then, microfinance has become a popular tool for promoting economic development and poverty reduction in developing countries. I added this in a separate category because it was initially a *good* yet risky business to add more people to the financial market and provide them with products they could not access otherwise. The real success story of social impact and empowerment came later on.

Microfinance was typically provided by nonprofit organizations or social enterprises, rather than traditional banks. Nowadays there are special types of financial institutions that specialize in microfinance for small enterprises and individuals alike. The loans are usually small, ranging from just a few hundred dollars to a few thousand dollars, and are intended to be used for income-generating activities such as starting a small business, purchasing livestock or farming supplies, or investing in education or training. Though some criticize microfinance as a potential path trap in poverty, its availability makes it an invaluable benefit in today's uncertain world. With families needing access to money when their earnings are inconsistent, microfinance can provide much-needed support in times when families may not make as much income.

Though microfinance has been on the market and improving for a while now, some aspects are still criticized. One key aspect is the overindebtedness. Critics argue that the high interest rates associated with microfinance can lead borrowers into a cycle of debt, especially when coupled with inadequate financial literacy and limited income-generating opportunities. In some cases, borrowers may take out additional loans to repay existing ones, creating a burden that can be difficult to escape. This cycle of debt can have negative consequences on the financial well-being and livelihood of borrowers.

Microfinance institutions typically charge much higher interest rates than banks offer, due to the fact that they borrow from banks and then lend it to their customers. The high interest rates can also be explained by the high risk of the transaction due to the limited collateral available.

Many question the ethical implications of providing financing to the poor, given the high interest rates.

Another important aspect relates to the impact on vulnerable groups, particularly women. While microfinance is often promoted as a tool for women's empowerment, there are concerns that the focus on women borrowers may reinforce gender inequalities and burden women with additional responsibilities. Critics argue that without addressing broader social and systemic barriers, microfinance alone may not result in meaningful empowerment or transformative change for women. Furthermore, the emphasis on repayment rates and financial sustainability in microfinance institutions may divert attention from addressing the root causes of poverty and inequality.

The list of limitations goes on, citing inflated claims about poverty reduction. Some argue that while microfinance may provide short-term relief or enable individuals to meet immediate needs, it may not address the underlying structural factors that contribute to poverty. Without access to complementary resources, such as education (especially financial education), healthcare, or market opportunities, microfinance alone may not lead to sustainable poverty alleviation. Indeed, in my work with microfinance institutions, this was the key thing to discuss. What other services could be provided to people to educate them on aspects of business planning, structures, marketing, and financial literacy? Very few can make it out of the micro-enterprise category if there's no support with the business-planning aspects to help the companies grow. Especially in the social development context, there's room for a more holistic approach that combines access to finance with comprehensive development strategies and support systems to address the multifaceted dimensions of poverty.

Now that we've got the negatives out of the way, we can move on to the benefits. It's worth noting that criticism has spurred ongoing discussions and efforts to improve microfinance programs and make them more effective and sustainable. Several social impact products have been deployed to support microfinance institutions in these efforts. Organizations and practitioners continue to explore innovative approaches and complementary interventions to ensure that microfinance can genuinely contribute to poverty reduction and inclusive development. The potential of microfinance has been widely recognized, and there's a relative consensus on its key benefits:

- *Financial inclusion.* Microfinance plays a crucial role in promoting financial inclusion by providing access to formal financial services to those who are traditionally excluded from the mainstream banking system. These institutions typically charge much higher interest rates than banks offer, due to the fact that they borrow from banks and then lend it to their customers.

- *Poverty alleviation.* Microfinance is often seen as a tool for poverty reduction, despite the counterarguments we just discussed. By providing small loans to low-income individuals, microfinance enables them to invest in income-generating activities, start or expand microenterprises, and generate sustainable livelihoods. This access to capital empowers people to lift themselves and their families out of poverty, reducing the reliance on informal moneylenders and improving their long-term economic prospects.

- *Women's empowerment.* Both mentioned as a criticism and an opportunity, microfinance has demonstrated a significant impact on women's empowerment. Women are often the primary recipients of microfinance, as it enables them to start businesses, increase their incomes, and gain greater control over their financial resources. By participating in economic activities, women experience enhanced decision-making power, improved self-esteem, and increased social status within their families and communities. Microfinance programs often incorporate financial education and skill-building components, further contributing to women's empowerment and economic independence.

- *Entrepreneurship and job creation.* Microfinance fuels entrepreneurship and stimulates economic growth at the grassroots level. By providing capital to aspiring entrepreneurs, it enables the establishment and growth of small businesses, leading to job creation within local communities. Borrowers not only become self-employed but often employ others, generating income opportunities and fostering economic development in their surroundings.

- *Social and community development.* Microfinance has the potential to drive social and community development by fostering social capital and supporting local initiatives. As these programs prioritize close relationships with borrowers, they often involve community-based lending models and group-lending approaches. These mechanisms encourage peer support, cooperation, and collective responsibility, promoting social cohesion, trust, and community development.

I'd like to share some personal experiences and viewpoints on microfinance. These are all based on projects I worked on. My aim is not to diminish the achievements of microfinance or to shame organizations for operating in some grey areas. It is merely to contribute to the discussion and potential development of this sector so it can further address the criticisms. I want to start by stating that microfinance institutions are generally for-profit enterprises that risk lending to people who have low credit scores, nonexistent or limited credit history, and little collateral. Yes, this is typically lower-income groups in society who, as we stated earlier, are not eligible to obtain other commercial bank financing for their operations. These organizations exist to make a profit and support people on their entrepreneurial journey or through other financial challenges. Microfinance institutions are often compared to loan sharks, but I wouldn't go there. Microfinance is a game-changer in some places, supporting the communities and businesses so they may thrive. What we don't often talk about is how microfinance helps repeat customers build their credit history and eventually qualify for commercial bank loans, thus helping them evolve out of the "micro" credit world into bigger loans that can make more meaningful impacts on their businesses.

I've noticed that most microfinance institutions have a limited ability to measure, define, and demonstrate their social impact. It's unclear whether we should expect them to operate on a social enterprise model or whether they already are social enterprises based solely on the products and services they provide. In my work with them, I had to design easy questionnaires for environmental and social risk assessment, focusing on the operations of the business or the new project funded by the microloan. The people attached it to their credit risk questionnaire and filled it out for each applicant. Note that these people had no education, training, or experience in environmental and social risk management. They operated on the assumption that if the business had the relevant permits, it was operating in a way that would protect the environment. Any questions regarding labor and working conditions were met with disbelief and the answer that they operated in line with the law, so there were no issues. I know from experience that even larger businesses often struggle with workforce and contractor management.

The other issue is the potential to finance informal businesses. In several countries, there are significant barriers to registering a business, and it's not even standard practice—especially for smaller, family-run enterprises. Financing these informal businesses can be seen as positive because they are often operated by marginalized individuals or people for whom obtaining other financial support is a challenge. Microfinance fills this gap by including these individuals and businesses and putting them on track to grow and potentially register their businesses formally. Microfinance is traditionally a fast way to obtain money, often with same-day approval. This flexibility helps entrepreneurs seize time-sensitive opportunities and address urgent business needs. On the other hand, financing informal businesses contributes to the maintenance of the grey economy and the impacts on taxes being paid. Without proper screening and business registration, there's a risk that a business is carrying out activities without a permit or compliance with the legislation. This can lead to fraudulent activities or misuse of funds, which can undermine the credibility and effectiveness of microfinance programs.

The issue with informal businesses is especially pressing when a development finance institution (DFI) provides loans to microfinance institutions for lending purposes. This is where I'm coming from. The IFI or DFI comes with a set of environmental and social requirements that should be applicable to the operations of the microfinance institution. This includes standards for labor, amongst other things. In theory—and often in practice—an IFI or DFI could finance an informal business with informal employees, working without a contract through a microfinance institution that doesn't enforce the IFI standards.

Another issue that's discussed behind closed doors is whether the low interest rate from the IFI or DFI should translate into lower rates for the beneficiaries of the microfinance institution. Since the money is going into a large pot and we can't really tell who should benefit from it and it's really hard to follow what loans are funded by the IFI. Is it a reasonable expectation for some end beneficiaries to get more advantageous rates while others pay the full price? How would we determine who's eligible and who isn't? I honestly have no good answer to that, but I see the potential for trouble there.

In my view, the added value of the IFI or DFI would be to facilitate the provision of training and to educate entrepreneurs on growing their businesses—or at least making it more streamlined, profitable, and sustainable. Not everyone wants to grow their businesses; I've met some entrepreneurs who only wanted to continue business as usual.

This one was a tailor in a Balkan country. This one-woman show specialized in evening gowns, wedding gowns, and special occasion dresses. She'd used many microloans to purchase equipment, stock up on supplies, and cover the cost of marketing. The business was dependent on her and her ideas. Sometimes she worked based on photos that clients provided, but she also had her own designs. Each dress was special and beautiful. The business was not yet scalable as it depended solely on her ability to work. She could work eight to ten hours a day, yet she knew that if it was high season, there was no way for her to complete more than a few orders. This was not due to the lack of equipment or technology. This was because she was the business, and she only had so many hours in a day. Some machines did help her work faster, especially those that did the stitching or embroidering more efficiently. Yet the issue remained that she was the only one working. Would training in entrepreneurship or financial literacy help her? What were her goals with the business? Did she want to just design her own line and not work in the made-to-measure business? Would she be open to discussing business models that outsourced certain tasks so she could deliver more products? These are all ideas from people educated in Western Europe and always looking for a business to scale. She said she was currently happy with her life. She liked to have the flexibility to take care of her daughter; she liked to serve customers personally and be there for the special moments in their lives. She found it creatively stimulating to recreate dresses based on magazine photos and photos online. She was happy with where she was at the moment. Microfinance gave her the opportunity to grow the business to a certain extent, and she would figure out the next steps when she got there.

Microfinance has the potential to be a scalable and sustainable solution to poverty reduction and economic development. While microfinance organizations may start out small, with a limited number of borrowers and limited funding, they have the potential to grow and expand their impact over time. This can be achieved through partnerships with local governments, other NGOs, or private sector businesses, as well as by developing new financial products and services that meet the needs of underserved communities. We have seen some incredible examples of this.

Next up, I'm bringing you Rwanda's first microfinance institution, Duterimbere. Jacqueline Novogratz, the founder and CEO of Acument as we saw in the previous chapter, initiated the creation of two microfinance institutions in Rwanda: Duterimbere and Urwego Bank. These institutions aimed to provide accessible and affordable financial services to the country's low-income population.

Duterimbere, meaning "let us develop ourselves" in Kinyarwanda, was established in collaboration with local partners. It started as a savings and credit cooperative (SACCO) and gradually expanded its offerings to include loans, savings accounts, and other financial products. Duterimbere focused on serving rural and peri-urban communities, supporting agriculture, and promoting entrepreneurship among women. Through its customer-centric approach and commitment to social impact, Duterimbere became a pioneer in microfinance in Rwanda, setting the stage for further developments in the sector.

Urwego Bank, also founded by Novogratz and Acumen, aimed to provide financial services specifically tailored to the needs of the poor. Urwego Bank adopted innovative practices to reach remote and underserved areas, leveraging technology and mobile banking solutions to facilitate financial transactions. The institution focused on promoting financial inclusion, supporting small businesses, and empowering women. By combining financial services with capacity-building programs and training, Urwego Bank aimed to holistically support its clients in their entrepreneurial endeavors, contributing to economic growth and poverty reduction in Rwanda.

The establishment of Duterimbere and Urwego Bank marked significant milestones in the development of microfinance in Rwanda. These pioneering institutions, driven by Jacqueline Novogratz's vision and impact-driven approach, laid the foundation for a more inclusive financial sector. Their success paved the way for the growth of microfinance and the emergence of subsequent microfinance institutions, expanding access to finance and creating opportunities for entrepreneurship and economic empowerment among Rwanda's underserved populations.

Global Reporting Initiative

The Global Reporting Initiative (GRI) is a nonprofit organization that developed a widely used framework for sustainability reporting in 1997. This framework is designed to help companies and organizations of all sizes and sectors report on their economic, social, and environmental performance in a standardized and transparent way. The GRI framework provides guidelines for reporting on a range of sustainability issues, including governance, human rights, labor practices, environmental performance, and community engagement. The guidelines are structured around a set of principles, which include stakeholder inclusiveness, sustainability context, materiality, completeness, and accuracy. Sounds like ESG? Well yes and no. While they share some similarities, they differ in their focus and scope. ESG is a broader framework that considers a company's environmental, social, and governance performance, considering a wide range of factors that may impact its sustainability. ESG assessments typically evaluate how a company manages risks and opportunities related to environmental impact, social practices, and governance structures. On the other hand, GRI is a specific reporting framework that provides guidelines for disclosing sustainability information. It focuses primarily on reporting, outlining a structured framework and indicators to ensure consistent and comprehensive sustainability reporting across organizations. GRI helps companies identify, measure, and report on their environmental, social, and economic impacts, enabling stakeholders to understand their sustainability performance in a standardized manner.

One of the key features of the GRI framework is its emphasis on stakeholder engagement. The guidelines encourage companies to connect with their stakeholders, including employees, customers, suppliers, investors, and communities, in order to identify and prioritize the sustainability issues that are most relevant to their business. This way, companies can better understand the expectations and concerns of their stakeholders and use this information to inform their sustainability reporting.

Another important aspect of the GRI framework is its focus on materiality. Furthermore, it adopted the concept of double materiality after the European Commission first described it within a proposed directive context in 2019. Double materiality essentially means that materiality is defined both from the perspective of the organization's impact on people, as well as the financial materiality influencing the value of the business. In my world, we mainly focus on the previous aspect (the company's operational impact on people), however, adding the calculation of the company's value increase by operating in a sustainable matter seems like a good way to persuade businesses to integrate such considerations.

The GRI framework has become widely adopted by companies and organizations around the world. With it, companies can demonstrate their commitment to sustainability and transparency, as well as their ability to manage and mitigate the social and environmental risks associated with their business. The framework can also help companies identify areas in which they can improve their sustainability performance, as well as opportunities to create value through sustainability initiatives.

One of the benefits of the GRI framework is that it allows for comparability and benchmarking. By using a standardized framework, companies can compare their sustainability performance to that of their peers and industry standards. This can help drive innovation and improvement in sustainability practices across industries and sectors. The GRI framework is also flexible as it is designed to be adaptable to the unique circumstances and needs of different organizations, allowing companies to report on the sustainability issues that are most relevant to their business and stakeholders. The GRI also provides sector-specific guidance to help companies in different industries report on the issues that are most material to their business. Another benefit of the GRI framework is its alignment with other sustainability standards and frameworks. The GRI guidelines are associated with other widely used sustainability standards, such as the UN SDGs, the Paris Agreement on climate change, and the ISO 14001 environmental management standard. This alignment can help companies demonstrate their commitment to sustainability and integrate their sustainability reporting into their overall business strategy.

However, there are also criticisms of the GRI framework. Some argue that the guidelines are too vague, making it difficult for companies to know which issues to prioritize and report on. Others argue that the framework does not go far enough in addressing systemic issues such as climate change and inequality. I have very limited personal experience with reviewing GRI reports for my social due diligence and impact assessment purposes.

In terms of reporting, the GRI framework provides guidance on how to meaningfully present sustainability issues that are often difficult to quantify, such as human rights and community engagement. They encourage companies to use qualitative information, such as case studies and narratives, to report on these issues, in addition to quantitative data.

The Global Impact Investing Network

The Global Impact Investing Network (GIIN) is a nonprofit organization that's dedicated to increasing the scale and effectiveness of impact investing around the world. The GIIN was founded in 2009 by a group of impact investors and has since grown into a global network of over 360 members, including investors, asset managers, and service providers. The network is dedicated to promoting collaboration and knowledge-sharing among impact investors, as well as advocating for policies and practices that support the growth of the industry.

One of the key activities of the GIIN is its work to develop and promote industry standards and best practices for this purpose. The organization has developed a set of principles for impact investing, outlining the key characteristics of impact investments, including intentionality, transparency, and the measurement of social and environmental performance. Remember, we briefly mentioned this in the impact investing chapter. The GIIN also operates a range of programs and initiatives to support the growth and effectiveness of the industry around the world. These programs include training and capacity-building for investors, the development of market infrastructure and tools, and advocacy for policies and regulations that support the growth of the impact investing industry.

The GIIN also plays an important role in promoting transparency and accountability in the impact investing industry. The organization has developed a set of metrics and standards for measuring and reporting on the social and environmental impact of impact investments. The GIIN is working to develop new approaches to impact investing to maximize impact. The other important role of the network is the capacity building of impact investors and asset managers around the world. By providing training and guidance notes, the organization can help investors develop the skills and knowledge needed to make informed decisions.

Moreover, the GIIN has helped increase the visibility and legitimacy of impact investing as a viable approach to addressing social and environmental challenges. The organization has developed partnerships with leading global institutions, such as the World Bank and the United Nations, and has helped drive the development of impact investing policies and practices on the national and international levels.

The main scope and focus of the GIIN is to remove the barriers to entering the impact investing field. I had limited exposure to the GIIN prior to writing this book, however, I was familiar with some of their tools and publications. In 2018, they published the Roadmap for the Future of Impact Investing where they share similar sentiments I included in this book: a world where social (and environmental) aspects (mitigation and proactive positive impact creation) are mainstreamed into business and investment decisions, where we have a standardized way to measure impacts, where we agree on the demonstration tools for impacts and where businesses are held accountable to their impacts (double materiality). The action tools target a variety of stakeholders from academics to wealth advisors. I can't wait to get a chance to be more involved in their work.

Legislation and Approach to Modern Slavery

Modern slavery is a term used to describe the exploitation of individuals for financial gain, often involving forced labor or human trafficking. This is an issue that affects millions of people around the world, and it is a violation of basic human rights. In my world, we use tools around labor standards and working conditions to manage issues related to potential bonded labor, forced labor, exploitation, and contractor management.

There are many other forms of modern slavery, including forced labor in factories, mines, and farms, as well as domestic servitude, sex trafficking, and debt bondage. Victims of modern slavery are often vulnerable individuals, including women and children, who are forced into situations of exploitation and abuse. Modern slavery has a devastating impact, and it is also a major obstacle to economic and social development. It undermines the rule of law and human dignity, and it perpetuates poverty and inequality. As we have seen throughout this book, employment and labor are repeat topics for the majority of the social impact products. Doing it well and doing it lawfully is crucial. While many social impact products use voluntary standards to demonstrate their labor-related achievements, legally binding tools also govern the terms and conditions of employment.

There are many organizations and initiatives working to combat modern slavery around the world. These efforts include raising awareness about the issue, providing support and services to victims, and advocating for stronger laws and regulations to prevent and punish modern slavery. One important initiative in the fight against modern slavery is the United Nations Sustainable Development Goals (SDGs). Goal 8 of the SDGs specifically addresses the issue of forced labor and modern slavery and aims to promote decent work and economic growth while eradicating all forms of forced labor and human trafficking. In addition, many companies are now recognizing their responsibility to address the issue. Legislation introduced in certain countries requires companies to report on the actions they've taken to prevent modern slavery in their supply chains.

It's important to recognize that modern slavery is a complex issue that is often linked to other social and economic challenges. For example, poverty, lack of education, and gender inequality can all contribute to the vulnerability of people to exploitation and forced labor. Addressing these underlying issues is critical. Modern slavery is often a hidden problem, and it can be difficult to identify and assist victims. It is essential that individuals and organizations be trained to recognize the signs of modern slavery and know how to report it to the appropriate authorities. In addition, it's important to address the demand for goods and services that are produced through modern slavery. Consumers have a responsibility to be aware of the ethical practices of the companies they support and to demand that goods and services are produced without exploitation.

The fight against modern slavery has gained significant attention globally, resulting in the introduction of key legislation aimed at combating this pervasive crime. Here are three examples of important legislation regarding modern slavery:

- *Modern Slavery Act 2015 (United Kingdom).* The Modern Slavery Act is a landmark legislation in the United Kingdom. It requires large businesses operating in the UK to disclose the steps they have taken to address modern slavery in their supply chains and operations. The Act includes provisions for transparency in reporting, supply chain due diligence, and the establishment of an Independent AntiSlavery Commissioner. It has helped raise awareness, drive corporate responsibility, and encourage companies to take action to prevent and address modern slavery. In a previous role, we had to do a detailed assessment of labor conditions within the supply chain because the Modern Slavery Act applied. It was in the early days of its application, and we had limited practical guidance as to how exactly the client is supposed to ensure us that they comply with the legislation.

- *California Transparency in Supply Chains Act (United States).* The California Transparency in Supply Chains Act was enacted in 2012 and was the first of its kind in the United States. It requires companies operating in California with annual revenues above a specified threshold to disclose their efforts to eradicate human trafficking and slavery from their supply chains. The Act emphasizes the importance of transparency and public reporting, aiming to empower consumers and stakeholders to make informed choices and encourage companies to take responsibility for their supply chain practices.

- *Modern Slavery Act 2018 (Australia).* The Modern Slavery Act in Australia requires entities operating in Australia with an annual revenue above a certain threshold to report on the risks of modern slavery in their operations and supply chains, as well as the actions taken to address those risks. The Act aims to enhance transparency, encourage due diligence, and drive collaboration between businesses and governments in the fight against modern slavery. It establishes an annual reporting requirement to increase awareness and foster continuous improvement in supply chain practices.

These legislations represent significant efforts to combat modern slavery. They underscore the importance of collaboration between governments, businesses, and civil society in addressing this complex and global issue. As we will see, there are overlaps between labor management in supply chains and other recent initiatives here in the European Union (EU). In practical terms, many of the labor-related performance standards cover issues related to bonded labor, forced labor, and child labor. The new supply chain management initiatives and working groups recognized the issue and have now developed an approach that is the international best practice for the management of labor risks in the supply chain. I'd also like to mention that we require gender-based violence, sexual exploitation and abuse, and harassment policies to be developed by clients. My job as a social performance practitioner does have its limits, but working with creative and inspiring people made it relatively easy to come up with practical ways to incorporate these into our everyday operations.

Sustainable Development Goals 2030

The SDGs 2030 were adopted by the United Nations in 2015 as a comprehensive and ambitious plan to end poverty, protect the planet, and promote prosperity for all. No social study would be complete without including the SDGs because they are widely adopted by institutions. In a previous role of mine, we did a study on benchmarking our standards against the SDGs, so we could include in our reporting how our operations contributed to achieving the goals. While they might seem ambitious, they are easy to translate into practical action. The one thing that always bothered me a little bit was the reluctance of clients to discuss social safeguard issues (compliance based), but they were oh-so-quick to jump on the SDG bandwagon (voluntary set of standards). I would argue for compliance first and the extra mile second, but in this case, we would end up in the "whose social impact is better" argument. After all, the SDGs were designed to be a blueprint for peace and prosperity for people and the planet. Who wouldn't want to contribute to that?

The SDGs in numbers: 17 goals, 169 targets, 3,572 events, 1,341 publications, and 6,724 actions. The SDGs are a universal and integrated agenda, which means that all countries and stakeholders are responsible for achieving them, and progress on one goal can have positive impacts on others. The SDGs are also grounded in the principles of human rights, sustainability, and social justice, and aim to leave no one behind. Achieving the SDGs by 2030 is a major challenge, but it is also an opportunity to create a more just, equitable, and sustainable world. The SDGs offer a roadmap for governments, businesses, civil society, and individuals to work together to address some of the most pressing challenges facing humanity today.

The SDGs cover a wide range of issues, collected into seventeen goals:

1. *No poverty.* End poverty in all its forms everywhere.

2. *Zero hunger.* End hunger, achieve food security and improved nutrition, and promote sustainable agriculture.

3. *Good health and well-being.* Ensure healthy lives and promote well-being for all.

4. *Quality education.* Ensure inclusive and equitable quality education and promote lifelong learning opportunities for all.

5. *Gender equality.* Achieve gender equality and empower all women.

6. *Clean water and sanitation.* Ensure availability and sustainable management of water and sanitation for all.

7. *Affordable and clean energy.* Ensure access to affordable, reliable, sustainable, and modern energy for all.

8. *Decent work and economic growth.* Promote sustained, inclusive, and sustainable economic growth, full and productive employment, and decent work for all.

9. *Industry, innovation, and infrastructure.* Build resilient infrastructure, promote inclusive and sustainable industrialization, and foster innovation.

10. *Reduced inequalities.* Reduce inequality within and among countries.

11. *Sustainable cities and communities.* Make cities and other settlements inclusive, safe, resilient, and sustainable.

12. *Responsible consumption and production.* Ensure sustainable consumption and production patterns.

13. *Climate action.* Take urgent action to combat climate change and its impacts.

14. *Life below water.* Conserve and sustainably use the oceans, seas, and marine resources for sustainable development.

15. *Life on land.* Protect, restore, and promote the sustainable use of terrestrial ecosystems, sustainably manage forests, combat desertification, and halt and reverse land degradation and biodiversity loss.

16. *Peace, justice, and strong institutions.* Promote peaceful and inclusive societies for sustainable development, provide access to justice for all, and build effective, accountable, and inclusive institutions at all levels.

17. *Partnerships for the goals.* Strengthen the means of implementation and revitalize the global partnership for sustainable development.

As you can see, the SDGs are really a joint effort among many stakeholders with rigorous reporting requirements on adoption. Annual reports on the implementation process have been prepared since 2016 with country-level actions for each goal. The latest I looked at is from 2022. In addition to this, every four years they publish the Global Sustainable Development Report written by an independent group of scientists to review deliberations at the general assembly. The latest report covering 2023 is currently being developed, but the advanced, unedited version is already on the website. Chapter 1, titled "Half-way to 2030," basically tells us that our joint efforts for the implementation of the SDGs resulted in unexpected positive outcomes. Even in 2015, it was acknowledged that the SDGs with the timelines provided were rather ambitious, but there was a sense of optimism because everyone seemed to understand that we simply have to do this. We still have seven years to go, and there's a significant global push to make progress.

To achieve the SDGs, it is important for all stakeholders to work together and to prioritize collaboration, innovation, and transformative change. Governments have been creating policies and incentives that promote sustainable development; businesses have largely adopted sustainable practices and invested in new technologies; and civil society has been very vocal about raising awareness, holding stakeholders accountable, and advocating for change. We seem to be going in the right direction, even if the pace is slower than expected.

What's interesting to see is the interlinkages between different goals and targets. For example, addressing climate change (Goal 13) can have positive impacts on poverty reduction (Goal 1) and health (Goal 3), while promoting gender equality (Goal 5) can contribute to economic growth and decent work (Goal 8). The SDGs also recognize the importance of partnerships and collaboration between different stakeholders, including governments, businesses, civil society, and academia.

One of the challenges of achieving the SDGs is ensuring that progress is equitable and leaves no one behind. This requires addressing systemic inequalities and discrimination based on factors such as gender, race, ethnicity, income, and location. It also means ensuring that marginalized and vulnerable groups have access to the resources and opportunities they need to thrive, such as education, healthcare, and decent work.

Measuring progress toward the SDGs was recognized as an important step to ensure accountability and identify areas that require additional attention and resources. The United Nations has developed a framework of indicators for each SDG, which provides a standardized way to measure progress and identify areas that need improvement. In addition, there are several tools and initiatives that aim to promote transparency and accountability, such as the GRI and the SDGs Index. Perhaps unsurprisingly, the leading countries on the SDG Goals Index are Finland, Sweden, Denmark, Germany, and Austria. My home country, Hungary, is twenty-second on the list, and my other home country, the UK, is eleventh.

In thinking about the SDGs and the significant efforts the UN has already made to improve global human rights, I did wonder how SDGs compare to human rights since—according to my knowledge—they fundamentally target the same issues. I went on a few reputable websites to find some answers and the official narrative on this. UNDP's (United Nations Development Program) Sara Rattray published an article in 2019 that stated they are "two sides of the same coin." She argued that SDGs are based on human rights with over 90 percent of the goals and targets corresponding to human rights obligations.

The United Nations Office of the High Commissioner for Human Rights (OHCHR) created a document to demonstrate how human rights are integrated into the SDGs. If human rights have been around for so long and are inalienable, then why do we need another set of the same goals instead of an action plan with practical steps to achieve the desired outcomes? The roles and responsibilities of government, NGOs, and the private sector could be better clarified so we could each manage the impacts that are in scope for us. At this point, the SDGs are not legally binding, and while we can translate some of them into contractual obligations under different agreements by requiring compliance with certain standards, the question of whether we need separate assessments of human rights risks will always be there. Using the same logic, there could be better uses for the legally binding human rights conventions and legislation through which the roles and responsibilities of companies in the safeguarding of human rights could be managed. To a certain extent, this is what we do with the social safeguards, despite not using the term human rights explicitly. This is the result of years and years of discussions. The tides are turning when it comes to the legislation that references human rights risks in supply chains. But more about this later.

As I said, the world is changing, and clients who were previously reluctant are now more than happy to get involved and manage their human rights risks. This was not always the case. I remember sitting in meeting rooms with various clients, trying to explain the benefits and make a case for going beyond compliance and proactively engaging with critical stakeholders. Sometimes, it was a very hard sell, to say the least. The SDGs brought awareness back to the issues with more targets presented in a relatable and pragmatic way.

Human rights and SDGs go hand in hand. My research in this topic took me to the website of the Danish Institute for Human Rights. They created a video on this subject with useful visuals and an online tool. The interesting thing about human rights and SDGs is that they should be applicable to each and every project, as most of the UN member states are signatories to them. However, the SDGs and the Universal Declaration of Human Rights (UDHR) are not legally binding documents. Since its adoption in 1948, the UDHR has inspired legislation around human rights in several countries globally.

The SDGs are a powerful tool that encourages collaboration amongst various stakeholders to achieve common goals. It's a very comprehensive framework that aims to address the most pressing social, economic, and environmental challenges as identified by experts, governments, stakeholders, and international organizations. The SDGs recognize the interconnectedness of these issues as opposed to separating them into environmental and social categories as we do in my field. The need for collective action, international cooperation, and inclusive development is mainstreamed in each goal. They're ambitious goals, so achieving them requires a shift in our thinking, policies, and practices. These shifts are already visible halfway through the implementation, but as new challenges emerge, we must think of ways to innovate and recalibrate our targets and expectations.

The EU Environmental Impact Assessment Directive

Though not social in nature, The EU Environmental Impact Assessment Directive (EIA) is another legal tool social performance practitioners within the EU can use to address some key aspects of the new construction of high-risk projects. The directive is a legal requirement for all projects that are likely to have significant effects on the environment according to Annex II. The directive came about in 1985 and was revised in 1997, 2011, and 2014. It aims to ensure that all projects requiring development consent must be subjected to a comprehensive and detailed environmental assessment.

The directive follows the objectives of Article 191(1) Treaty on the Functioning of the European Union, stating the emphasis on preserving, protecting, and improving the quality of the environment and human health. It is further informed by some internationally agreed-upon principles, such as the principle of rectification and source polluter pays principle. The principles of transparency, certainty, accountability, and cost-effectiveness are also taken into consideration when looking at the whole EIA process.

While the EIA covers a lot of ground regarding the environment (pardon the pun), it does reference stakeholder engagement (as understood by an SIA practitioner) and capturing impacts on human receptors. The main issue is that in comparison to an SIA, the level of depth for the assessment of human beings and the social environment is very weak. It must be noted, though, that the EU has stringent legal frameworks; high standards of social protection; and enforceable directives on human rights, labor, worker protection, health, and safety—both in the workforce and for the general public. During my work, I noted that several projects that follow the EIA directive alone miss out on capturing the social impacts due to the significant gaps between what should be an ESIA directive and international best practices. We had countless arguments with clients who were reluctant to understand the importance of adequate social impact assessment for their projects. The argument was always that the legislative framework was strong and that they would comply with it.

The differences between the EIA directive and SIA requirements could really make or break a project:

- *Screening and categorization.* The first step for any new project is to screen and categorize it to determine whether it falls under the directive and requires an EIA. Annex II provides the list of activities and types of projects that would fall within this scope. In the SIA world, we have the scoping stage, where we look at potential impacts on social receptors. While both instruments include a similar approach, the scope of recognizing social impacts is different. The EIA would typically deal with land and livelihood impacts separately under national legislation. Furthermore, it would not go into detail about the topics to be covered.

- *Social topics covered in the SIA.* Obviously, the EIA looks at the environmental aspect, while the SIA looks at the social aspect. This is where we find the largest gap between these two reports. Social issues that are typically covered in an SIA include labor standards, working conditions, occupational and community, health and safety, public consultation, stakeholder engagement, grievance management, and any impact on indigenous people and cultural heritage. If you need a refresher, check the SIA chapter.

- *Social baseline data.* EIAs under the directive that I have read so far had little to no social content other than identifying some of the major cultural heritage sites that might be affected, archaeological finds that might be present on the site, and some of the obvious basic risks to community health and safety. Primary data, collections, or surveys to gather site-level information and social information from the project area of influence is very limited under the EIA directive. The social baseline that should guide the impact assessment ideally covers a variety of different topics, including the administrative divisions, the governance structures, the economic situation, employment in the project area of influence, demographics, and community health and safety. It also includes any sort of social maladies, including crime, child or forced labor, or lack of education.

- *Stakeholder engagement.* While some aspects of stakeholder engagement are incorporated in the EIA, these are usually limited to two public hearings and an EIA disclosure. A stark contrast to the SIA, which encourages project sponsors to have an ongoing two-way dialogue with their affected and interested stakeholders and to set up a grievance mechanism to record any complaints, questions, or queries. Disclosure requirements under the SIA are also different, with more meetings—even with smaller groups or vulnerable groups, as appropriate—and the sharing of project documents in multiple languages. The EIA directive leaves the management of complaints to the official channels available in the member states.

- *Labor and resettlement.* Without going into more detail, I want to emphasize the importance of addressing labor and resettlement issues in any E(S)IA. These are crucial aspects for which, despite legislation, there's often a lack of supervision and implementation monitoring. Labor issues for which I have seen the most legislative gaps include stronger oversight of contractors, occupational health and safety, agency or third-party workers, and supply chain management. Supply chain management will be covered under the next directive, and I'm less worried about that because of the increased attention it's received in recent years. But managing vulnerable workers, including migrant workers, and providing them with accommodation are important aspects of any new construction project. Relying on contractors to follow national legislation is not enough without a presence on-site to supervise implementation.

Resettlement is a whole other topic, and I made a conscious effort to not let it overpower this book. This is another area I am very passionate about, but it would probably take another book to cover all the details and scenarios. In this section, I want to highlight that the requirements for eligibility, compensation, and management of resettlement are probably where the biggest gaps lie between international best practices (i.e., IFI standards) and national legislation. Missing out on baseline data collection and managing this process separately from the EIA process is a huge miss in my view. Even when national legislation is stringent, there are gaps in terms of resettlement planning, consultation, information disclosure, acknowledgment of informal landowners and land users, and calculating the impacts on livelihood and access to natural resources. I leave it at this for now. Who knows, maybe I'll write a book about this too?

I want to conclude this section with something I've been advocating for: to update the EU EIA Directive and turn it into an ESIA directive to capture some of the key social impacts of the high-risk projects that are being constructed within the EU. It is ignorant to think that there are no vulnerabilities regarding community, labor, health, and safety here in the EU. Speaking from personal experience, every company is better off if they supervise the activities of their employees and contractors, especially on large construction projects where there is a significant potential for things to go wrong. If an impact or risk is unnoticed, there will be no plan to manage it.

Nonfinancial Reporting Directive

The NonFinancial Reporting Directive (NFRD) is an EU edict that requires large companies to disclose information on their ESG performance. While this directive was upgraded in 2023, it is worthwhile noting the key features of this pioneering initiative. The directive aimed to increase transparency and accountabili-ty for companies in areas such as climate change, human rights, and anticorruption. There are several reporting requirements for ESG, but I wanted to talk about this one because paved the way for the CSDDD and CSRD, which has the potential—in my humble opinion—to revolutionize social risk assessment and management. I'll talk about this in more detail soon.

The NFRD was first introduced in 2014 and was amended in 2017 to align with the EU's broader sustainability agenda, including the SDGs and the Paris Agreement. The Paris Agreement is a landmark international treaty adopted in 2015 under the United Nations Framework Convention on Climate Change. Its primary goal is to address climate change by limiting global warming to less than two degrees Celsius above preindustrial levels.

Under the NFRD directive, companies that meet certain criteria, such as having more than five hundred employees or a turnover exceeding €40 million, must report on a range of ESG issues, including their policies, risks, and outcomes. From my SIA practitioner perspective, this covers labor, working conditions, and to some extent, stakeholder engagement. The directive also requires companies to provide information on their business models, strategies, and risk management approaches.

One of the main benefits of the NFRD was that it provided investors, consumers, and other stakeholders with access to more comprehensive and comparable information on companies' ESG performance. Here we need to mention that the directive is focusing on the reporting of impacts, not the creation. Now, I don't know how familiar you are with EU directives, but they have a mandatory section that needs to be transposed into national legislation. There is also an optional but recommended section for companies to comply with voluntarily. The directive may appear ambitious, but not the whole directive is mandatory to be transposed into legislation by Member States.

However, the NFRD has also faced criticism for its lack of clarity and consistency, particularly around the scope and level of detail required in its reporting. Some stakeholders argue that the directive doesn't go far enough in requiring companies to report on their impacts. In response, the European Commission has proposed a revision, which would strengthen the reporting requirements and harmonize reporting standards across the EU. The other issue is whether the competent authority who's required to review it is actually competent. We will talk more about this later on, but the reporting on ESG and NFRD has two dimensions that need to be understood: a competent authority reviewing whether the report meets the requirements in terms of format and timing, and a competent authority reviewing whether the report's content is appropriate and adequate from a technical perspective. My argument is that it's not enough to have a stakeholder engagement policy document if the engagement process isn't meaningful and doesn't meet requirements. Later, we will see how the issue of capacity within the EU will play a bigger role in determining the extent to which new directives can bring real change to social and human rights risk management.

Overall, the NFRD represented a very important step toward greater transparency and accountability on environmental and social issues. My slight issue is not with the directive or its reporting requirements but with the lack of standardized frameworks for assessing risks and impacts. The difference should be widely understood between mitigation of adverse impacts, *doing good* as required by law, and going the extra mile. The NFRD also reflected a broader trend toward greater environmental and social reporting and disclosure requirements around the world. In recent years, many countries have introduced regulations or guidelines that require companies to report on their ESG performance, often with the aim of increasing transparency and accountability. This trend reflects a growing recognition of the importance of sustainability in business decision-making, as well as the role that companies can play in addressing global challenges such as climate change and inequality.

However, some critics argue that the NFRD may impose additional costs and administrative burdens on companies, particularly SMEs. They also note that reporting requirements may vary across different countries depending on how they transpose the directive into their national legislation, thus creating additional complexity for multinational companies that operate in multiple jurisdictions. In response, some stakeholders have called for greater harmonization of reporting standards and simplification of reporting requirements, particularly for SMEs.

Corporate Sustainability Reporting Directive

Corporate sustainability reporting has emerged as a crucial tool for fostering transparency, accountability, and sustainable practices within the business sector. Recognizing its significance, the EU has taken substantial steps to strengthen sustainability reporting and disclosure through the Corporate Sustainability Reporting Directive (CSRD). As we have seen, this is one of many EU directives that require greater transparency and accountability in the operational impacts of companies.

The CSRD represents a key legislative proposal that was approved by the European Commission in 2023. I was fascinated when I first read it because of its ambitious scope regarding both the range of companies it covers and the technical requirements they're meant to follow. It aims to amend and expand upon the existing NFRD and align it with the global sustainability reporting standards, including those of the GRI and the Task Force on Climate-related Financial Disclosures. The CSRD seeks to enhance the quality, comparability, and reliability of any sustainability information disclosed by companies across the EU. With this proposal, a broader range of companies will be subject to mandatory sustainability reporting requirements. The companies need to meet two of the three requirements to fall within the scope of the CSRD: i) EUR 43 million in net revenue, ii) EUR 22 million in assets, and iii) 250 or more employees.

The CSRD will introduce a more standardized reporting framework, setting out specific disclosure requirements on sustainability matters such as human rights and environmental risk assessments. Additionally, the CSRD aims to address the issue of greenwashing by introducing strict audit and assurance requirements to ensure the accuracy and reliability of sustainability information. The Directive is already applicable to companies that were reporting under the NFRD (five hundred or more employees) with the first reports due in 2025 covering the financial year beginning on or after January 1 2024.

From my understanding, the reason for this new directive is largely to push EU companies to review the management of their supply chains and integrate human rights due diligence into their policies and management plans. I was happy to see the term management plan used in an official, legally binding EU document because this is the practical implementation that many other policies miss. It's going to bring us one step closer to approaching sustainability in a more holistic manner, stepping away from perfectly crafted policies into the practical act of managing risks and impacts.

From a social impact assessment perspective, the highlights of the directive include references to human rights, mitigation measures for adverse human rights impacts, and the integration of sustainability into management systems. Another highlight is the requirement for companies to have grievance mechanisms accessible to workers in the supply chain. Not only will these bring immense social benefit, but they will also require an alignment with IFI standards and international best practices. The implementation guidance note was not on the website at the time of writing this book, so I can't comment on the level of depth required for the assessment. I'm familiar with the consensus on the most recent best practices for supply chain management, but that's a topic for the next book! Typically, the instrument required is the Supply Chain Management System, which involves a set of procedures to map supply chains and gather data from suppliers through a self-assessment, media search, and where appropriate, on-site audit. This is adjusted to reflect the risk profile of the company, project, sector, supplier country of operations, and other aspects.

I see that a lot of what we require as *best practice* in this new directive also highlights the responsibility of the companies to take action—beyond a simple policy stating that contractors are obliged to follow national legislation. How many times have I heard this? I've lost count over the years. The directive references the OECD Due Diligence guidance for responsible business conduct to guide the human rights due diligence process. It largely follows what we implement for SIAs— another welcome addition! I'm quite excited to see how this directive will be implemented, starting as early as January 2024 for certain companies. I do have questions regarding the capacity of the EU and the competent authority to review the reports and look closely at the due diligence process that was undertaken. I could ask the same question I asked before: what makes someone a supply chain expert? Of course, it comes down to experience in implementing the *best practices* with a deeper understanding of social performance and risk management issues. Further thoughts on this would fill many pages, so I'll spare you for now. The other good question to ask is whether the SIA and SIA practitioners could help companies undertake the human rights risk assessment. There are significant overlaps, and the processes are largely the same. I guess we'll see if this directive brings more light to the work of people like me and recognizes subject matter expertise, rather than focusing on data for the reporting.

CSRD vs. CSDDD vs. ESRS

The book would not be complete without mentioning the CSDDD, the EU's Corporate Sustainability Due Diligence Directive, and the ESRS, the European Sustainability Reporting Standards. The EU has stepped up in a significant way in recent years to respond to public awareness and interest in improving sustainability reporting and assessments undertaken on a company level. Let's have a quick look at what these mean from the social impact perspective.

The CSDDD aims at "establishing a European framework for a responsible and sustainable approach to global value chains, given the importance of companies as a pillar in the construction of a sustainable society and economy." Sounds very similar to the CSRD right? While the CSDDD is a framework and requirement to undertake the assessment, the CSRD is the disclosure of the information. In simple terms, CSDDD provides the requirement to assess impacts and the CSRD is the tool to demonstrate the impacts using a unified metrics system. The applicability of the CSDDD is broader when compared to the CSRD as even non-EU companies that have a revenue of over EUR 43 million within the EU fall within the Directive's scope. The due diligence needs to be repeated every twelve months. In terms of the topical scope, it is almost identical to the CSRD: looking at human rights and environmental management issues within the supply chain. Timelines for implementation align with that of the CSRD as well.

The ESRS is more of a set of guidelines covering topics, metrics, and indicators that companies can add to their sustainability reports. The ESRS is inspired by other standards such as the GRI we looked at earlier in this chapter. The topical scope covers the issues you are very familiar with on the social side: labor and supply chain, diversity and anticorruption, and human rights. Other environmental topics and indicators are also included. The concept of double materiality appears here as well, hence the need to include supply chain–related issues in the scope of the reporting. The reporting starts between 2024 and 2026 for companies that meet the requirements and fall under the standards.

The EU also proposed a new directive to ban products from the EU markets that were made with forced labor. The new proposed legislation is called Prohibiting Products Made with Forced Labor on the Union

Market Regulation. Updates on the proposed Regulation's approval are yet to be disclosed, but it definitely sounds like we are moving toward taking forced labor and supply chain a lot more seriously than before. From a social impact perspective, this is very much in my area of expertise as we safeguard and mitigate adverse impacts. But supply chain management is for the next book, where hopefully I can flesh out the implementation of these new standards, directives, and regulations.

All the Limitations

Despite efforts to address social and human rights risks and impacts with large-scale initiatives and pioneering legislation, several limitations and criticisms remain. I have briefly mentioned some of these in the summary sections, but there are some repeated systemic issues that I want to address:

- *Greenwashing and social washing.* One of the biggest challenges with social branding is the risk of greenwashing and social washing. I use both terms here because greenwashing is the more widely used term, but social washing has been reported for at least a few years now. Reporting on impacts can be a powerful way to demonstrate a company's sustainability efforts, but it may not necessarily reflect the company's actual contribution to the creation of impacts. The impacts and claims of impacts can be direct and measurable, but we have seen several social impact products whose impacts are indirect or implied, without any scientific or reliable way to measure the role they played in the creation. With Grameen Bank, we saw how the report included statistics on the poverty decrease in Pakistan, implying that it was largely due to the bank and its operations, when in fact international aid, IFI, and private sector investments had been actively supporting poverty reduction and socioeconomic development for decades.

- *Lack of accountability.* Several of the initiatives presented here are voluntary, which means there are no legal requirements or consequences for failing to deliver on sustainability promises. We looked at some mandatory requirements and legislation as well, so this limitation is mostly true for voluntary initiatives. In the case of voluntary initiatives, there's often a lack of competent authority to supervise the delivery of the program and keep it on track. The lack of legal tools to manage such instruments is also leading to a broadened scope with no harmonized industry standard for performance indicators, reporting requirements, or benchmarks. However, this limitation seems to be addressed through the efforts to hold companies to the same standards by the increasingly informed and aware shareholders and public.

- *Who are the experts and specialists?* While researching this chapter, the question of who the experts and specialists are popped up over and over again. Several of these initiatives are geared toward investors so the majority of impact investment experts are people with limited background in development. When I say development, I don't just mean social, human, or economic development in a developing country context, as we have seen that impact investing specifically often targets developed country markets. Looking at the EU directives and regulations, I raised the issue of capacity building on the competent authority level to be able to process the new reports that are expected from next year. Will there be human rights experts and supply chain experts involved in the review of the reports? What will the sector-specific guidance notes look like? The SDGs are probably the one area where I personally know social development specialists working on implementation. I was honest about how someone ends up as a social development specialist—mainly through field experience -, however, having the relevant educational background to understand the complexity of social issues is essential. I am eager to see how the industry will evolve and what expertise will be useful to contribute to the successful implementation of these initiatives.

- *Lack of standardization.* The issue with standardization has been mentioned countless times in this book. The context I offer here is this: we could only standardize what we require on a product-by-product basis. The difference between legal, mandatory, and voluntary requirements should define the level of standardization. However, the standardization should at a minimum cover the level of assessments undertaken, the definition of the scope, and the demonstration of the impact within the given context. For instance, one company's CSR initiative can be wildly different from its competitors, but if the reporting includes the scale and scope of the initiative, the company's involvement in the initiative, and the metrics used to demonstrate the impacts, it will make it more comparable with other similar initiatives. As an example from my line of work: Despite the consensus of academics and practitioners on the scope and content of the SIA, the lack of legal requirements (in general) means it is up to the project developer or the financing institutions to set the standard.

- *Resource intensive.* This is one of the biggest issues I hear from clients. The money and time it takes to assess impacts, design programs, and cover the implementation costs. The legal requirements will not spare smaller businesses in the EU from having to hire people or companies to do the mandatory reporting on the new due diligence they need to undertake. I mentioned my dilemma on exactly what new expertise will be required here, but one thing is for certain: whether a person is an expert on the social topic or an expert in the reporting requirements, good specialists are costly. Support from these specialists is expected regularly on a long-term basis. The due diligence and assessments take time, especially when there are requirements for on-site audits of the suppliers. I have done this before, even in politically sensitive areas of the world and the minimum time for a more detailed assessment from planning to final report is a minimum of two months.

- *Balancing increased stakeholder scrutiny.* Every shareholder and stakeholder comes with their own set of expectations, often with disregard for the limitations and budgetary constraints of the company. I also feel that expectations and criticism are often unfair, especially for voluntary social impact products. Think of a family launching a small philanthropic initiative to support a cause that's close to their hearts. Whether the criticism of their activities is warranted depends on the lens we use to examine their actions. Several companies use voluntary social impact products to distract from the fact that they don't follow mandatory standards. It is no longer a distinguishing factor and a competitive advantage for a company to have an ESG rating or a CSR program because they have become common practice. The rules of the social impact game seem to have changed as the general public got more educated and interested in the intersection between social sustainability and businesses. Increased expectations put a budgetary, time, and prioritization burden on several businesses, and it often feels like a zero-sum game for them.

These challenges of other social impact products should not be an excuse for any company to avoid acting on social responsibility. Rather, they should be used to frame discussions on how to improve work methods and develop a common understanding of each social impact product. My prediction is that with the new regulations and increased awareness of the social aspects of businesses, the social impact product market will be regulated and standardized a lot more. The hope is that these updates will bring more credibility and transparency to reporting, a more effective and meaningful assessment of impacts, and pragmatic actions to mitigate adverse impacts.

CHAPTER 10

THE END AND THE BEGINNING

This is the end of this book and the beginning of many discussions about social impact products. I hope this book is a valuable resource for understanding and defining social impacts in different contexts. When I started this journey, I had different ideas about what this book would say, but as I refreshed my knowledge and completed my research, I grew a lot more hopeful for social impact creation in general. I've seen amazing initiatives that are changing the lives of so many people. I've seen that we are surrounded by this *care* from companies, organizations, and people around us. Almost everyone I talked to on this journey participates in social impact creation to a certain extent. Many people are SIA or social performance practitioners, so their situations were a bit more straightforward. I talked to people who donate to charities, who participate in their company's CSR initiatives, and who go to great lengths to calibrate their investments and businesses to benefit their communities. I've seen hundreds of social enterprises that target people who are vulnerable because they can't access jobs or services. I've seen the kindness, the good intentions, and the love. I know how this sounds, and I'm aware the world is not always so rosy. Yet after completing these chapters and looking at the tools we have today with a critical lens, I have a newfound inspiration from the people, companies, and stories I've gotten to know over these past few months. It seems that the world is full of ways to do good while making money, and the innovation never stops.

At the beginning of the book, we saw how social development, social impact, and social value may mean very different things in very different contexts. I knew that there were ways to categorize social impact products, yet I was surprised how similar they seemed, with all these overlaps and hybrid models. What is the social impact? I gave this title to the book because I wanted to show the diverse ways to explain this and the many things it could mean to people within the context of their operations. The big conclusion is that social impact can be almost anything. It is around us every day. It can be the choice to buy products from a social enterprise or a donation that gives homeless people access to a shelter with showers and laundry. It can be a scholarship that makes one person's dream come true. It can be a quality job with an employer that doesn't exploit its workers but provides them with everything the law requires—and maybe even a bit more. It can be a consultation with the communities around the operational factory, who have concerns about emissions or discharges. It can be a requirement for contractors and suppliers to follow the highest standards in terms of labor and working conditions. The list can go on and on, but you've read enough about it already.

The key concepts presented in this book are only a fraction of the social impact products that are out there. Every day, someone comes up with a new way to make the world a better place. In some cases, it will be a better place for a well-defined selected group of people. In others, more of us would feel the benefits. While looking at this, I tried to balance facts and theoretical insights with personal observations and opinions. This book really is a product of the many conversations I've had with inspiring colleagues from the broader social impact field, who each represented their own unique specialization and opinions. The integration of case studies and examples was very important to me because looking at things we've all come across made a difference in understanding the concepts.

I remember the first time I moved to the UK and got a letter inviting me to a community consultation. Many people I asked about it said they weren't going because their opinion didn't matter, but I thought about what I'd been preaching to my clients, so it would've been hypocritical not to attend. Companies genuinely want feedback and to understand how to do better, and I want to know about initiatives that affect me and to provide my opinion. I know it doesn't always happen like this though, but it is reassuring that companies follow the requirements.

My other main intent with this book was to provide these insights and analysis from the perspective of an SIA or social performance practitioner. I noticed that we keep writing books for each other instead of providing our wealth of knowledge to wider audiences. It is true though that a lot of people had no idea what we do or how we fit into the broader sustainability market. It used to be very funny when I tried to explain to people what I do and they had no idea. In fact, several of my close friends and family could not understand what I did for many years. Now that ESG and other social impact–related topics get more attention from the mainstream media, people are more aware of this field. The perspective of people like me can support the categorization, definition, and scoping of the different social impact products. I was thinking about whether the world was ready to listen to someone with my background, yet I urged others to step up and speak up whenever they could—not to bring other products down but to initiate these important conversations that can have a really significant effect on how we approach social impacts. While many people have field experience by definition, their lens for assessment is different than mine. I am a researcher who is there to gather information, observe, and understand. I love spending time visiting clients and projects; to me, this is the best part of the job. I know I'm not alone in this, and many people working in philanthropy or even CSR have done the same. Social entrepreneurs dedicate their whole lives and work to impact creation, and several impact investors visit their investments to see the changes they make in people's lives. My perspective might be unique because I've worked with several social impact products and have an in-depth understanding of their strengths and weaknesses. I had a big dilemma about whether it's the creation or the demonstration of the impact that matters more, but this was quickly answered by the legal requirements and prioritization of ESG ratings. I refuse to believe that the key aspect of social impact creation is to demonstrate our impacts within the frameworks to boost bankability for investors. I've found the opposite to be true: people want to do good but don't have a resource that provides them with clear options or ways to explain their narrative and demonstrate their contribution. I look at this book as a starting point to push for a mainstream understanding of the social impact market.

I hope that people who read this, especially people working with any of these products, will examine their company practices and potentially recalibrate those to maximize their impact. This would mean that they start by looking at the desired outcomes, and once that's figured out, they look for tools to achieve those outcomes. I also hope that people with my background will have more opportunities to support the work of companies in social impact creation. We have a wealth of experience in the field and can provide pragmatic solutions. In a way, this book is also an opportunity to acknowledge and appreciate SIA practitioners, who have been working tirelessly behind the scenes to standardize approaches and come up with useful solutions to mitigate adverse social impacts. I have a special appreciation for SIA practitioners who look for ways to enhance the positive impacts of projects and who work with their clients to develop tools and programs that are not mandatory but an add-on.

Sustainability is more than ESG and reporting on macro-level practices. Sustainability begins with the approach each company takes to manage its operations. I've spoken to a lot of clients who never thought of developing an ESMS on a corporate level. Yet once they were pushed to do so, their whole operational model changed for the better. New projects were delivered faster and with fewer issues from international lenders—at least, on the environmental and social risk management side.

There's a lot to campaign for in terms of social impacts. I want to see the EU EIA Directive updated to include a basic set of social impact assessment requirements that would prescribe management plans to address those impacts. I want to see companies taking the time to develop corporate-level ESMS. It might not bring the benefits we see with the different sustainability ratings, but who knows? Maybe one day we'll rate companies based on their ESMS too. The tendency is definitely to move toward more responsibility and accountability with real impacts reported. In my view, the era of incredible but empty promises is over now that the social impact market has started to mature and more ESG rating agencies come under the ESMA (European Securities and Markets Authority) for regulation and standardization. This is no longer a new market, and while many investors feel disillusioned, lost, or overwhelmed, there's a strong push to continue and evolve. The intention to improve the world may be ambitious, but we can break it down into tasks and standards that will eventually contribute to that.

The world is complex and interconnected. It's more important than ever to understand that our daily decisions influence our communities and, indirectly, this world we live in. What we place value on will get the chance to evolve, and what is nurtured will bloom. Hopefully, placing value on society, communities, and people is a no-brainer for us, so we can make efforts to create positive social change. How do we do that? Well, hopefully, this book has given you some ideas. In the meantime, I'll continue to do my thing and innovate in the field of social impact creation and management.

What's Next for Social Impact Products?

I must admit, I was a bit surprised to see the lack of technology used to simplify data collection, analysis, and management—especially for social impacts. So my prediction (and this will be funny to read in a few years) is that the market for social impact products will mature in several different ways. For one, there will be more clarity and better definitions for each product. For instance, we'll understand that a company might have a great sustainability rating, but that doesn't mean that it is a *good* company if we examine its operations from another angle. Hopefully, we'll all approach the issue of mandatory and extra mile–type impacts differently, and we won't give bonus points to companies who do what is mandatory under the legislation where they operate. This should incentivize them to go even further and implement international best practices throughout their operations, especially if these requirements are more stringent than what is prescribed by law. I do see how corporate-level ESMS will be the standard for any self-respecting company that wants to take charge for its environmental and social impacts.

Legislation is also likely to change to incorporate more on the social impact assessment aspects, especially for the construction of new greenfield projects. We have seen that some countries already follow this, and it's likely to become more widespread. Especially if we change the EU EIA Directive to add aspects of SIA. The only issue I see is the international best practice regarding involuntary resettlement, impacts on livelihoods, and access to natural resources. The biggest gaps here—amongst many— are typically the lack of recognition for informal landowners and land users under national legislation, and the required compensation. As I said before, this is very much one of my main areas of interest, but I didn't want this book to be too heavy on this topic. There are other very interesting books, articles, blog posts, and studies published by many of my wonderful colleagues. The current environmental impact assessment tools and practices are also not sufficient to manage this aspect efficiently, we would need to deploy a full SIA for that. That would cost time and money, and these are the most valuable resources for new projects and companies.

The next improvement I see is more honesty about the impact created by the company or that the company contributed to. The current social washing contexts allow for wild, farfetched claims. I think that the standardization and context provided for these social impact products will result in more honest reporting. It should be acceptable for a company to say that they can't change the world but that they can provide access to healthcare and subsidize glasses for communities in need within a defined area. Does it contribute to increased access to healthcare in general? Sure, because these villages will have access, but also not so much because the impact is localized and will not scale. When I write my reports, I report facts, not aspirations. Aspirations can go into the policies and strategies. And, please, spare no ambition when you write these because I am a strong believer in aiming high. The magic is in the implementation. What's often missing is a plan to implement actions to achieve the goals under the strategy or the policy. And an ESMS is exactly this plan for company operations. It tells you exactly what will happen, when, how often, who is responsible, what the completion indicators are, and how often they're reported. Every company and every project I had, had some surprise issue that no one suspected. I wish more companies would understand how beneficial it is to invest in these E&S risk management tools for any operation. The reality of any operation is that some impacts will be outside the scope of the company, and it should be acceptable to acknowledge this. Other social investment opportunities highlighted by locals may not be a priority for a company, and it will be acceptable to admit that. I sincerely hope that with this new level of honesty, we will be able to refine our strategies to focus on the priority issues, impacts, and scope of any company.

I do hope that the technological advancements will not spare the social impact market. There are tasks that could be simplified for professionals with the use of AI technology, for instance. There was a boom in using new software and technology across all major fields—even the monitoring of bird movement—yet this has not translated into anything related to social impacts. When I was researching this, all I could find were databases that make data collection and reporting easier. While this is a real benefit, I think we can do better. Here are some of the products I've come across:

- Salesforce Philanthropy Cloud is a platform that enables organizations to engage employees, track volunteerism, and manage philanthropic initiatives. It provides tools for employee giving, matching donations, and volunteer management, allowing organizations to measure and communicate their social impact. This is best used for CSR activities and philanthropy.

- Socialsuite is an impact management platform that helps organizations measure and manage their social outcomes. It provides tools for data collection, web scraping, project management, blockchain integration, data analysis, and reporting, allowing organizations to track progress, assess program effectiveness, and demonstrate the social value they create. It works together with Contrib.com, a digital platform that aims to facilitate crowdfunding for social impact projects and initiatives. This platform provides a space for individuals, organizations, and communities to connect, collaborate, and raise funds to support a wide range of social and environmental causes. Contrib.com allows project creators to create fundraising campaigns and share their stories, highlighting the impact they aim to achieve. It also enables individuals and businesses to discover and support projects aligned with their interests and values by making financial contributions. Pretty cool, right? Crowdfunding is an interesting subcategory of impact investing, but it can also fall into the SIB or CSR category, depending on the type of project and whether it has financial returns.

- Impact Cloud is a comprehensive software solution for impact measurement and management. It offers a range of features, including outcome tracking, stakeholder engagement, data visualization, and impact reporting. Impact Cloud enables organizations to streamline their impact management processes and align their activities with the SDGs. This can be used for SIA, CSR, philanthropy, impact investing, SIBs, and SOCs, but is also useful for social entrepreneurs tracking their impacts.

- OpenFn is an integration platform designed for social impact organizations. It enables seamless data integration and automation across various systems and platforms, facilitating efficient data management and analysis. OpenFn helps organizations improve data quality, reduce manual data entry, and enhance the effectiveness of their programs. While the website says it helps governments and social sector organizations, the tools could be useful for other social impact products as well.

- The Social Value Portal provides a digital platform for organizations to measure and manage their social value. It offers tools for measuring social impact, calculating SROI, and reporting on social value outcomes. The platform enables organizations to assess the social value of their activities and make data-driven decisions to optimize their impact.

- ImpactMapper is a web-based software that allows organizations to track, analyze, and report on their social impact. It provides features for outcome measurement, data visualization, storytelling, and impact reporting. ImpactMapper helps organizations map their impact, communicate their achievements, and improve program effectiveness.

- Sinzer is a social impact measurement and management software that helps organizations assess and manage their social and environmental impacts. The software allows organizations to define impact frameworks, set indicators, and collect data to measure their social outcomes. It offers a range of data collection methods, including surveys and automated data imports, making it easier to gather relevant information. Sinzer also provides data analysis and visualization capabilities, enabling organizations to gain insights into their impact performance and communicate their results effectively.

The End—for Real

As we bring our exploration of social impacts to a close, let's reflect on the transformative potential that lies within each of the products and the collective responsibility we share to shape a sustainable future. Throughout this book, we have delved into the myriad dimensions of social impact and witnessed the profound ways in which individuals, organizations, and communities can drive positive change. Now, as we reach the end of our journey, it is crucial to remember the key lessons we've learned and the actions we must take to create a more equitable, inclusive, and sustainable world.

First and foremost, we must recognize that social impact is not a singular endeavor but a collective pursuit. It requires collaboration, empathy, and an unwavering commitment to the common good. If we come together, share knowledge and resources, and amplify our collective voice, we can effect meaningful change on a global scale. We must foster partnerships across sectors, bridge divides, and engage diverse perspectives, all while understanding that the challenges we face are complex and multifaceted, requiring holistic and collaborative solutions.

Moreover, to shape a sustainable future, we must adopt a long-term mindset and embrace the principles of social responsibility. We must be mindful of the social and environmental consequences of our actions, recognizing that our decisions today have far-reaching implications for future generations. It is incumbent upon us to integrate sustainability into all facets of our lives, from business practices to public policies, from education to innovation. We can all act as agents of social impact, as we must continuously strive for growth, learning, and self-reflection. The challenges we face are ever evolving, and our understanding of social impact must adapt in tandem. We must remain open to new ideas, challenge existing paradigms, and embrace innovation as a catalyst for progress. Fostering a culture of continuous improvement can push the boundaries of what is possible, finding creative and effective solutions to the pressing social issues of our time.

As we conclude this book, let us remember that social impact is not a destination but an ongoing journey—a journey fueled by passion, purpose, and the relentless pursuit of a better world. It is a journey that each of us can embark upon, regardless of our background or circumstances. Through small acts of kindness, conscious consumer choices, responsible business practices, or active participation in civil society, we can all contribute to the collective momentum of social impact. So, let us go forth with determination and hope, knowing that the choices we make, the actions we take, and the impacts we create today have the power to shape a brighter and more sustainable future for generations to come. Together, let us be the change we wish to see in the world, and may our social impacts reverberate for generations, inspiring a legacy of positive change.

SOURCES, BIBLIOGRAPHY, AND REFERENCES

1. Acumen: https://acumen.org/investment-principles/

2. ADB India Social Enterprise Landscape Report: https://www.adb.org/publications/india-social-enterprise-landscape-report

3. Ashoka: https://www.ashoka.org/en-us/people/william-drayton

4. Australia Social Impact Assessment Guideline under State Development and Public Works Organization Act 1971: https://www.statedevelopment.qld.gov.au/__data/assets/pdf_file/0017/17405/social-impact-assessment-guideline.pdf

5. Backes DS, Toson MJ, Ben LWD, Erdmann AL. Contributions of Florence Nightingale as a social entrepreneur: from modern to contemporary nursing. Rev Bras Enferm. 2020 Oct 19;73(suppl 5):e20200064. English, Portuguese. doi: 10.1590/0034-7167-2020-0064. PMID: 33084809. https://pubmed.ncbi.nlm.nih.gov/33084809/

6. Barefoot College: https://www.barefootcollege.org/about/

7. Ben & Jerry's Activism: https://www.benjerry.com/values

8. Better World Books: https://press.betterworldbooks.com/about/

9. Bornstein, D. (2004). *How to Change the World: Social Entrepreneurs and the Power of New Ideas*. Oxford University Press.

10. Boston Consulting Group: www.bcg.com

11. British Council: Social Enterprise in a Global Context: The Role of Higher Education Institutions, Country Brief: Canada: https://www.britishcouncil.org/sites/default/files/canada_-_

social_enterprise_in_a_global_context_-_final_report.pdf

12. British Council: Social enterprise in the UK: https://www. britishcouncil.org/sites/default/files/social_enterprise_in_the_ uk_final_web_spreads.pdf

13. British Council: Social Enterprise, An overview of the policy framework in India: https://www.britishcouncil.in/sites/default/ files/social_enterprise_policy_landscape_in_india_0.pdf

14. British Council: The state of social enterprise in Bangladesh, Ghana, India, and Pakistan: https://www.britishcouncil.org/sites/ default/files/social_enterprise_in_the_uk_final_web_spreads.pdf

15. Calvert Impact Capital: https://calvertimpact.org

16. Cancer Research UK: https://www.cancerresearchuk.org/ about-us/our-organisation

17. Carnegie Corporation of New York. (2021). About Us. https:// www.carnegie.org/about-us/

18. Carroll, A. B., & Shabana, K. M. (2010). "The Business Case for Corporate Social Responsibility: A Review of Concepts, Research, and Practice." *International Journal of Management Reviews*, 12(1), 85–105.

19. Cen, Xiao and Qiu, Yue and Wang, Tracy Yue, Corporate Social Responsibility and Employee Retention (June 23, 2022). Available at SSRN: https://ssrn.com/abstract=4144689 or http:// dx.doi.org/10.2139/ssrn.4144689

20. Coca Cola sustainability: https://www.coca-colacompany.com/ sustainability

21. Connection at St. Martin's: https://www.connection-at-

stmartins.org.uk

22. Contrib.com: https://www.contrib.com

23. Cost Benefit Analysis: https://www.investopedia.com/terms/c/
cost-benefitanalysis.asphttps://online.hbs.edu/blog/post/
cost-benefit-analysis

24. D.C. Water Social Impact Bond: https://www.
quantifiedventures.com/dc-water

25. d.light: https://www.dlight.com

26. Dees, J. G. (2001). "The Meaning of Social Entrepreneurship."
Stanford Social Innovation Review, 1(1), 1–8.

27. Duterimbere: https://duterimbere.org.rw

28. Ecofiltro. (2021). About Us. Retrieved from https://www.
ecofiltro.com/about-us/

29. Embrace Innovations: https://www.linkedin.com/company/
embrace-innovations/https://fellowsblog.ted.com/
how-i-m-making-my-social-enterprise-sustainable-73b4d7cadc8c

30. Embrace Innovations. (2021). About Us. Retrieved from https://
embraceinnovations.com/about-us/

31. Equator Principles: https://equator-principles.com

32. ESG related articles:

   a. https://www.zerohedge.com/markets/blackrock-faces-leftist-
   backlash-it-votes-fewer-esg-proposals

   b. https://www.zerohedge.com/markets/esg-dying-its-
   inevitable-death

c. https://www.zerohedge.com/markets/hundreds-funds-brink-losing-esg-ratings

d. https://www.zerohedge.com/markets/morningstar-says-anti-esg-fund-hype-might-be-over-it

e. https://www.zerohedge.com/markets/vanguard-ceo-abandons-esg-investing-alliance-not-game-politics

f. https://www.zerohedge.com/political/long-term-negative-effects-esg-will-be-catastrophic

g. https://www.zerohedge.com/markets/esg-investing-boom-already-over

33. EU Ban on products made with forced labor: https://ec.europa.eu/commission/presscorner/detail/en/ip_22_5415

34. EU Corporate Sustainability Due Diligence Directive: https://eur-lex.europa.eu/legal-content/EN/TXT/?uri=CELEX:52022PC0071; https://www.europarl.europa.eu/RegData/etudes/BRIE/2022/729424/EPRS_BRI(2022)729424_EN.pdf

35. EU CSRD, CSDDD and ESRS: https://www.greenbiz.com/article/csrd-csddd-esrs-and-more-cheat-sheet-eu-sustainability-regulations; https://www.supplyshift.net/blog/supply-chain-management/csddd-and-csrd-whats-the-difference/

36. EU EIA Directive: https://environment.ec.europa.eu/law-and-governance/environmental-assessments/environmental-impact-assessment_en

37. EU Nonfinancial Reporting Directive: https://www.europarl.europa.eu/RegData/etudes/BRIE/2021/654213/EPRS_BRI(2021)654213_EN.pdf

38. EY Sustainable investing: the millennial investor(2017—accessed in July 2023): https://assets.ey.com/content/dam/ey-sites/ey-com/en_gl/topics/financial-services/ey-sustainable-investing-the-millennial-investor.pdf

39. Fidelity Charitable: Millennial investors drive growth in impact investing (2021—accessed in July 2023): https://www.fidelitycharitable.org/about-us/news/millennial-investors-drive-growth-in-impact-investing.html

40. Fischer, F., & Forester, J. (Eds.). (1993). *The Argumentative Turn in Policy Analysis and Planning*. Duke University Press.

41. Food for Life: https://www.foodforlife.org.uk/~/media/files/evaluation%20reports/4foodforlifelcssroifullreportv04.pdf

42. Forbes: What the rise of the millennial investor means for a sustainable world (2021—accessed in July 2023): https://www.forbes.com/sites/worldeconomicforum/2021/02/08/what-the-rise-of-the-millennial-investor-means-for-a-sustainable-world/?sh=35cb906465cc

43. Forbes. (2018). "The 10 Biggest Philanthropic Gifts Of 2018." https://www.forbes.com/sites/stevenbertoni/2018/12/11/the-10-biggest-philanthropic-gifts-of-2018/?sh=3e9a9bdf6c01

44. Gibson-Brandon, Glossner, Krueger, Matos, and Stefan (2019), Responsible Institutional Investing Around the World.

45. Glasson, J., Therivel, R., & Chadwick, A. (2012). *Introduction to Environmental Impact Assessment*. Routledge.

46. Global Entrepreneurship Monitor: 2020/2021 Global Report: https://www.gemconsortium.org/report/gem-20202021-global-report

47. Global Reporting Initiative: https://www.globalreporting.org

48. Global Sustainable Development Report: https:// sustainabledevelopment.un.org/globalsdreport

49. GOGLA Standardized Impacts Metrics: https://www.gogla. org/what-we-do/business-services-and-standards/gogla-impact-metrics/

50. Grameen Foundation: https://grameenfoundation.org/about-us/ leadership/muhammad-yunus

51. Guide to Human Rights Impact Assessment and Management, IFC, UN Global Compact and Business Leaders Forum (2010): https://d306pr3pise04h.cloudfront.net/docs/issues_ doc%2Fhuman_rights%2FGuidetoHRIAM.pdf

52. IFC Performance Standards: https://www.ifc.org/wps/wcm/ connect/topics_ext_content/ifc_external_corporate_site/ sustainability-at-ifc/policies-standards/performance-standards

53. IFC Social Bonds (access July 2023): https://www.ifc.org/wps/ wcm/connect/corp_ext_content/ifc_external_corporate_site/ about+ifc_new/investor+relations/ir-products/socialbonds

54. IKEA Sustainability: https://about.ikea.com/en/sustainability

55. ImpactMapper: https://www.impactmapper.com

56. India CSR legislation: https://www.legalserviceindia.com/legal/ article-774-all-about-csr-regulations-in-india.html

57. International Association for Impact Assessment. (2002). Principles of Environmental Impact Assessment Best Practice. International Association for Impact Assessment.

58. International Labor Organization conventions: https://www.ilo.

org/dyn/normlex/en/f?p=NORMLEXPUB:12200:0::NO:::

59. ISO 26000: https://www.iso.org/iso-26000-social-responsibility.
html

60. ISO: https://www.iso.org/about-us.html

61. Khan, M. H. (2021): Ethnography: An analysis of its advantages
and disadvantages, Global Journal of Management and Business
Research Vol 21. Issue 5 Version 1.0: https://globaljournals.org/
GJMBR_Volume21/4-Ethnography-an-Analysis.pdf

62. Kotler, P., & Lee, N. (2005). *Corporate Social Responsibility:
Doing the Most Good for Your Company and Your Cause.* John
Wiley & Sons.

63. Li-Wen Lin: Mandatory Corporate Social Responsibility
Legislation around the World: Emergent Varieties and National
Experiences: https://blogs.law.ox.ac.uk/business-law-blog/
blog/2020/11/mandatory-corporate-social-responsibility-
legislation-around-world

64. London homelessness social impact bond evaluation: https://
www.gov.uk/government/publications/london-homelessness-
social-impact-bond-evaluation

65. Lufthansa Group Sustainability Reporting: https://www.
lufthansagroup.com/en/themes/sustainability-reporting.html

66. Lusch, R. F., Vargo, S. L., & Tanniru, M. (2010). "Service, Value
Networks, and Learning." *Journal of the Academy of Marketing
Science*, 38(1), 19–31.

67. Made in Marylebone: https://www.maryleboneproject.org.uk/
our-work/made-in-marylebone/

68. Magatte Wade Ted Talk: 2017: https://www.ted.com/talks/ magatte_wade_why_it_s_too_hard_to_start_a_business_in_ africa_and_how_to_change_it

69. Mair, J., & Marti, I. (2006). "Social Entrepreneurship Research: A Source of Explanation, Prediction, and Delight." *Journal of World Business*, 41(1), 36–44.

70. Massachusetts Juvenile Justice Pay for Success: https://www. bostonfed.org/publications/communities-and-banking/2017/ spring/a-pay-for-success-opportunity-to-prove-outcomes-with-the-highest-risk-young-people.aspx

71. Microsoft CSR: https://www.microsoft.com/en-us/ corporate-responsibility

72. Modern Slavery Act 2018 Australia: https://www.legislation.gov. au/Details/C2018A00153

73. Neumeier, M. (2017). *The Brand Flip: Why Customers Now Run Companies and How to Profit from It. New Riders.*

74. New York Times: Cafeterias Built on Honesty Fail: https://www. nytimes.com/1963/11/09/archives/cafeterias-built-on-honesty-fail-exchange-buffet-which-let.html

75. O'Reilly, N., & Haines, N. (2008). "A Review of the Corporate Reputation Literature: Definition, Measurement, and Theory." *Corporate Reputation Review*, 11(1), 3–21.

76. OpenFN: https://openfn.org

77. Patagonia as a non-profit: https://hbr.org/2022/10/ what-happens-when-a-company-like-patagonia-becomes-a-nonprofit

78. Patagonia CSR & Impact Investing: https://www.patagonia.com/
how-we-fund/; https://www.patagonia.com/social-responsibility/;
https://www.theguardian.com/commentisfree/2022/sep/20/
patagonia-billion-dollar-climate-initiative-philanthropy;
https://www.theguardian.com/environment/2022/sep/21/
how-investments-in-the-earths-future-should-be-made-by-
patagonia-and-others

79. Petts, J. (2009). "A Review of Social Impact Assessment
Methodologies." *Environmental Impact Assessment Review*, 29(5),
286–311.

80. Rikers Island Social Impact Bond: https://www.mdrc.org/
project/social-impact-bond-project-rikers-island#overview

81. Salesforce Philanthropy: https://www.salesforce.com/blog/
what-is-philanthropy-cloud/

82. Salesforce Sustainability: https://www.salesforce.com/solutions/
philanthropy/corporate-social-responsibility/

83. Salt Lake County Pay for Success: https://utahcf.org/
community-impact/pay-for-success; https://www.forbes.com/
sites/sorensonimpact/2022/05/13/pay-for-success-the-social-
impact-model-mitigating-homelessness-and-incarceration-in-
salt-lake-county-part-two/?sh=529828856693

84. SDG Index: https://dashboards.sdgindex.org/rankings

85. Sen, S., & Bhattacharya, C. B. (2001). "Does Doing Good
Always Lead to Doing Better? Consumer Reactions to Corporate
Social Responsibility." *Journal of Marketing Research*, 38(2),
225–243.

86. Shaping Impact Group, SI2 Fund: https://shapingimpact.group/

en/funds/si2-fund

87. Shaping Impact Group: https://shapingimpact.group/en/

88. Sinzer: https://www.sinzer.org/en/home

89. Skoll Foundation. (2021). What Is Social Entrepreneurship? Retrieved from https://skoll.org/what-is-social-entrepreneurship/

90. Social Bond Principles: https://www.icmagroup.org/sustainable-finance/the-principles-guidelines-and-handbooks/social-bond-principles-sbp/

91. Social enterprise scandals: https://www.cbsnews.com/news/goodwill-head-who-makes-164000-fired-disabled-workers-after-minimum-wage-hike/https://www.chicagoreporter.com/after-goodwill-controversy-spotlight-on-subminimum-wage/https://www.countryliving.com/shopping/a18198848/is-goodwill-a-nonprofit/

92. Social Enterprise UK: https://www.socialenterprise.org.uk/evidence-policy/about-our-policy-and-influencing-strategy/

93. Social Entrepreneurship Canada: https://www.bdc.ca/en/articles-tools/sustainability/environment/what-is-social-entrepreneurship

94. Social Finance India SIB: https://socialfinance.org.in

95. Social Impact Bond at HMP Peterborough: https://www.gov.uk/government/publications/social-impact-bond-at-hmp-peterborough

96. Social Outcomes Partnerships and the Life Chances Fund: https://www.gov.uk/guidance/social-impact-bonds

97. Social Value Portal: https://socialvalueportal.com

98. Socialsuite: https://socialsuite.com

99. Sopact Impact Cloud: https://www.sopact.com/impactcloud

100. SROI: https://neweconomics.org/uploads/files/
aff3779953c5b88d53_cpm6v3v71.pdfhttps://www.investopedia.
com/ask/answers/070314/what-factors-go-calculating-social-
return-investment-sroi.asphttps://www.betterevaluation.org/
methods-approaches/approaches/social-return-investment

101. Starbucks CSR: https://stories.starbucks.com/stories/2022/
starbucks-global-environmental-and-social-impact-report-2021/

102. Task Force on Climate-Related Financial Disclosures: https://
www.fsb-tcfd.org

103. Teasdale, S., Bellazzecca, E., de Bruin, A., & Roy, M. J.
(2023). The (R)evolution of the Social Entrepreneurship
Concept: A Critical Historical Review. Nonprofit and Voluntary
Sector Quarterly, 52(1_suppl), 212S-240S. https://doi.
org/10.1177/08997640221130691

104. The Bike Project: https://thebikeproject.co.uk

105. The Bill & Melinda Gates Foundation. (2021). About
Us. https://www.gatesfoundation.org/Who-We-Are/
General-Information/About-Us

106. The Body Shop sustainability: https://www.thebodyshop.
com/en-gb/about-us/brand-values/sustainability/sustainability-
commitments/a/a00063

107. The California Transparency in Supply Chains Act: https://oag.
ca.gov/SB657

108. The Chan Zuckerberg Initiative: https://chanzuckerberg.com

109. The Danish Institute for Human Rights—Data explorer: https://www.humanrights.dk/our-work/sdgs-human-rights

110. The Danish Institute for Human Rights: https://www.humanrights.dk

111. The Fair Chance Pledge: https://unlock.org.uk/project/unlocking-students-with-criminal-records/fair-chance-pledge/

112. The Felix Project: https://thefelixproject.org

113. The Ford Foundation. (2021). Our Work. https://www.fordfoundation.org/work/

114. The GIIN Roadmap: https://roadmap.thegiin.org/our-vision/

115. The Global Fund: https://www.theglobalfund.org/en/

116. The Global Impact Investing Network: https://thegiin.org

117. The Halifax Food Policy Alliance: https://www.nefconsulting.com/wp-content/uploads/2016/09/SROI-Report-HFPA-16Aug2016.compressed.pdf

118. The MacArthur Foundation: https://www.macfound.org

119. The Omidyar Network. (2021). Our Approach. https://omidyar.com/our-approach/

120. The Open Society Foundations: https://www.opensocietyfoundations.org

121. The Paris Agreement: https://unfccc.int/process-and-meetings/the-paris-agreement

122. The Rockefeller Foundation. (2021). Our Work. https://www.rockefellerfoundation.org/our-work/

123. The Skoll Foundation. (2021). Our Approach. https://skoll.org/about-us/our-approach/

124. The Social Pantry: https://socialpantry.co.uk/about/

125. The William and Flora Hewlett Foundation. (2021). Our Focus Areas. https://hewlett.org/our-focus-areas/

126. TOMS: https://www.toms.com/us/impact.html

127. Tripple Bottom Line: https://online.hbs.edu/blog/post/what-is-the-triple-bottom-line

128. UK Government: Setting up a social enterprise: https://www.gov.uk/set-up-a-social-enterprise

129. UK Modern Slavery: https://www.gov.uk/government/collections/modern-slavery

130. UN Sustainable Development Goals, Global Sustainable Development Report: https://sustainabledevelopment.un.org/globalsdreport

131. UNDP Sara Rattray: https://rolhr.undp.org/content/ruleoflaw/en/home/stories/story-2.html

132. Unilever CSR: https://www.unilever.com/planet-and-society/

133. United Nations Environment Programme. (2015). Guidelines for Social Life Cycle Assessment of Products. United Nations Environment Programme.

134. United Nations Office for the High Commissioner for Human Rights: https://www.ohchr.org/en/sdgs

135. United Nations Sustainable Development Goals: https://sdgs.un.org/goals

136. Urwego Bank: https://www.urwegobank.com

137. Warby Parker: https://www.warbyparker.com/buy-a-pair-give-a-pair

138. WE Charity: How Canada became a hub for social enterprise: https://www.we.org/en-GB/we-stories/opinion/canada-leading-the-way-for-social-enterprises

139. Western Journal: Google Employees Lose Adult Daycare Amenities as Company Cuts Costs https://www.westernjournal.com/google-employees-lose-adult-daycare-amenities-company-cuts-cost-list/

140. Worcester SIB Massachusetts: https://www.forbes.com/sites/annefield/2014/02/07/biggest-social-impact-bond-in-the-u-s-targets-stubborn-recidivism/?sh=3b8af7fe15b9

141. Yunus, M. (2010). Building Social Business: *The New Kind of Capitalism That Serves Humanity's Most Pressing Needs*. PublicAffairs.

INDEX

Note with regard to acronyms: full wordings are used in main headings whereas acronyms are used in subheadings e.g. Social Impact Assessment (SIA) as the main heading, SIA in subheadings.

Cap de Nice Press